Disposable Children

America's Child Welfare System

RENNY GOLDEN

Northeastern Illinois University

Foreword by
JONATHAN KOZOL

Wadsworth Publishing Company
I T P ® An International Thomson Publishing Company

Belmont, CA • Albany, NY • Bonn • Boston • Cincinnati • Detroit • Johannesburg
London • Madrid • Melbourne • Mexico City • New York • Paris
Singapore • Tokyo • Toronto • Washington

For my sister, Katy Golden,
who has been a child welfare caseworker and advocate for twenty-five years.

Criminal Justice Editor: Sabra Horne
Assistant Editor: Claire Masson
Editorial Assistant: Kate Barrett
Marketing Manager: Mike Dew
Project Editor: Vicki Friedberg
Print Buyer: Karen Hunt
Permissions Editor: Jeanne Bosschart

Cover Design: Andrew Ogus/Book Design
Cover Photograph: © Nubar Alexanian/
  Stock, Boston
Copy Editor: Donald Pharr
Compositor: Thompson Type
Printer: Edwards Brothers

Printed in the United States of America
  2 3 4 5 6 7 8 9 10

For more information, contact Wadsworth Publishing Company, 10 Davis Drive, Belmont, CA
94002, or electronically at http://www.thomson.com/wadsworth.html

International Thomson Publishing Europe
Berkshire House 168-173
High Holborn
London, WC1V 7AA, England

Thomas Nelson Australia
102 Dodds Street
South Melbourne 3205
Victoria, Australia

Nelson Canada
1120 Birchmount Road
Scarborough, Ontario
Canada M1K 5G4

International Thomson Publishing GmbH
Königswinterer Strasse 418
53227 Bonn, Germany

International Thomson Editores
Campos Eliseos 385, Piso 7
Col. Polanco
11560 México D.F. México

International Thomson Publishing Asia
221 Henderson Road
#05-10 Henderson Building
Singapore 0315

International Thomson Publishing Japan
Hirakawacho Kyowa Building, 3F
2-2-1 Hirakawacho
Chiyoda-ku, Tokyo 102, Japan

International Thomson Publishing Southern Africa
Building 18, Constantia Park
240 Old Pretoria Road
Halfway House, 1685 South Africa

Library of Congress Cataloging-in-Publication Data
Golden, Renny.
   Disposable children : America's child welfare system / Renny
Golden.
      p. cm. — (Wadsworth contemporary issues in crime and justice
series)
   Includes bibliographical references and index.
   ISBN 0-534-26466-2
   1. Child welfare—United States. 2. Child welfare—Government
policy—United States. 3. Family services—United States.
4. Social work with children—United States. I. Title.
II. Series: Contemporary issues in crime and justice series.
HV741.G59 1997
362.7'0973—dc20   96-30784

Contents

I   WHOSE FAMILY VALUES? WHOSE BEST INTERESTS?

II ADVOCATES AND PATHFINDERS

A Note from
the Series Editor

We live in the wealthiest nation in the world. Yet we also live in a paradox: In this wealthy nation, more children grow up in poverty than in virtually any other Western democracy. Children who grow up impoverished represent an enormous social problem. They are less likely to be gainfully employed as adults and less likely to raise their own children successfully. In particular, they are more likely to experience abuse and thus to need our protection. If we fail to protect them effectively, they are more likely to end up in prison or on welfare themselves. The cost of "disposable" children is extraordinary, not only in tax dollars but in the loss of their potential contribution to our society. Not least, our moral standing among nations is damaged.

We deal with poor and vulnerable children—children at risk—through a welfare system that has its roots in long-standing traditions of paternalism and intrusiveness. We see these people as problems to be managed rather than as untapped human resources to be released. The result is a monumental failure—more poor people, greater inequality in life circumstances, and increasing frustration about the prospects of meaningful changes in social policy about the poor.

I am proud to introduce *Disposable Children: America's Child Welfare System,* by Renny Golden, as the latest addition to the Contemporary Issues in Crime and Justice Series. This series provides students and professionals interested in crime and justice with detailed discussions of important, topical problems and issues in our field. This book discusses one of the most pressing problems in today's society, and it addresses the reasons why we must rethink our child welfare system.

I am particularly proud to introduce this addition to our series because the issues it covers go beyond the subjects we often think of as central to crime policy. This book helps us to see, as we have shown elsewhere in this series, that crime is not merely a problem of criminals and what to do about them. To be effective, crime policy must be topically comprehensive, addressing economic, educational, and—as this text makes explicit—welfare policy.

Students using this book are in for a triple fascination. First, they will hear about the problem of America's child welfare system from the perspective of the people who are affected by it—the children who grow up in poverty and disadvantage. Next, they will see why today's approaches are bound to fail because they rest on untenable assumptions about effective social action. Finally, they will read about better approaches to the problem of poverty, approaches that empower communities to become better places for families of poor members. Readers may disagree with some of what they read in this volume, but they cannot help but be challenged by the overall power of the author's central point: We must stop treating America's children as though they were disposable.

Todd R. Clear
Florida State University

Foreword

In the winter of 1995, the nation was shocked to learn of the death of Elisa Izquierdo, a child in New York whose apparently addicted or mentally ill mother was subsequently blamed by law enforcement officers for having murdered her.

The case elicited a tide of outrage at the child's mother and indignation at the way the child's case had been mishandled by the city's child-protection agencies. As so often happens in these situations, little was changed after the news attention had subsided. What remained, perhaps, was only a vague, generalized, and rancorous belief that the mothers of the poor are every bit as irresponsible, immoral, and unworthy as some of our hard-nosed sociologists have told us. Little was learned from this experience, but prejudices hardened and new cries were heard from those who favor the removal of poor children from their parents altogether.

Renny Golden takes a deeper, wiser, longer look at the entire question of how a nation can, or should, or someday might make sane, responsible, and humane decisions about the disposition of the children who, for good or ill, may be entrusted to its care.

Without the venom and forensic fireworks that often characterize discussions of this question, Golden gently draws us into the real lives of children and into the dilemmas of their families and of the people in the social work arena who have sought to find solutions to seemingly insoluble challenges. Building her reflective passages around the narratives of children and adults who have admitted her into their confidence, she poses the ultimate questions for professionals and nonprofessionals alike: Does America regard these children as "disposable"? Do we really wish to salvage life and the integrity of families? Is our goal in social work to build a "service industry" or is it to build good and strong communities?

Drawing on some of the most enlightened advocates and scholars of our times—including many like Kip Tiernan, the prophetic and inspiring streetworker who has fought so hard for women and their children in my own hometown of Boston—Golden makes the issues come alive because she lets the living speak for themselves and sees the inner moral strength of those who, though they live at the rock bottom of our economic pecking order, nonetheless reveal resilience, courage, and resources frequently unrecognized by those who far too easily condemn them.

Disposable Children is a complex work—too complex to be reduced to a simplistic summary. But it has the kind of balance between anger and reflection, edginess and calm, that I have always found in the best social workers, who must operate in the crisis mode that is too often necessary in the world of the very poor, the sometimes sick, and the often homeless.

I first met Renny Golden nearly twenty-five years ago and subsequently followed her persistent pilgrimage among the poorest of the poor, among those of our immigrants who are still known as "illegals," among the mothers, the children, the saints, the radicals, the priests and activists from Arizona to Chicago. Her moral energies have never been subdued. She still burns with a lovely steady flame of quiet hope and gentle empathy relieved at times by the best kind of irony and humor. It all comes through in the pages of this book. Let us hope that a new generation of good, angry, tender, loving, and impatient social workers have an opportunity to learn from the important lessons she brings us.

Jonathan Kozol

Preface

Thousands of maltreated children pass through juvenile court into state care each year, and it as if they disappeared into a sinkhole. This book argues that child welfare practice in the United States is not so much a child protection system as a child removal and family regulatory system. The families to be regulated are often poor, single-mother-headed families, the majority of whom are nonwhite. Although there has been a *policy* of family preservation since the child-saving movement of the Progressive era prompted the first White House Conference on Children in 1909, the child welfare *practice* has been removal of children from families.

This book describes and illuminates the myriad forces that have historically undercut America's child welfare policies of family preservation: enforcement of social norms that are based on mainstream racial and middle-class standards of nuclear family life; legal policy that objectifies children as possessions of their parents or the state; a child welfare system without a long-term plan; a foster care system driven by federal contracts; and a child welfare and juvenile court system that blames mothers for failure to control male sexual or physical violence against children. All parties claim a legal, political, and moral interest in protecting the child's "best interests." Yet the child is systematically gagged; the child who is not pushed back into conformity is a unique survivor.

Woven throughout this book are the first-hand accounts of those touched by the child welfare system—the children whose fate is decided by the system, the social workers and psychologists who attempt to establish a workable solution, the judges who are forced to make difficult decisions. The narratives of youth, parents, and child welfare advocates, told in their own words, subvert the institutional discourse of child welfare by revealing the human cost of bureaucratic practices.

The last chapters of this book offer examples of youth, family, and neighborhood development projects that rebuild shattered communities through an inclusive process that restores to communities their creativity, skills, dignity, and capacity to identify and solve their own problems. These initiatives reclaim creative communal power, and in so doing, interrogate the child welfare professional service model of care. It is my wish that these chapters will provide some hope for the future.

Renny Golden

Acknowledgments

I wish to thank all those who taught me about child welfare in the United States, especially Prentis and Lois Caudill, Tammy, Johnny, Justin, and Jacob Daniels, Paul Dennis and Jackie Rivet-River, Desiree Maurer, Elizabeth and Lamond, Joan, Angelica, Donna, Jatayn, Melinda, and Samir and Hanaan. I also wish to thank the following dedicated advocates for children and families: Denise Plunkett, Gail Smith, Joanne Archibald, Camile Odeh, Juliet Dinka, Peter Schmiedel, Diane Redleaf, Jan Ereth, Bruce Boyer, Ben Wolf, Karl Dennis, Ivan Medina, Patrick Murphy, Chuck Golbert, Pia Menon, Seth Donnelly, and Rich Cozzola.

I'm grateful to my friends who critiqued this book early on and gave suggestions: Michael McConnell, Cinny Poppin, Tom and Carol Montgomery-Fate, Sheila Collins, Judy Wittner, and to John Hagedorn, who provided helpful final suggestions. Thanks to Northeastern Illinois University students Mike Rich, Cristina Perez, and Melvin Shabazz for assistance, and to my colleagues Kingsley Clark and Shelley Bannister for their support, as well as to my colleague Dragan Milovanovic for pushing me into this book. Thanks to Millie Juskevice and Marlene Stern of the Citizens' Committee on Juvenile Court, Jack Wuest of the Alternative Schools Network, Maria Whelan of the Chicago Community Trust, and Juancho Donahue of the Chicago Coalition for the Homeless for their unswerving support of the "voiceless." So many helped me connect with families or young people who were state wards—thanks to Linda Abernathy of Best Interests of Children, Sam Guardino, Cindy Clark of the Public Guardian's Office, Kerry Gilfoyle, and Brigid Lowery.

I especially want to thank Maureen "Mo" Hickey for her willingness to rescue me from an endnote snarl and for putting up with FedEx shipments back and forth while I was in Guatemala and El Salvador. Mo and Jolie Chabot were a wonderful help!

I want to thank my editor, Sabra Horne, for her willingness to advocate for this book and to endure the pressures of getting it to an early press. To editorial assistant Kate Barrett, project editor Vicki Friedberg, and copy editor Don Pharr, thank you for your support and hard work as well.

My thanks to the following reviewers for their helpful comments and suggestions: Jerald C. Burns, Alabama State University; Dean J. Champion, Minot State University; Mary J. Clement, Virginia Commonwealth University; Arlene Kaplan Daniels, Northwestern University; Philip D. Holley, Southwestern Oklahoma State University; Anthony M. Platt, California State University at Sacramento; Beverly D. Rivera, Central Missouri State University; Jill Rosenbaum, California State University at Fullerton; Herman Schwendinger, State University of New York at New Paltz; Julia Schwendinger, Institute for the Study of Social Change, University of California at Berkeley; Alan Spector, Purdue University-North Calumet; Judith Wittner, Loyola University, Chicago; and Jeanne Payne Young, Sam Houston State University (retired).

Thanks to my friends in Boston: Alice Hageman for her usual incredible hospitality in giving me a place to do major writing; Roxanne Cumming for giving me *two* places to write and not minding *two* dogs; Brinton Lykes for providing me with access to Boston College's Social Work Library; and Eva Pytowska for telling me about Dr. Korczak, an advocate for children, whose story was inscribed in her childhood memories of Poland. To Jonathan Kozol for his kind support, but especially for his unwavering and passionate advocacy for children for more than twenty-five years. And to writer Carolyn Paige for her inspiring story and for affording me peaceful writing space.

Finally, to my dear friend Mary Ann Corley, thank you for your unassuming kindness and generosity throughout this project. I couldn't have done it without your support.

Introduction

I first learned to do field research in a war zone in El Salvador. Peasant women taught me. I'd come to El Salvador in the mid-1980s to learn more directly about the war conditions that refugees faced in order to report back to Chicago church and synagogue congregations that were "harboring" exiled Central American refugees in sanctuary. "Tell me your story," I would say, rarely more than that. Then the mothers constructed a narrative of family history and the social history of peasants that revealed the tortured fate and courageous resistance of ordinary people in extraordinary circumstances. This experience prepared me for my research about the tragic lives of maltreated children in the United States and the ways we are distanced from those lives. When I interviewed young people and families for this book, I sometimes saw the same inexpressible grief in their eyes, and I reexperienced the spirit of resistance and impossible hope that I first encountered in the dusty, bomb-cratered fields of Morazan, Chalatenango, and Usulatan.

It is hard not to notice the reported abuse that children suffer at the hands of parents or guardians in the United States. Those hideous stories fascinate. They sell news. What is hard to believe, because it is not reported, is that when abused or neglected children are taken into state protective services, they begin another experience of betrayal that will be as destructive as their original abuse or neglect—if, indeed, there actually was neglect. The great majority of children taken out of their homes are removed because of neglect charges. And how is neglect linked to poverty? According to a 1991 U.S. Committee on

Ways and Means report, the majority of children in foster care are from families receiving aid to families with dependent children (AFDC), and 46 percent of the foster care population are minority children.[1] Single mothers are the majority of the parents who were supporting their children before they entered state care. One of the most egregious examples of this trend happened in Cook County, Illinois (Chicago and environs), where a class-action suit filed on behalf of widower James Norman was necessary to stop DCFS from removing children from their homes for reasons of poverty alone.

PERSONAL NARRATIVES:
THE "SERVICED" AS TEACHERS

At the end of each chapter in Part One of this book, I have included the boxed narratives of youth and families who are survivors of abuse by both parents and child welfare's "protection." These stories represent the survivor's will to refuse acquiescence. In every case, however, someone loved them fiercely enough for them to believe in themselves. In the case of Samir, his immigrant mother and his brothers, as well as a Palestinian community organization, fought for his return home; Paul, the five-year-old who slept in a closet and on the streets, had a "mother" who befriended him; and ten-year-old Prentis Caudill had a twelve-year-old sister who promised him that the sodomy and beatings he experienced in their home would end and that she would love him always.

There are also families who refuse to be serviced and who act to recover dignity and some control of their fate and their child's fate, in spite of having their children removed. In the case of Hanaan, Samir's mother, it was the organized Arab community that helped spark the resurrection of her shattered will and accompanied her in her year-long process of getting her son and two infants returned to her. The Palestinian community helped her by identifying the cultural ignorance of American child welfare practices, thereby allowing her to deconstruct the power of U.S. child welfare authority rather than internalizing its judgments. This is not to say that Hanaan's stressed parenting behavior should remain uncriticized. But the needed changes and interventions took place within the context of the Arab community.

Another mother, Tammy Daniels, still continues a struggle to have one of her two young sons returned by the Illinois Department of Children and Family Services (DCFS). Tammy's evolving sense of empowerment has resulted from her ability to direct anger not at herself, but at the system that allowed her two-year-old son to be sodomized by an older boy in a foster home without admitting that it happened. At the same time, the ongoing healing of Tammy and her husband, Johnny, was possible because of the services that child welfare offered. This family used counseling, parenting classes, and alcohol recovery services to confront their floundering family life and troubled marriage. In this regard, Tammy continues the historical practices of immigrant mothers in the nineteenth century who used the services of the Massachusetts Society for the Prevention of Cruelty to Children (MSPCC) to deal with alcoholic or violent husbands and also to carry them through periods of abandonment or impoverishment.

Linda Gordon's research, using MSPCC casework records, reveals the ingenuity of poor mothers with little social power who, nevertheless, used state services as best they could to assist their families. The immigrant mothers of Boston risked opening their lives to the social judgments of standard-bearers who lacked solidarity with the pauperized immigrant classes. Today, poor mothers also take advantage of child welfare's services and meet or fail to meet class and cultural standards of family life.

Just as the Society for the Prevention of Cruelty to Children agencies in Boston and New York saw their task as maintaining middle-class standards of American culture (as opposed to the "inferior" cultures of the foreign Italian and Irish), so today's "family values" defenders have targeted unwed teenage mothers, in particular African Americans and Latinas, as the causes of the breakdown of American family life. By family life, they mean a male-headed nuclear family. Unwed teen mothers are portrayed by the "family values" proponents as welfare dependents who will produce a scourge of future youth who lack a work ethic, and in the case of African American males, become predators who pose a dangerous social threat. When the more moderate President Clinton joined—in fact, sponsored—a national campaign to end teen pregnancy, there was bipartisan consensus.

REGULATING THE CHILDREN AND FAMILIES OF THE UNWORTHY POOR

Caseworkers are assigned the conflicted role of supporting troubled families, on the one hand, and functioning as state-mandated investigators with the legal power to take children from their homes and bring charges of abuse and neglect against their parents, on the other hand. The contradictory nature of the caseworkers' task is linked to child and social welfare's historical distinction between the worthy poor and the unworthy poor. Social work has, since its inception in the nineteenth century, been invested with the legal investigative powers to declare a mother "fit" or "unfit." Both child and social welfare agencies, which are intimately linked, function as social regulators that apply family fitness norms to the services and interventions they offer.

My sister Katy, who has worked as a child welfare caseworker for almost twenty-five years, struggles with the conflicted nature of her role, but she works to keep the enforcement mandate from undercutting her support of families. We have never agreed about the reason that child welfare fails—or, as she would put it, why the troubled families she works with so often fail to pull their lives together. Years of working in the black and Latino communities of Chicago's poor Westside, and then working with Guatemalan and Salvadorean refugees, has taught me to analyze the larger forces that shape the destinies of those who lack social power. It was while I was in El Salvador that I learned from peasants, who knew far more than I about the effects of market globalization, what social destruction can result when impoverished majorities are written off as surplus populations. Katy, on the other hand, is a pragmatist interested in results for the families she currently serves. She's defensive about "critiques" that blame social workers for a system that can barely deal with the human wreckage that is to be "serviced." Her eyes glaze over when I suggest that the problem runs deeper than either the liberal solution of more money for services or the conservative solution of cutting spending on social welfare programs that "don't work."

Katy agrees the system needs fixing but holds little hope that substantial reform, let alone transformation, will be accomplished. She has worked almost always with families with multiple, often catastrophic problems—such as mentally ill or retarded parents with children who have been victims of physical or sexual abuse, or emotionally distraught mothers trapped with abusive mates and abused children. After twenty-five years, she's more interested in the programs that might make the lives of some children and families less brutal, less tragic. That's all she hopes for.

We do agree on a few things. First, we agree that the clients of child welfare systems, whether public systems or private county services like my sister's, are exclusively impoverished or working poor families. Second, we agree that society has abandoned these families to the supposed protection of child welfare. Third, child welfare's response is almost always damage control rather than prevention. Fourth, we agree that the services provided are fragmented and that there is a lack of continuity of care.

My sister, like many caseworkers, is dedicated to the families she serves. To relax from the endless pressure of triage, Katy leads canoeing workshops on the Wolf River in Wisconsin. She uses the analogy of paddling upstream with a strong wind in your face to describe her advocacy for troubled families. I do not believe the "wind" or "racing waters" are fate. At the local level, I believe that caseworkers have been given an impossible dual task that undercuts their effectiveness with families. Caseworkers function as regulators of the poor by virtue of the power they have to remove children from their families, but they also function as caring advocates who want to support families' efforts to find their way to security and independence. On a larger level, I believe that my sister cannot discern "the killers of the dream" because she is too involved with the wounded and dying.

She, along with many of her profession, has been given a job few of us would desire. Caseworkers are like the mythic villagers who lived by a river where one morning they saw a dead body floating by. The villagers fished the body out and gave it a burial, praying for the soul of the corpse. The next day, two bodies were floating down the river, and the villagers again dug graves and held religious services for the deceased. The third day, three bodies. By week's end, there were so many bodies that the villagers had divided into service committees: one to dig graves, one to offer prayers, and one to fish the bodies out of the river. Intensely focused on the tasks designated by the institution they had constructed, the villagers became involved in the functions of caretaking. No one went upstream to see what was killing the people.

This book is an effort to find out why some children and families are expendable and to identify the forces that are killing them. It presents my argument to Katy, and to the future caseworkers, lawyers, and criminal justice workers whom I teach. It is a book for those on the front lines, who see the effects of a social war on children. But it is not for only those in the field. It is for all who care about the fate of children, especially the most vulnerable ones.

In the years that I taught courses on juvenile justice, my students—fed by sociologists' and criminologists' preoccupation with the "delinquency" side of juvenile court—expressed little interest in what happened to the youth and children who passed through the abuse and neglect side of juvenile court. They wanted to know about gang violence. Myriad textbooks treat the topic with sometimes elaborate theories to "explain" gang violence. Yet thousands of children pass through juvenile court into state care each year, and it as if they disappeared into quicksand. There is a presumption that the majority are safe in foster care or residential care. When I suggested that these children's lives under state protection were not safe, I had little data, besides the personal experience of a few child welfare advocates or lawyers, on which to base these claims. Social work research has documented the excessive caseloads and lack of training of caseworkers, as well as the failure of child welfare systems to offer effective family support services, but few books presented the scope of the tragedy of child welfare in America. Only recently have researchers such as Lisbeth Schorr presented alternatives to child welfare's failures.

This book seeks to tell that untold story. Its audience is not only those future caseworkers who will be enveloped in the desperate effort to support children and families in crisis in much the same way that Hans held his finger to a dike threatening to break apart. The book is also intended for anyone concerned about the fate of wards of the state who grow more numerous, more voiceless, and more endangered than any sector of U.S. society. This is the story of the children of the state and of their advocates.

METHOD

I originally intended a book that would be primarily based on the narratives of children who were (or had been) state wards. But I soon learned that children have not yet developed the critical, reflective ability of adults. Children may indeed know, in a deep way, that the child welfare system has injured them, but they can't always articulate what they feel. Moreover, their gratitude to individual caseworkers who have cared about them overwhelms their total experience. Their actions of running away, acting out, and withdrawing "say" much more than the life narrative might.

Furthermore, access to children in care is almost impossible. Child welfare agencies are protected by a legal wall of confidentiality supposedly there to protect children from exploitative interest. Of course, discretion and a rigorous ethic of care are essential in asking wounded children to talk about their lives. However, children have rarely been listened to or had the opportunity to "tell their story."

A final reason that the exclusive subject of my research changed from children in state care was that I discovered another narrative that needed to be told. Parents who lost children to protective services had a story to tell that was critical to my research purposes.

For all these reasons, I chose to interview former state wards who had recently been emancipated, as well as families whose children had been removed by child welfare. I have used these interviews as narratives in the first five chapters. These narratives stand on their own. This book is thus not a primarily ethnographic study of children in care, with historical/political contextualization, but a socio-historical analysis of America's child welfare system with ethnographic and life narrative research that exemplifies the human response to child welfare's practices.

These voices, I believe, imbue this research with an ethical claim and urgency that a critical analysis lacks. These narratives interrogate us: What will we do to stop the systemic maltreatment of children and troubled families? This is the "point" of this research, far more than contributing a comprehensive description of child welfare functions, processes, or policies. It is difficult for most Americans to imagine the devastation wrought by modern inheritors of the "child-saving movement" of the nineteenth century and early twentieth century, or by the conservative defenders of nativist, male-dominated family life. These narratives, told in the context of globalization's spiral of surplus workers, reveal the stories of children whose lives are disposable, as well as child advocates and families who are challenging those practices.

These narratives offer the authority not of experts, but of those who have experienced child welfare's services and interventions. In telling their story, silenced recipients of services confer a different meaning upon their lives and their casework record. Their text deconstructs the official record as well as child welfare's policy canons.

Youth and mothers construct an account of their lives that was not developed by academics, psychologists, or doctors in policy centers or offices. Their stories were produced and interpreted, by them, in their homes or in restaurants. These are accounts of multi-foster care placements, of survivors of psychiatric wards or quiet rooms, of the grief that has no name, of the terror of being in a shelter, of broken promises: it is the account of children's spiritual breakdown when life becomes a process of waiting and waiting and waiting. Finally, these texts document the resilience of those who refuse to become "cases," and they reveal the ingenuity of mothers and children who challenge the labyrinth of social services for their survival.

The youths and families I interviewed were—with the exception of a young man in Maine and the mother of a neurologically impaired young woman in Maine—from Illinois, primarily Chicago. I chose Illinois's Cook and Champaign counties because I live in Cook County and have numerous contacts with advocates working in child welfare and, through them, access to families and youth who had been serviced by DCFS or by a private child welfare agency. I also chose Illinois because, as in New York, DCFS is one of the most dysfunctional, overwhelmed, and publicly pilloried of state child welfare systems. In 1989, for example, the American Civil Liberties Union brought a comprehensive class-action suit against DCFS demanding massive changes that have yet to be implemented. Examining one mammoth child welfare system within both a national and global context provides a window into a complex world.

Cook County is also distinctive because, along with New York, it has become nationally known for sensational stories of hideous child deaths at the hands of known abusive parents to whom children were returned by caseworkers. Cook County Public Guardian Patrick Murphy has gained national attention for his virulent criticism of DCFS and private agencies, who in their zeal to reunite families, allow these tragedies. Patrick Murphy's attack on family preservation advocates, in spite of his passionate defense of children, exemplifies the contradictions of a modern day "child saver." The child savers of the late nineteenth and early twentieth centuries upheld a progressive policy of family preservation but practiced "saving" the children of poor, immigrant classes by removing them to institutions or reform schools. Murphy has so despaired of DCFS, and most private contractors' ability to protect children, that he is championing the return to orphanages.

THE INTERVIEWEES

The Public Guardian's office gave me access to numerous case histories of children who had been mistreated by parents, foster caretakers, and DCFS. Additionally, interviews with Public Guardian lawyers and caseworkers (and their arrangements with former wards who expressed a willingness to be interviewed for the purposes of this research) were a rich source of ethnographic material. The Cook County Public Guardian's office is unique in its refusal to guard information.

Another person who linked me to youth workers and former wards was a caseworker who works with drug-exposed infants and HIV-positive infants at Columbus–Maryville Children's Reception Center in Chicago. Columbus–Maryville, affiliated with Catholic Charities, is contracted by DCFS to receive all Cook County children entering state care.

Additionally, I was able to draw from a number of sources: I talked to youth who lived in independent living apartments; a downstate organization, "In the Best Interests of the Child," contacted me after reading a *Chicago Tribune* editorial I wrote about child welfare in Cook County, and through them I was connected with Tammy Daniels, whose sons had been taken by DCFS; Jackie

River and Paul Dennis, a state ward, were contacts I made through friends; Desiree Maurer, who has worked with the Chicago Coalition for the Homeless, is a friend; Seth Donnelly of the Hull House Youth Program provided access to young people in an innovative independent living program; and I interviewed youth formerly affiliated with Association (Settlement) House, the largest Latino child welfare agency in the Midwest. I also interviewed youths from various other venues whose stories challenged and shaped my assumptions but whose narratives are not included herein because many stories duplicate each other. The narratives chosen were for the purposes of providing illustrative texts, not those indicating the most egregious examples of state abuse. Public Guardian investigators had thick files of children's cases that read like horror stories from the Middle Ages. Rather, the narratives that I chose are relatively typical cases. In one or two cases only do the narratives touch on the exceptional.

The interviews were open ended. I told interviewees I considered them "teachers" who had a particular contribution to make by virtue of their experiences with child welfare's processes. I asked them simply to tell their story. I have used pseudonyms for interviewees with the exception of the Daniels family, Jackie River, Paul Dennis, Desiree Maurer, and Prentis Caudill.

In addition to the narratives of former wards, I have included, in Chapters 7–9, the narratives of advocates who work in child welfare. The criterion for the selection process was simply that the professionals interviewed worked *for the interests of children* (rather than a system, court, or agency) as advocates.

After several interviews, common themes emerged from among the professionals that illustrated the collective wisdom of advocates. However, I have let the advocates speak for themselves rather than summarize their reflections because each works within different aspects of child welfare, yet most of their strategies are relatively similar. This is not to suggest a consensus. Certainly the Public Guardian on one side and most of the lawyers and investigators on the other side disagree about family preservation.

I did not interview DCFS officials, but not because I consider them all nonadvocates for children. In fact, Jess McDonald, the director of DCFS, is probably the most progressive of the DCFS directors in years. But public bureaucracies tend to thwart or paralyze reform efforts. Additionally, agency budgets and policies are driven by legislative political interests more than by an agency director. Only those child welfare advocates actively working to transform destructive bureaucratic procedures (or, at least, present alternatives) offer a critique that *may* change practices rather than rearticulate compromised policies of child care and protection.

I have presented two final chapters that offer examples of innovative programs, applied at both local and state levels, exemplifying the vanguard initiatives of reformers who affirm that programs of care must be preventive, results driven, community based, and affirming of families' strengths rather than deficits, and believe that plans for services must be made *with,* not *for,* families. Finally, the last chapter presents the story of a depressed and fragmented neighborhood region that has reinvented itself through a courageous initiative of diverse community residents in partnership with supportive foundation outsiders and academics who endorsed the notion that poor people, not experts, know how to solve their own problems and rebuild shattered communities.

CHAPTER OVERVIEWS

The book has been divided into two sections: Part One (Chapters 1–5) is an analysis of America's child welfare system that includes a historical analysis of child welfare; Part Two (Chapters 6–11) is an analysis that uses Illinois, and in particular Chicago's Cook County child welfare system, as a case study that employs the narratives of child welfare advocates to reveal the system's dysfunction.

Chapter 1 identifies child welfare as a regulatory system with policy commitments to family preservation but a practice of family disruption. Chapter 2 reveals the link between charges of neglect and family poverty. Chapter 3 links a hidden economic trend of job expendability to child welfare's role as "warehouse" managers for the troubled children of former semiskilled and unskilled workers. Chapter 4 examines child welfare's regulatory role in the nineteenth century, when private charity agencies labeled the "cruelty police," such as the Societies for the Prevention of Cruelty to Children (SPCC), sought to rescue beggar and vagabond children from the "dangerous classes."

Chapter 5 highlights the development of the "child-saver" movement in the Progressive era, the historical impact of differential (class) entitlements of the Social Security Act of 1935, and the 1960s discovery of the "battered child syndrome." Chapters 6–9 present Chicago as a case study of child welfare's practices in the late twentieth century. These chapters present the narratives of child welfare advocates, reflecting, in their own words, on their reform efforts within the specific arena of their advocacy.

Chapter 10 claims that a strategy of community restoration as a component of child welfare practice moves beyond preventive measures toward transformation of the conditions that cause poverty and the social disruption of childhood and family life. The community is presented as the caretaker and as an extension of family life as well as the producer of identity, authority, belonging, and meaning. Chapters 10 and 11 both offer numerous community-based youth development and child welfare models of alternative care in the United States as well as a nationally successful community-based child welfare reform initiative in New Zealand.

In addition to the story of the resurrection of the Dudley neighborhood area bordering Roxbury in Boston, Chapter 11 presents, perhaps, an unusual ending for a book such as this—it is the story of the remarkable experiment of one child welfare advocate, Dr. Janusz Korczak, who created a children's community in Poland just before World War II. Out of Korczak's understanding of community arose a solidarity with children. He rejected the prevailing model of charity and instead developed a model of "accompaniment" of children that was liberating. And while Korczak was unable to prevent violence against those considered to be socially disposable, his story stands as an example to history of one man's extraordinary commitment to accompaniment that was stronger even than death.

NOTE

1. Nora Gustavsson and Elizabeth Segal, *Critical Issues in Child Welfare* (Thousand Oaks, CA: Sage, 1994): 94.

PART I

Whose Family Values?
Whose Best Interests?

1

❀

Who Is Saved?

An American child is reported abused or neglected every 11 seconds; is born into poverty every 32 seconds; is born to a teen-age mother every 62 seconds; is arrested for a violent crime every four minutes; and is killed by guns every two hours.[1]

MARIAN WRIGHT EDELMAN

The system is broken and needs to be fixed, but no one has the political will to do it....What possible good does it do to call for the death penalty for the mother, string up the judge and hang the caseworker?[2]

GAIL NAYOWITH, EXECUTIVE DIRECTOR,
CITIZEN'S COMMITTEE FOR CHILDREN IN NEW YORK

first met Prentis in a homeless shelter in Maine. He was 18, lanky and lithe. His body had the muscled grace of a tennis player. His brown eyes were wistful. He told goofy jokes like any teenager, but when he talked about what children suffer, he became old and philosophical. He was a kid from rural Maine and Kentucky whose mother was a welfare recipient. He'd been raped since he was six by a stepfather who was also his stepbrother.

However, he had fists, and the ferocity of a survivor. Prentis was a local lightweight boxing star. Although he danced when he fought, his blows were hammers. His physical helplessness was a memory that he slammed away with each blow. An opponent could weave and bob, but not escape.

His soulfulness found expression, too. He was a poet. For Prentis, imagination was holy, and language gave his spirit a way to be present in the world solely on his terms, with his fragile, powerful, and mysterious words. He published two books of poetry: *Gather Me No Stones* and *Such Darkness,* both after he finished high school.

His voice fell to a whisper, and his long, knotty fingers trembled when he told me of being sodomized, or beaten if he objected, and of his mother's refusal to believe him. When he was eight years old he told his twelve-year-old sister, Lois, that he couldn't take any more, that he wanted to die. The child took her brother into her arms, cradling him like an infant, and promised him that he would always be loved and that the suffering and abuse would end. In spite of his shame, in spite of a helplessness burned like a "Born to Die" tattoo on his spirit, Prentis trusted that promise. It was, he says, what saved him.

The betrayal that unraveled him was not caused by his abusive parents. It wasn't even personal, really. It was the common practice of child welfare protective services: separation of siblings. For many abused children, such separation is like a death. When child welfare services removed Prentis and Lois from their home after Lois attempted suicide, they assured the children that they would stay together.

However, they were separated. She was sent to a foster home, he to a treatment center. Prentis was heartbroken. The group treatment center staff promised him that Lois could visit. One of his poems, "And They Had to Do It," reads: "We, me and my childhood…waiting for scientists to analyze us for 13 years…grew violent when my love, dimm, dimm with a blanket over the cage so we could still hear my sister's cries."[3] A year passed, and he pleaded again. For his Christmas wish list he wrote down the only gift he wanted: to see his sister. But it wasn't granted. A phone call was allowed, nothing more. When the psychiatrist at the treatment center in Ohio asked about his fears, longings, and worries, he'd repeat again and again, "If you let me see Lois, I'll be OK. Don't you get it? I want to see my sister. She is everything to me."[4]

Confronted with the power of professionals at the treatment center, especially facing the authority of the psychiatrist, Prentis was seemingly powerless. He had been socialized to social welfare culture, with its myriad professionals, very early on. After his mother was left with five children, she claimed he was "mental" in order to get SSI payments from Kentucky public assistance. The psychiatrist who examined him said he was normal, and payments were refused.

He remembered the questions, though, and his fear. Later, as a ward of the state, he learned to use diagnosis on his own terms. He was labeled mentally retarded, which suited him, because he thought it ensured that he wouldn't be returned home. Also, little was expected of him in the various treatment programs.

When he was finally adopted by a minister's family and entered high school in Maine, he was placed in a special education class for slower learners. After a few months an English teacher reviewed his records but didn't accept the retarded diagnosis. She argued and cajoled administrators into giving him a chance in regular classes. That's when Prentis began to write poetry and also to act in school dramas. Prentis Caudill was one of his teacher's bright and deeply thoughtful students. (For Prentis's account of his childhood, see pp. 33–37.)

What are the stories of dependent children? How does the story of their lives subvert the protective service "narrative of care"? What are their forms of resistance that enable them to survive? Unlike peasant cultures, in which collective practices of community building serve as the basis of cultural identity and resistance, children in the U.S. child welfare system must broker their survival individually, often facing the colossus of a state bureaucracy, "homes" and guardians they did not choose, their own family's tragedies, and regulations that silence them.

These are the children of the state: sassy and sullen, silent and lost, in your face loud or speaking barely above a whisper. They are troubled and difficult. Sometimes a parent's betrayal or the state's betrayal by removing them from a family they love drives them to traumatic stress so deep that they seem, or are, unreachable. They are children whose human development depends on their ability to transform individual or social processes that reinforce their victimhood. To become whole, dependent children must reinvent themselves. And they must accomplish this within a child welfare system that penalizes initiative and rewards compliance. How do they make it through?

Developmental psychologists tell us that maltreated children can heal if there is one person who is crazy about them. Sometimes it's an aunt, a grandmother, an uncle, a teacher, a caseworker, a coach. For eight-year-old Prentis Caudill, it was his twelve-year-old sister. Thousands of children have caseworkers, foster care parents, public guardians, group workers, and psychologists who care about them. But the regulatory nature of a child welfare bureaucracy shapes the relationships of all its constituencies—workers, children, and families. In spite of the caring or advocacy of individual child welfare workers, or even private agencies, child welfare regulatory procedures circumvent support services that keep children in their homes or in foster homes where somebody "is crazy about them."

Each child welfare worker, from abuse hotline complaint takers to intake workers to investigators, performs a different function. The fragmentation produced by this specialization precludes any illusion about the nurturing or supportive role played by agency social workers. Not only do vulnerable children enter a system that will fail to protect them; their damaged sense of worth will actually be reinforced. Yet it is inaccurate to blame caseworkers. Rather, the work structure of child welfare systematically thwarts intensive, holistic, collaborative interaction with and support for troubled children and families. Frontline workers—caseworkers—are mandated to spend endless hours in court, provide cartons of paperwork, and function as investigators with the power to remove children from their families.

As it is, the child is special to no one. After the first or second placement in a foster home, youngsters see to it that no one can come close enough to hurt them again. Caught in the undertow of legal and institutional regulations, caseworkers also learn to cut loose quickly for their own sake and for the sake of children they know they cannot maintain bonds with. Collaborative team approaches that allow caseworkers to work in a supportive, sustained, holistic manner with a troubled family are structurally impossible as public child welfare systems are currently organized. Protective services, which are essentially investigations, substantiation of charges, and removal of children from their homes into placements, is the procedural reality of public child welfare. Disruption, not permanency, is the functional process that shapes legal and social service outcomes for maltreated children.

It is true that removal of children from a foster home is often because children "disrupt"—that is, they act out, resist, or run away so that the exasperated foster family tells the caseworker to remove them. However, such behavior is usually a child's effort to return to a home that the state has deemed abusive or neglectful without consulting the child or the family. Disruption is primarily an act of resistance, even though its consequences may be painful for all involved with the life of the child.

There is an alternative to removal of children from their homes and placement in foster care homes: family preservation. Intensive family preservation services focus on shoring up the entire family rather than focusing on the maltreated child. The process of supporting the family is more conducive to a healing outcome than are the services themselves. At its best, the family preservation process creates a plan of intensive individualized services that is made *with*—not *for*—the troubled family and can include friends, relatives, or community members.

For ninety years the stated policy objective of child welfare has been family preservation. The most current federal reiteration of that policy was made legally binding in 1980, when the federal Adoption Assistance and Child Welfare Act was passed. But the practice of family preservation is effectively practiced only in a minority of states. The contradiction between *policies* of family preservation and *practices* of child removal is the Gordian knot that has tangled America's child welfare system from its inception.

It is necessary to explore that conflicted history—and its current expressions—in order to explain today's child welfare crisis. Additionally, I present examples of innovations and community initiatives beyond the minimal standards of family preservation that are rebuilding shattered communities through an inclusive, democratic decision-making process that is in the control of neighborhood residents and social service residents.

CONFLICTS BETWEEN
POLICIES AND PRACTICES

According to the National Committee to Prevent Child Abuse, one million of the three million reported cases of child abuse or neglect in 1993 were substantiated. In that same year, close to half a million (464,000) children were under the care of child welfare in foster homes, group homes, or residential treatment centers.[5] The majority of children removed from their homes were taken because of neglect. According to a 1991 U.S. Committee on Ways and Means report, the majority of children in foster care come from families supported by Aid to Families with Dependent Children (AFDC), and 46 percent of the foster care population are minority children.[6] The majority of these families were headed by single mothers.

Some states, such as Michigan, Washington, Utah, and Alabama, have made both the policy and practice of family preservation unified. These states have developed support services to keep families together and reunite children with their families, thereby reducing their foster care caseloads. In spite of these encouraging examples, a full eight years after the watershed Adoption Assistance and Child Welfare Act there was "confusion among the states as to what constituted literal compliance with the act.... Such federal oversight as there was, was eccentric and entirely superficial, relying on what the agencies wrote in the case record."[7]

In spite of a federally mandated policy of family preservation, the removal of children from their families has increased. For example, in Illinois the caseload of the Department of Children and Family Services (DCFS) was 8,000 in 1965 but 45,000 by 1994.[8] Policy and practice are in contradiction. Child welfare has two policy objectives—prevention of child abuse and support to preserve families intact—that have been stated objectives since their declaration in the first White House Conference on Children in 1909.[9] But in the more than ninety years since, the practice has been state intervention and removal of children.

A myriad of issues and forces have come to bear on the objective of family preservation, to such a degree that this objective has been almost transformed into the opposite. Those social forces determine the fate of a child taken into custody by the state far more than do policy intentions. The forces include the following:

- Expansion of Child Protective Services (CPS)

Public child welfare bureaucracies' work is dominated by child abuse and neglect investigations that function to fiscally justify an expanding child welfare system, yet the increased funding has done little to service families. Rather, foster care populations in many states have exploded, and more caseworkers and supervisors have been hired to remove more and more children. For example, according to Natalie Pardo, "Illinois, New York and California show a disproportional growth in urban foster care."[10]

■   Child Welfare Bureaucracies' Self-Serving Mission

Work is structured toward more punitive, investigative, and child removal procedures because doing so is politically and fiscally expedient for bureaucratic survival. Agency work culture, which is centralized and hierarchical, is so alienating that caseworker morale is low and worker turnover is high.

■   Racial and Class Prejudice

One basic decision of the child welfare system is whether a child is being intentionally neglected by parents or whether the family is living in such poverty that they are doing the best they can under the circumstances. Judging that situation can unleash the forces of racial and middle-class prejudice. Too often it is not the actual family that is being "saved" but the ideal of the white middle-class nuclear family. When families living in poverty do not conform to that standard, especially families of color or families headed by single mothers, then they do not "deserve" preservation.

■   Children as Possessions or *In Loco Parentis*

The state simply does not ask the children for their preferences. Children are considered possessions of their parents and then the state. Children are systematically excluded from any long- or short-term plan for their lives. Prentis's life exemplifies this situation. He knew what he needed, but no one asked. When he explained, no one listened.

■   Fragmented Services and Lack of Continuity of Care

Child welfare has become a system of short fixes, emergency plans that, for the children, turn into boomerang journeys from shelter to foster family to shelter to another foster family. Children are "informed" about changes minutes or hours before they take place. Children never feel wanted, never feel "home."

■   Federal Funding Distortions

The public and private agencies that carry out child welfare policy depend upon federal funds. There is federal money to support foster care but not adequate funds available for family preservation such as "wrap-around" services (coordinated, comprehensive, child/family/agency collaborated arrangements) or sufficient support for relatives willing to take the children.

■   Reactionary Myths About Welfare

The social welfare system could support and enhance the child welfare system. The New Right in this country has unleashed an old mythology about welfare recipients that has distorted the truth and led to policy changes that will severely damage millions of children. Teen mothers are stigmatized, and "illegitimacy" has again become a weapon to blame the victims and make them ineligible for assistance.

■   Mother Blaming

Women as mothers are the targets of attacks by "family values" standard bearers. Both the courts and child welfare hold mothers responsible for any fate that befalls their children. Whether the mother herself is a victim of abuse is rarely a consideration in removing children from abusive situations. If a child is sexually abused by the mother's male partner, the mother is usually blamed for not stopping the abuse, whether she knew about it or not.

■ Shattered and Atomized Communities

Extended family support systems and neighborhood and community institutions have all but disappeared as a result of economic and social transformations occurring as the century draws to a close. If child welfare does bring services to the community, local community councils are rarely the decision makers. Rather, they function in delegated and advisory roles.

Neglect Versus Poverty

The director of California's child welfare system, Peter Dirge, links neglect to poverty. When Aid to Families with Dependent Children (AFDC) was cut 6 percent in 1992, Dirge says that "child abuse and neglect immediately rose. Families get caught in a downward spiral: first their utilities are cut off so they can't keep the baby bottles cold. Then they get behind in the rent and move in with friends or relatives who may have a criminal history. Forty percent of our families cannot find housing. Half can't find day care, so they can't work. Two-thirds have drug problems."[11]

Forcing child welfare programs to distinguish neglect from poverty often requires a class action suit. In order to stop Illinois' Department of Children and Family Services (DCFS) from removing children from impoverished families on charges of neglect, the Legal Assistance Foundation of Chicago had to file a federal class action suit against DCFS on behalf of James Norman, a widower raising two children. When DCFS took Norman's ten- and twelve-year-old daughters (because of a hotline tip that they were wandering through the neighborhood begging and that they were left alone too often by their father), the Normans were a family just getting by in a one-bedroom apartment. After the state took the girls, Norman lost his public assistance of $96 a month and his Social Security dependent payments of $200 a month. Without this meager assistance he lost his insurance and his job. After that, he lost his apartment. Still, he was willing to fight DCFS for his children.[12]

In 1991 James Norman won the right to be reunited with his girls. DCFS settled the case, agreeing to provide housing and cash assistance to poor families. This was a small victory for Chicago's poor, but it was too late for James Norman, who died one week before being reunited with his children, four years after the state took them from him.[13]

If some children are endangered by removal from their homes, others are endangered by remaining in them. An "epidemic" of child abuse reports has so flooded protective services that casework has become unending investigative-surveillance-demanding procedures that prevent workers from trusting their intuitions or judgment. An "at-risk" child might never be identified by an overwhelmed caseworker. Or, even when a worker knows a child may be in danger, the worker is forced to make triage decisions on which endangered child will receive help.

Child welfare workers are caught between the role of being sympathetic supporters of vulnerable families on the one hand and state-mandated investigators who can legally charge parents and remove children from their homes on the other. Historically, this dual, inherently contradictory function of support and enforcement intervention has been America's child welfare practice.[14] It is, in fact, this dual role that reflects the nation's ambivalent "charity and punishment" attitude toward poor families. The poor and dependent are to be regulated. Their children are to be saved.

Hard Decisions for Everyone

It is not just caseworkers who have to make heartrending decisions about the fate of children; so must their mothers. Special education teacher Carol Montgomery Fate condemns conditions that compromise a mother's protection of her child from sexual abuse: "In situations I've been involved with, the parent usually has a logical reason for choosing to ignore or minimize what their child is telling them—such as the abuser is paying the rent and they have nowhere to go. The mother I knew was faced with protecting her children from homelessness or sexual abuse, but not both." Those of us who enjoy a margin of security cannot imagine ever being desperate enough to sacrifice our child's safety. Yet fear of homelessness and fear of an abuser can silence a mother.

LISTENING TO THE SILENCED

There are two primary sources of revelation about America's child welfare system: history and the subjects of that history. The narratives—of youth who have been wards of the state, of mothers and foster mothers, as well as of lawyers, caseworkers, and administrators who are child advocates—are not "proof" of any claim. But listening to these voices in the context of the history of child welfare presents a perspective that has been silenced but that reveals both the human cost of those practices and the continual resistance to those practices that has been carried forth to this day. Conventional history may reveal the social and cultural forces that have shaped the contradiction between child welfare policy and practice, but life narratives allow us to truly understand the consequences for children and their families.

Children are silenced because of Western ideological assumptions about childhood. Under the law of *parens patriae,* children are considered possessions of their biological parents; however, if that right is forfeited through maltreatment as defined by the state, they become the state's property. Since the nineteenth century a notion of protection intended to "save" children has the actual result of silencing them. Children who plead to remain with their families, in contradiction of the child welfare worker's assessment, are ignored.

By the 1990s, "family values" congressional leaders launched major attacks on family preservation policies that "coddled" unwed mothers and drug-addicted mothers who neglected their children. According to Dr. Jan Ereth, the Milwaukee County director of Juvenile Court,

> the 1990's child welfare policies are vengeful. The state seeks to punish poor parents and there's no punishment worse than taking your kids. To the state these families are just resource gobblers. The state says, "We've invested in these children, so we're going to fix them.".... Parents have hope for their children; the state [child welfare system] is an industry.[15]

Child welfare's client families are indistinguishable from the mothers and children who are the targets of congressional campaigns to "end social welfare as we know it." Because of the flawed and fragmented implementation of family preservation policies by overwhelmed and overworked caseworkers, the "family values" politicians have been able to find sensational examples of infants and children united with hideously abusive or murderous parents. Conservatives have been joined by a liberal press that fears a dangerous "underclass" and seeks to discipline it.

Child welfare officials, seeking to dodge public criticism, have tightened regulations. This has led to deeper procedural rigidity rather than open consultation with children and families. According to Louise Armstrong, "to make known publicly the specific reasons you have removed a child from a parent could constitute grounds for libel: could be attacked as false and damaging. Yet the removal of the child in itself—keeping the reason and records entirely secret from the community and sometimes from the parent herself—is perfectly correct."[16]

America's child welfare system silences children, families, and caseworkers; moreover—by virtue of its confidentiality code—it silences itself. The confidentiality code intended to protect families and children does the opposite by sealing off public institutions and agencies from public scrutiny. As Armstrong asks, "Can we tolerate a system that operates entirely without public monitor, without review, without checks of any kind? Or can we only tolerate that so long as the system does not bother us, and continues to tell us it's being fixed?"[17]

Who Speaks for the Child's Best Interests?

Those who produce the policies that shape the treatment of children whose young lives have been tragic enough for the state to intervene are legal and sociological professionals who attempt to interpret *the best interests of the child.* "The child's best interest," says Bernadine Dorhn, director of Northwestern University Law Clinic's Children and Family Justice Center, "means how would we treat our own children."[18] This is a rigorous ethical standard, but it is rarely used. Rather, what constitutes the child's best interests depends on your point of view. Conservatives blame the poor for their lack of family values and consider it in the child's best interest to be removed from such a home and cultural environment. Liberals, seeking to save the child and family, consider the best interests of the child to be treatment and counseling and, for the parents, classes in parenting skills. Liberals also support child removal but with an adequate *permanency plan* (a long-term plan as opposed to emergency placement and then multiple foster care homes). Yet, when consulted, families state over and over again that their best interests (and their child's best interests) are housing, day care, jobs, decent schools for their kids, and health care.

For Dr. Jan Ereth, of the Milwaukee County Juvenile Court, there are only two approaches to the child's best interests standard: (1) "saving" the child from the family, or (2) assuming the best place for a child is with the family (with, of course, some exceptions): "The first interpretation assumes that troubled families or women of color with 'illegitimate' kids are too dysfunctional to stay intact as a family—the state must save them.... It's pure paternalism."[19] The second assumption believes that "no one will care more about kids than their parents."[20] According to Ereth, it's "easier to set up a whole institution (at triple the cost) than to pay a parent $28,000 a year to keep their kids in the community."[21]

Not only would it be fiscally cheaper to respond to those concrete needs of families; it would also respond to the best interests of the poor rather than to professional interpreters of their interests. For example, the Norman decision forced the Illinois Department of Children and Family Services to return more than 800 children to their families in 1994, saving the state about $20,000 in annual foster care costs for each family reunited.

If a child does need to be removed from an abusive family, the need for a workable permanency plan that will prevent "foster care drift," in which caseworkers often lose track of a child, is critical. "But there are no plans," says Jan Ereth. "There are no standards for measuring the quantity or quality of services delivered."[22] In states where permanency planning has been adequately implemented, children have been spared the cruelty of languishing in state care from infancy until adolescence. But the implementation of such planning is uneven and thwarted, and the proliferation of new abuse and neglect reports has halted the process. So children drift—babies grow to school age and float through four or five foster placements. Children whose parents consistently abandon them because of crack cocaine habits they can't or won't beat do not tend to want to have their parental rights terminated in order for the children to be adopted. And in other cases, a relapsing mother who could recover with adequate drug rehab support and effective parenting skills support classes loses her children to the state in a situation where they will be separated from their siblings and their mother for their youthful years if not their entire lives.

Intensive family support programs with services the family has identified as needed are frequently not implemented. Categorical services that comply with agency regulations are offered over and over in spite of their failure. A social worker gives an example:

> Parenting classes are a joke. Instead of helpful classes or direct work with parents and the child, the parent is sent to a classroom. There's no criteria for evaluating these classes. Any subcontractor can offer parenting classes. They don't have to present evidence of success.[23]

A long-term plan for a child works only if everyone involved in the child's life takes part (including the child). Such a "front end" process reverses child welfare procedures. "The system is backwards," says Richard Cozzola, program director of Civitas, Loyola University's Child Law Center. "Where we can impact is in the beginning. But as lawyers we were taught the issue is the trial rather than paying attention to the long term plan and bringing in parents to be part of that planning."[24] If child welfare lawyers focus on the trial, child welfare workers focus on policy injunctions. Not only are the child and family silenced by juridical and federal regulations, but child welfare personnel subjugate their best instincts to those procedures. Even good policy, such as family preservation, becomes bad practice if the implementors (a) fail to include those who will be affected by the decisions or (b) subjugate their own initiative and intuition to procedures.

Richard Cozzola tells one story that illustrates the punitive nature of DCFS procedures before the beleaguered Family Preservation mandate was implemented in Illinois. Cozzola worked for the Cabrini Green Legal Aid Clinic in the late 1980s, where he represented a mother from the Cabrini Green housing projects.

Interview: Richard Cozzola
Hanging in a White Neighborhood Could Cost You Your Kids

She wasn't hooked on drugs. She went to a white nightclub where she and her girlfriend were sitting on the steps outside—where they probably "shouldn't" be because it's a white people's place—and they get arrested for theft. They're thrown into Cook County Jail. The mom has left her kids with her mother. Because she doesn't immediately plead guilty, but says she is innocent, she sits in jail for weeks waiting for the case to go to a preliminary hearing. Her mom gets tired of handling these kids after three weeks and turns them over to the police, which then causes a neglect petition to be filed on the mom for leaving the kids.... The mom hears about this and pleads guilty to the crime she didn't commit, according to her.

She gets out and says to DCFS, "I want my kids back."

"No, you neglected them, you left them alone."

She fights very hard for her kids. But [DCFS feels] she's not visiting the children enough.... DCFS has placed them about twenty miles away, and they don't give her bus fare. So then she's cut off public assistance because she doesn't have her children with her. Next she fights with the Chicago Housing Authority (CHA) to keep her apartment.

She's so mad at the system that it's tough to get her to realize that her three kids really need to see her.... Her ten- or eleven-year-old starts doing some sexual acting out in the classroom. So DCFS places him at that wonderful children's spa—the Henry Horner Children's Home—which was, really, a rathole. At that point she has two kids on the farthest Southside, one kid on the farthest Westside, and she lives on the near Northside. She has to visit both sites. Somehow she was able to get two of the kids back.

It turns out the older boy who was acting out sexually had been molested by a babysitter with whom she had left him. So now they place him [downstate] in the Peoria Children's Home, a good four or five hours away, and she has two kids with her. In essence what DCFS was saying is—what we want to see from Mom is we want to see a real big effort to get her kid back—which is why she [should] visit her kid in Peoria. Now she has one kid who is five and one kid under the age of five living with her at home. She goes weekly to therapy sessions with a community mental health person in Cabrini Green, on her own [initiative]. She volunteers at Jenner School, which is where little Dantrell Davis was killed coming from the school. So it's a dangerous school but she's walking kids to and from that school. This is a mom who has a lot going for her.

[Still] DCFS says, "You have to visit this kid in Peoria."

She says, "OK, but I don't have any money."

DCFS says, "We'll give you one bus ticket there."

She says, "I have two kids under the age of five."

DCFS says, "Find somebody to leave them with."

Let's look at this woman's history. The last time she left her kids, it was with her mom, who she should be able to trust, and her mom turned them over to the police. And who was the person before that? The [babysitter] who molested the son. So what's her experience in leaving her children? Not good!

So she tells DCFS, "I have a boyfriend who has a job and for the same amount that it would cost you to send me there and back, we could buy gas to go in his car."

DCFS says, "No, we cannot buy gas for his car. We can only buy you one bus ticket."

I had to go in and make the biggest stink in the world at an administrative case review to get them to give her either the gas money or three bus tickets, which would allow her to visit her kid regularly for three months in order to get the kid back in her home![25]

Why Aren't Children Adopted?

Without an effective long-term plan, children don't stand a chance of being adopted. Less than 3 percent of adoptable children were adopted in Illinois in 1994. According to Dr. Jan Ereth, "of 5,000 children in foster care in Milwaukee County in 1993, only 50 were adopted."[26] Nor is the dismal number of adoptions resulting from the fact that children are reunited with their families in Milwaukee County. "We have 900 new cases per year," says Ereth, "but only 20 percent of the children are united with their families."[27]

To keep a family united, child welfare caseworkers—who are often young and inexperienced because few workers remain in such a stressful job long—must be willing to challenge the judgments of both juvenile judges and assistant public guardians, who invariably opt for removal of children from their homes. To press for adoption, on the other hand, requires endless commitment to a paperwork chase and the stamina to ride out state procedures. It's easier for a caseworker to leave kids in foster care. Caseworkers feel that the kids in foster care are, at least, safe, unlike the many kids who aren't.

But are they safe? Ben Wolf, who is the director of the Children's Initiative for the American Civil Liberties Union, the agency that sued DCFS for abuse and neglect of children in its care, says that the Illinois foster care system is "a laboratory experiment to produce the sexual abuse of children."[28] DCFS is so chaotic that they don't keep tabs on who or where "known sexual attackers" are, says Wolf.[29]

Wolf's indictment is directed less at foster care families' inability to control abuse than at DCFS's inability to monitor its own process. Foster care is topsy-turvy in its effects. It is a system driven by the trough of federal funds available rather than children's needs or the needs of foster families. Federal money pays a portion of the cost of every child placed in foster care. Private child welfare agencies that contract with the state public agency receive funds for every day they keep a child in foster care—and the money ceases if the child is sent home. Although both the private and public child welfare agencies are non-profit, they depend on these subsidies for operational existence. Where is federal reimbursement for keeping children *out* of foster care, for "front end" services that prevent family disruption?

Confronted with intense criticism for "losing" children through chaotic record keeping and foster care drift, New York has decided to cut off private providers' fiscal incentives to keep children in foster care. "If you're an agency now," reported State Commissioner Michael Dowling, "you don't get hurt if you sit around."[30] So New York developed a system of *managed care* (based on the health care model) in which the state pays a flat rate for each child. If the child remains in foster care after the flat rate allotment runs out, the agency receives no more reimbursement. This is a fiscal response, not a moral response, to the tangled fortunes of the 60,000 children under state care in New York. What is the evidence that managed care is anything more than regulated health care replicated for children? At least with managed health care adults can complain if the services provided are not meeting their needs. Children in state care cannot.

New York's managed care innovation, which is being partially adapted by Massachusetts, does not involve family and children input. It is an agency-to-agency fiscal solution. Already New York's Comptroller's Office has revealed that the foster care tracking system is so chaotic that one in five children *in its care* have the wrong address listed.[31] That's almost 12,000 children they can't immediately locate. In fact, New York is being federally investigated for record tampering. How is New York's accountability improved by managed care? New York and Illinois are just two of the troubled child welfare systems that "do not have citizen foster care review."[32]

A 1990 study by Chapin Hall Center for Children states that "actions taken in the interest of protection were often confusing, frightening, and dehumanizing" (see box, p. 26). With the exception of unambiguously abusive homes, how could a family be more harmful than a foster care system that is "confusing, frightening, and dehumanizing" to children? This is not an indictment of foster care parents who are woefully underpaid, undersupported, and unappreciated for the herculean task they take on in nurturing children whose sorrow, rage, and humiliation are raw and painful. Foster mothers, in fact, are

The Chapin Hall Study

A 1990 study that interviewed fifty-nine children in state foster care in Illinois by Chapin Hall Center for Children at the University of Chicago found the following:

- At least 40 percent of the children placed in foster care found that the reasons for placement were confusing.
- Sixty-one percent of the children "reported that they remember being told very little about the reasons for being moved from their former foster homes," and "over 60 percent of the children who had previous placements said they had little or no involvement in the decision to move."
- Although most of the children felt their caseworkers cared about them, one third didn't know why they had a caseworker.

- Forty-one percent of the children didn't know the purpose of the counseling they received, and 44 percent "described it vaguely as helping with problems."
- All but thirteen children thought the way they were removed from their homes or school could have been handled better: "Five children thought the abuser should have been removed instead of them." One quarter of the children who were taken from their schools with police present expressed anger at such humiliation.
- The children thought the foster parents should have been informed of their history before they came into the home.[33]

disciplined if they are too successful in nurturing children. The reason for this, according to the surreal and mechanistic regulation logic that propels child welfare procedures, is that children are *in the process of reunification with their families,* so attachment to the foster mother would disrupt the process. But a child can't wait years to find a home or attachment. If children do learn to protect themselves against the betrayal of their affectional trust, they will be labeled "attachment disordered" and sent to treatment centers.

One reason that child welfare systems fail to make "reasonable efforts" to keep families together is that the federal money for foster care flows like a river. While it is true that the Clinton administration committed billions for family preservation support services in 1993, the program has been so pilloried that it's not clear how long the money will be available. According to Richard Wexler, "The National Center for Youth Law, which favors family preservation efforts, has warned advocates they will have to fight to make sure that the money is not 'captured by politically powerful service providers.'"[34] One innovation, which is subject to the vicissitudes of state legislative decisions, is relative foster care. Although relative foster care "works" better than foster care, the test of its success lies, as with so many reforms, with whether or not there are supportive follow-up services provided to caretaker families. In California, for instance, relative foster care has limited success because the child welfare system places children with overwhelmed relatives and doesn't look back.

THE PROBLEM POSED
BY "FAMILY VALUES"

Child welfare policies seem to be less about protection of children than protection of society from "unruly" or "unfit" populations. Child welfare policies intend to curb or regulate poor families, in particular single mothers who are heads of households. Historically, when "family values" (which is a code for male family norms) are threatened, women tend to be held responsible for the breakdown of the family, and this breakdown is considered a barometer for all social ills, regardless of the economic or social crisis facing the nation. The middle class, white, male definition of *family* remains normative in these crises even while the *degree* of punitive policies is debated between conservatives and liberals.

Family traditionalists have reduced the causes of complex social problems to the breakdown of the family—by which they mean a male-headed nuclear family. Unwed teen mothers are particular targets because they live and act outside of these norms. "Illegitimacy" has been seen as responsible for society's ills, whether the proponents were nineteenth-century agents of the Society for the Prevention of Cruelty to Children (SPCC) or twentieth-century "family values" defenders. *Time* magazine's Nancy Gibbs holds unwed teenage mothers responsible for "a generation of young, pitiless men and boys.... When people ask where all these 16-year-old predators are coming from, one answer is chilling: from 14-year-old mothers."[35] It is teenage mothers, then, who are held primarily responsible for crime, lack of a work ethic, violence, and the rage of the dispossessed male. The assumption is that unless young women are married and hence attached to a male authority figure, their children will become a threat to society.

The link between social welfare (Aid to Families with Dependent Children, or AFDC) and child welfare is made by child welfare policy scholar Douglas Besharov of the American Enterprise Institute: "Today everyone recognizes that dealing with births out of wedlock is the central issue of welfare reform, so much so that the President's [Clinton's] draft plan makes dealing with illegitimacy the No. 1 priority."[36]

These teen mothers are stigmatized as social outlaws who have children in order to live off the government. Yet teens younger than 18 account for only 1 percent of the parents receiving AFDC: "fewer than 50,000 out of 4 million parents receiving AFDC nationwide."[37] Further, there appears to be no correlation between welfare payments and out-of-wedlock childbearing, according to a June 1994 study by 76 economists and social scientists.[38] Another myth implies a lifetime of dependency on AFDC by young mothers when, in fact, studies by the National Longitudinal Study of Youth and the Center for Law and Social Policy found that "40 percent of unmarried teenage mothers leave AFDC within 1 year, and 70 percent leave within 4 years.[39]

A national study links family income and teen pregnancy. The National Longitudinal Study of Youth found that the more family income increases, the more teenage full-term pregnancies decrease: "In fact, 4 out of 10 poor teens became mothers, compared with 1 out of 10 teens in the highest income bracket."[40]

Social welfare for poor mothers and child welfare are inextricably linked, even though policy makers have historically separated these two destinies. Commenting on the claim of the women's movement that "every woman is one man removed from welfare," Louise Armstrong insists that what is also true is that "every child is one father away from foster care."[41]

When mothers' pension laws were passed in 1911, a dispensing system was devised whereby caseworkers evaluated which mothers deserved government assistance and which were undeserving according to the dominant culture's class, gender, and race standards. Social work was invested not only with social investigative power—to declare a mother fit or unfit to receive public assistance—but with legal power to remove a child if the mother was unworthy enough. Although child welfare and social welfare systems became separate, the norms of family fitness and the surveillance/regulatory nature of those two systems have remained the same.

Historically, it has been women who have appealed to state agencies for help against male intra-family violence directed against themselves or their children. According to Linda Gordon, "Throughout eighty years in which there were periods of strong professional disinclination to acknowledge the existence of wife-beating, battered women kept up a remarkably steady level of complaints to child-protection agencies.... In some periods the experts confronted wife-beating and sexual assault, male crimes, while in others they avoided or soft pedaled these crimes and emphasized child neglect, which they made by definition a female crime."[42]

Even in cases of unambiguous male violence against a child, as in incest, the mother is held responsible for not stopping the abuse. If the mother fails to protect her child from incest, both will be punished by the child's removal rather than the removal of the abuser.

Both state child welfare agencies and social welfare (public aid) agencies service the same population, in fact, often the same family. Child welfare and public aid deal with poor women, primarily mothers, and poor children. Parental fitness is essentially about *mother* fitness.

President Clinton was unequivocal in confronting teen-age mothers: "We will say to teenagers: If you have a child out of wedlock, we'll no longer give you a check to set up a separate household."[43] Health and Human Services Secretary Donna Shalala, whether wrongly or naively, views teen pregnancy as the primary cause of problems within the entire social welfare system: "We will never successfully deal with welfare reform until we reduce the amount of teenage pregnancy."[44]

To Be Young, Black, a Mother, and a Ward of the State

Dickens House is a temporary home for teenage mothers and their children, who are all wards of the state of Illinois. The tiny tots' playroom bursts with giggles, squeals, and a swirl of running, twirling toddlers. Some mothers walk babies through the bobbing circles of two- and three-year-olds. In a quiet office away from the children's play, their young mothers speak of their own childhoods. They are somber and leery. Mostly they are sad. Speaking of her own abusive childhood, Angelica says, "I just wanted to get away. I'm not going to let my baby go through what I went through. I want her to have a life without being afraid like I was."[45]

When Donna came into state care, she was twelve. One evening her mother told her to pack her brothers' and sister's bags and go to her grandmother's. But her grandmother couldn't afford to feed them all and sent them back home. It was dark when the children arrived home, but nobody was there. Donna knew her mother was an addict and understood now that her mother had slipped so far she couldn't even deal with her children: "You know she left us outside for four days. And we had a little sister too, and she was hungry and stuff. I finally called the police on the fifth day, and DCFS came and got us."[46]

These teen mothers seem grave. Their babies brighten them up. The young women's attitudes seem to match the findings of studies that show that adolescent mothers may be exercising their best option in bleak circumstances when they latch onto older men who promise them a way out of homes characterized by poverty, violence and rape. Instead of being a mindless effort to cheat the state, these pregnancies are strategies of survival.

Having a baby is both an act of resistance against the violence and suffering they've experienced and an assertion of hope for the future. Melinda's story is an example. I met Melinda in an emergency shelter. She tells a not uncommon story of feeling betrayed by the father who sexually molested her, by a mother who wouldn't believe her, and also by a child welfare system that turned away from her. In all of this, it is her baby who has been her source of hope and impetus to achieve. It is her baby who has given her tragic life purpose and meaning.

Teen Mother's Narrative of Survival
Melinda

I watched my father beat on my mom. There's a lot of times my mother cried on my shoulder because she was scared. All my life I've felt guilty because I wish I could have helped my mother when he was beating her, but I was so young. Finally, my mom broke away and took me and my brother to live with my grandmother. He followed us there. My mom always took him back because he'd sweet talk her.

When I was twelve years old, he [biological father] sexually molested me nine or ten times. When I told Mama, she didn't believe me...kept calling me a liar. Me and my mom never got along after that. One day, I don't know why, she called me on the phone and said she was sorry she didn't believe me at first. Everything was going fine until my father was released from jail. He sweet talked her into letting him come back home. He told her to kick me out.

I was sixteen and my baby was five days old when my father kicked me out of the house at 2 A.M. I had no place to go. My baby and I moved in with my aunt and uncle, but I couldn't stay too long because the baby's father kept coming around and he beat on me. The same way my father beat on my mama. But I broke away from him.

I stayed with my grandmother for two weeks, but I needed a place to stay, so I called DCFS. They said there was nothing they could do because I was under Mama's custody. They said in order to get custody of me and my baby they would need a court order. So they sent me back to my home. My father jumped on me and hit the baby. So I called the police. But the police came and said there wasn't anything they could do unless they saw him do it. So the police took me back to the station, and they called DCFS. But DCFS told them there was nothing they could do. So I finally went to an agency on 80th and Ashland, and they called DCFS and explained my situation. So then DCFS said, "OK, we'll cite her mother and father for child abuse and neglect." So they brought me into the system.

It's hard living in places like this. DCFS, they shift you and move you from place to place. I don't even know where my brothers and sisters are, and they won't tell me. One of my brothers is here in the shelter. My sisters are somewhere in Gary, Indiana, in a foster home, and my little baby brother, he's in another foster home. But we don't know where any of them are at. They won't tell me until I get the facts from my caseworker, but the caseworker is not in her office.

Somebody's got to care for them. I've got my own baby, but when I go into independent living with DCFS—that's when you get your own apartment—I'm going to try and get custody of my brothers and sisters.... It's going to be hard, but I'm a strong black woman and I think I can do it. I been taking care of them since they were little babies, you know. I bathed and fed and clothed them. I done a mother role more than you could say my mother herself.

I feel it's a blessing I have this baby because I feel that God has given me a chance to start my life over with my baby. I don't shun no babies away. I don't believe in no abortions. I just believe in taking care of my responsibilities. You know I would never do my daughter the way I was treated.... If she ever came to me and told me a man touched her in the wrong way I would right off the bat believe her.... I would never take a man over my child; my baby comes first. You know a man is like a bus! They come, they stop, they go. But your baby is yours forever.[47]

Melinda has internalized society's expectation of her to be responsible for children. In her quest to "take care of her responsibilities" she hopes to care for her own child along with her brothers and sisters. If she fails, she will take on the humiliation and guilt reserved for unwed mothers. She has to care for a baby, successfully maneuver independent living arrangements, pass the GED, and find a job to support herself and her baby. She doesn't know yet that child welfare will not allow her siblings to stay with her, even if it were humanly possible for a high school dropout to support five kids alone!

In addition to the social opprobrium heaped upon unwed mothers, one must add the "race card." Can Melinda avoid the circumstances that trapped her mother? These young black mothers are despised by a culture that holds them responsible for social chaos and violence. Confronted with poverty and possible public aid dependency for at least a while, is it any wonder that

Melinda's future could turn sour? What happens when racial exclusion, lack of job opportunity, and the humiliation and frustration of not being able to climb out of the grip of poverty that surrounded her childhood crash in on her? If she turns to drugs or alcohol to numb her pain, she may lose the baby she cherishes, and she may even believe she deserves to lose her.

But Melinda's narrative also expresses resistance to the cultural forces aligned against her. Incredibly, her source of inspiration and hope is a two-month-old baby named Daphne. Contrary to the nightly news and afternoon talk shows, which would sensationalize the tragedy in the above scenario (because it sells), Melinda reminds us that the central characteristic poor black women must rely on is their own fierce determination to create life for themselves and their children in the midst of a war zone. Sitting in a shelter after years of physical and sexual abuse, not knowing where her brothers and sisters have been placed, Melinda understands herself as a "strong black woman" blessed by God, who "has given me a chance to start my life over with my baby."

COMMUNITY AND CULTURE
AS BASIS FOR IDENTITY AND CARE

There is a model of child rearing and child protection that child welfare advocates quote frequently. According to an African proverb, "It takes a whole village to raise a child." Such a notion of childrearing and child healing shifts the social contract between society and children. The community is responsible to each family and each child, and the child is accountable to the community, not just to his or her biological parents. The child's sense of identity and belonging is linked to a people even if biological parents fail or cannot uphold their responsibility. In belonging to a community, children are not, as designated in the *parens patriae* law, the property of their parents, or, if maltreated, they are not relegated to the state.

The notion of children as property presumes a power relation in which the powerful agent, the parent or the state, has a legal, moral, and political right to discern a child's best interest. While all cultures agree that adulthood carries an obligation to teach and care for children, responsibility is different than ownership, which is ultimate power and control over an object or subject.

However, the village community as a child's place of belonging doesn't address postmodern North America, where community has been shattered. How does the state respond to the brokenness and social chaos that mire masses of its people, and the particular burdens borne by its poorest families and communities? To answer this question requires an analysis of the social transformation, equal in magnitude to the Industrial Revolution, that is affecting America at the end of this century. Such an investigation reveals the underlying conditions of deindustrialization that have given rise to urban deterioration, youthful unrest, the potential eruption of poor, immigrant, former working-class communities—in summary, the devastating results of the globalization of the economy and congressional decisions to cut social spending in order to remain competitive in the new world market. Given global restructuring of the economy and government's inability to discipline international corporate power (some would say complicity with corporate power), can child welfare services meet the crisis provoked by increased stresses on the lower-class clientele whom they serve?

CONCLUSION

Children can survive horrifying treatment if there is one person who loves them deeply. Child development experts insist that a consistent, loving nurturer is as critical as shelter, clothes, and food to the child's future development. Yet child welfare cuts bonds and places children in the foster care shuffle intended to find them a "bed," as if that minimum human right "protected" an abused or neglected child.

Rather than helping troubled families stay together, child welfare splits them up through a policy of child removal. The legal standard that justifies this is "the child's best interests." The philosophy which informs decisions is that such families (low-income, single mothers) are unfit and need fixing. Thus, children are removed as a way to discipline a family not upholding traditional family norms, either because of neglect linked to the dissembling effects of poverty or to maltreatment of children linked to stress. In cases where parents are clearly dangerous to children, immediate action is not taken because overwhelmed caseworkers, with impossible caseloads, cannot respond appropriately.

In spite of a historical policy of family preservation, a practice of child removal drives the system. Agencies receive federal funds for placing children in foster care, but reciprocal money is not available for preventative initiatives to build community-based development projects aimed at empowering vulnerable families. Child welfare's policy of "confidentiality" does not protect children but does protect these public bureaucracies from exposure and legal redress. Lower-class children and families, who are the exclusive clients of child welfare, are silenced by the maze of juridical and bureaucratic regulations that they must navigate. "Reforms" change little or nothing because they do not aim at changing bureaucratic work structure and thus agency practice. Reforms remain only policy initiatives with little practical ability to decentralize bureaucracies and work with the strength and healing capacity of families and their communities. In summary, child welfare systems are attempting to "teach" families to be democratic and respectful by using an autocratic model.

Remarkably, some mothers have been able to resist these practices by using state services designed for the survival of their families. Development initiatives that build community in the shattered wastelands of urban desolation challenge punitive regulatory practices which treat families as problems that need to be fixed rather than as resourceful collaborators.

Personal Narrative
Prentis Caudill

Here is a narrative that reveals a spirit strong enough to endure not only an abusive childhood and parental betrayal, but also the state's protective placements in psychiatric units and residential group homes. Prentis describes a treatment process that "makes you feel like you're the one who did the thing that was bad and you're locked in a place you can't get out."

Prentis discovered his creative writing talent only after he left state care and entered a high school in Ellsworth, Maine, where he proved he was not retarded. What this story reveals, however, is that Prentis's imagination was always a powerful resource that allowed him to invent his own healing, often in spite of the therapy he received. Boxing, poetry, and the memory of his sister aided in his healing. With these he reinvented his life, in spite of the "placements" the state assigned. All along, he had Lois, who was family. Yet he was denied that connection over and over in the name of his "best interests."

I was about six years old and we were living in Kentucky when my father left my mother and us four kids. She tried to get disability for us, but she couldn't get SSI. So she saved bus money for us to go see Granny in Maine. When we left Granny's, my half brother who had never lived with us came back with us on the bus. He moved in and everything seemed OK. Then Mom told us he was supposed to be our dad or something, and they started sleeping together. It was weird. He got a job, and we were doing better. Then my mom worked at St. Paul's School as a cook in the cafeteria.

But then my brother [half brother who was his mother's sexual mate] started sleeping with me and being very abusive. He beat me, he beat my mom, he beat everybody except my brother Al who wasn't there, and my oldest brother.

My mother got angry if I left the house. For some odd reason she'd smack me around if I was five minutes late. I mean not just whip me if I was late, but literally beat the hell out of me.

When a friend asked me to their house I never went in. I was always afraid. She was very disciplined. That's what she called it, disciplinary. She tried to drown me once in the bathtub with my brothers because I was messing with my brother's car. Little kids are curious, and I was curious that day.

My sister got tired of this, so she tried to kill herself. She tried often, but this time they came and took her to the hospital. When the state came to take her, my mom told me not to say anything. My brother said not to say anything…that everything would be OK in the long run.

My sister used to take my beatings for me. Like if my mom was hitting me, Lois would just jump in the middle of it and say, "You're not going to hit him anymore." So then she and my mom started fighting. Lois did a lot for me. I told her I was afraid and couldn't stand it anymore, that I couldn't bear what my brother was doing to me. Lois just held me and told me not to worry, that things would get better. So I believed her.

Lois is my mom. Just because a man is born to a woman doesn't make her his mother.… Lois cut her wrist and took a bunch of sleeping pills. My mom was pissed off. My brother rushed her to the hospital, and then she came back. But one time she didn't come back.

The day she went to live with somebody for a little while was the scariest day of my life. To see the person you love walking away. I was begging her, "Please don't leave me." My sister hugged me and told me to stay strong, she'd be back. A little while later they took her to the hospital. They wanted to do an evaluation on me, and that's when my mom and my brother told me not to say anything. When I got in there, I didn't tell them anything. Then I saw my sister. She just hugged me and looked at me for a while. Then she said she had to tell.

"They're going to do it again," she said. Then she told me they had been doing it to her. When she told me that, I got mad, and I told them everything they had done to me. It just pissed me off that they had hurt my sister. So the cops came for my brother.

My mom came and looked at us and said, "You're lying, none of this happened." My own mom telling me none of this happened. That's what made me mad. It's like the one woman who everybody tells you is supposed to be there for you is sitting there denying everything that's true. That makes you so mad, doesn't it?

I was in the hospital for a while. My sister was in the hospital, and she kept coming to see me. I heard how good it would be to be in state custody. I had my thirteenth birthday in there. I remember I got a cake, and that felt weird. I couldn't go outside because I didn't have shoes because they thought I'd run away. Where in the hell was I going to run? It was the only safe place I knew.

I was in the psychiatric hospital for a half year. A lot of times my sister would "go off." I could hear her screaming, and staff would carry her down the hallway.

Everybody would "go off" every few days because they had so much built up they couldn't release and then the staff would piss you off. They just kept working with all the stuff that's in your past. They bring it up, and you can't get out and you can't do anything about it. It makes you feel like you're the one that did the thing that was bad and you're locked in a place you can't get out. They tell you when to go, to eat, to sleep, to get up, and they put

you in a little room where there's nothing, nothing around you. The room is called a "quiet room." You could be in there screaming, and all they would do would be to shove you to one side, walk away, and lock you in. You could bang forever, and no one would come for you.

I felt like I was on trial, but I didn't do anything wrong. All you have to do is act up and they give you drugs. The drugs were nice because they'd calm you down or put you to sleep for days.... They gave me Thyroxine. Sometimes your muscles twitch.

Some of the staff were nice, and my doctor was really nice. Being in there, it's weird. There's no one but you. It's scary, man. I was thinking, "Did I do the right thing?" I felt stupid because I told. Now all of the sudden I lose my sister [who went to stay with a big sister in a foster home]. I lost my sister, my family, I'm in a psychiatric unit, and I'm alone. Then a caseworker told me that the state had custody of me and I was going to a new place.

It was a Protestant home in Ohio. The kids there were constantly fighting. I learned fast if you want something, fight for it, steal it or, you know, whatever it takes. I had already started to learn how to box in the hospital in [Kentucky]. A guy gave me gloves, and I started hitting the bag. I liked it, I felt power. I had never felt power like that before—that I could use the anger inside me. So when I went to the Ohio group home I fought with everybody. They hurt me, and I'd punch them because it was either me or them and it wasn't going to be me.

The kids were always having sex with each other, and I had sex with one of them. I never felt sorry for this; to this day I still love him. He wasn't my lover but my best friend—he was always there for me. He made sure I wasn't alone and that no one bothered me. It wasn't for sexual favors. It was because we cared about each other. It meant something, and that's why we slept to-gether. Staff knew but never said any-thing. I guess they understood.

I started going nuts because I'd been through so much hell in my life. I was fourteen or fifteen, and the staff brought the psychiatrist to see me. They told me I was going to see my sister every freak-ing day, every freaking day. That was a little trick to get me to behave, to coop-erate. It was supposed to be a bargain—they help me, and I do what they want. But it didn't work. I never saw my sister.

Then it was Christmas, and they gave us a wish list to get whatever we wanted. The only thing I put on that paper was to see my sister. And I never got it. That just pissed me off. So every time I got a chance I was always in fights. The one thing I wanted they never gave. So then they put me in CPH, another hospital for kids.

It was a little more free. A guy named Chester would always put the gloves on and box with me. At that point I didn't give a damn. If they'd let me talk to my sister, I'd have [opened up] to the doctor and everybody. I never felt so alone. I felt like a rat in a cage sitting there begging. "Won't you please, please let me see my sister?" They said, "If you're good." So I did whatever they told me.

I finally got to see my sister. I hugged her in my arms, and that was it. It was for real this time because after a while you don't know if something is real or not, you know?

I was a lot crazier by then, than when I first started. The state puts work-ers there who don't care. Every time it's a different social worker. It's crazy. They kept mixing up their story—they'd say, "We're going to try a new thing, we're going to get you back with your family." Then they'd say, "Nope, nope, nope, I'm sorry but you can't see your sister, instead you'll have visitation with your mom." I was saying, "I don't want to see her, only Lois!" Here they are giving you what you don't want,

what got you put in there [in the first place]. They give you what you don't want instead of what you do want, which you're willing to die for. It drives you crazy.

My half brother was put in prison for ten years for child molestation. My mother still didn't believe he did any-thing. By then I'd heard that they'd put my sister in a hospital where she was being mistreated. I heard that girls were raped in there. Now that hospital has been shut down. It was in Kentucky. I don't think they did anything to her body, but they'd tie her down or some-thing, and to me, that is raping my sister.

When a new social worker came to work with me, I spit in his face. I was going to beat the hell out of him [I was so angry about Lois], but the staff came and stopped me. My sister asked them many times, told them what was hap-pening to her; the state ain't worth a damn if that's the way they treat my sister. They denied things were happen-ing to her, but if my sister says some-thing is true, then it's true.

When I was sixteen or seventeen they sent me back home to Kentucky. Eventually I went to live with Lois and her new boyfriend. Then I traveled to Maine, where my mother was going to a Baptist church and trying to get her life together. Then a minister and his wife asked me to stay with them. They started calling me their son, and they took me to school. They proved I was worth something. Mostly, they loved me. Then my father Tom found out he had cancer. He fought it for two years, and he died this June. That's how I came here [to a homeless shelter].

It was weird to see him die. His last days are still in my memory, you know? But you get hardened; you don't let nothing get to you. If someone says they are leaving you just say "Yeah, OK, it was nice to know you." You never re-ally have faith you'll see them again.

I've got a girlfriend I met in class, and I love her deeply. I'm going to

Bangor, and I hope she'll wait for me. Since I was six years old I've waited for boxing, and now that I'm going to Bangor for boxing, it feels weird.

Where it catches you is at night—all this stuff, these years, come crashing through. It grabs you, and there's nothing you can do. The rapes are over with, but in your sleep, you're raped a million times and there's nothing you can do. I wake and think—"You're not dead yet; it's time to survive." When I was [in the group home] I faked that I was mentally retarded, but I never faked being insane. I just wouldn't do homework. I'd act like I just couldn't do it. It was easy—I was afraid if they knew I had my wits [I'd be sent home]. I figured they'd think that was the only place for me.

A year before my father died I started writing down the voices I heard inside. I wrote about everything. I figured that if they won't look at me and listen to my words, that I'll write and leave it where I know people will find it. It surprised me that I could write. I had faith in myself because of Lois. My sister kept me alive all these years because she kept telling me I was worth something. I figured if one person can believe in me, then many can.

It's up to me to change everything. What will the kids I'm going to have do if I don't stay strong for them? That's my faith and hope—to stay strong for other people. Some people are selfish, but I want to share with everybody. Most people don't believe me, but I learned this in the seclusion room. That's where my poetry came from. You just have to pay close attention, and the words will come.

Lois is in Elkridge. If she wanted my life, I'd give it to her—anybody that could go through that hell for me, I could surely give them something back. That's what the world should do, but this world isn't like that. My sister is very proud of me. She tells her friends—

she introduces me to everybody like I'm a celebrity. I love it.

Some people think, well, it's over now. It's not over because now you have to regain what you've lost. I've lost my entire childhood. I lost my teenage years. And now I'm twenty-one, and what have I got? I've got what I have now. I have me. And it's like you're born twenty-one and now you just go on. And it sucks. I don't want to be an abusive father. I want my kids to look at me and say, "God, you know my father is great. He's a good man." I'd do anything to have my kids say that to me. Because when I say I love them I want them to feel my love, not to wear my love. I believe that therapy is good for people. But I don't believe that it works for all people. I don't believe in judges and courts that say that therapy will help you.

Because it didn't help me. All it does is bring it up in your mind and make you mad. So I started my own therapy with myself. [Society] keeps us in place—just the way fables like Mother Goose and Cinderella were supposed to keep people in their place, by keeping people in fear. You want to die, but you don't want to. I'm not afraid of death.

If I meet a kid along the way—there's a kid at work right now that thinks he's not going to make it. He feels all alone. So I turned to him and said, "I'm with you. I understand." I put my hand on his shoulder and said, "How do you feel? Do you want to go get something to drink or eat?" I'll do anything in the world for someone like that because I have been there. I know what they want, or I should have said "what they need" because your wants and needs are different. Everybody needs to be loved. It's not a want. No. Who can survive without love?

I fight every day. I fight for power. Some abused people don't fight, or they fight as abusers. But those who are strong fight every day to break the chains. You have to break your own chains. Sort of like Harriet Tubman. She tried to free all the slaves. I want to free people from themselves. My power isn't through abuse or even through boxing. I know where to draw the line. I never question myself—am I doing this right? I believe my spirit knows where it is going.

Some people ignore their spirit. I listen to mine. Some say their spirit is

God, but mine is a spirit from the grave. I thank my spirit for my creativity.

I try to give kids who are abused my faith because when I was in fourth grade I thought about suicide, but my sister Lois's faith in me held me, saved me. I may be homeless, but I've still got heart, and you're not homeless if you got heart—a place to be.

NOTES

1. Marian Wright Edelman, qtd. in *The State of America's Children Yearbook 1995* (Washington, DC: Children's Defense Fund), 3.

2. Jill Somolowe, "Making the Tough Calls," *Time* (Dec. 11, 1995), 44.

3. Prentis Caudill, *Gather Me No Stones,* (Washington, DC: Federal Department of Education Office of Special Education and Research, 1994), 2.

4. Interview with Prentis Caudill, Aug. 20, 1995.

5. *The State of America's Children Yearbook 1995,* 72.

6. Nora Gustavsson, and Elizabeth Segal, *Critical Issues in Child Welfare* (Thousand Oaks, California: Sage, 1994), 94.

7. Louise Armstrong, *Of "Sluts" and "Bastards": A Feminist Decodes the Child Welfare Debate* (Monroe, Maine: Common Courage Press, 1995), 47.

8. David Reed and Courtney O'Malley, "The Orphanage Debate: Making Sense of Complex Issues" [discussion paper] (Chicago: Children and Family Justice Center, Northwestern University Law School, 1996), 42.

9. Leroy Pelton, *For Reasons of Poverty* (New York: Praeger), 1989.

10. Reed and O'Malley, 42.

11. Peter Dirge, qtd. in Margot Hornblower, "Fixing the System," *Time* (Dec. 11, 1995), 45.

12. Natalie Pardo, "State Neglects Cook County's Poor Kids," *Chicago Reporter* (January 1995), 8.

13. Ibid.

14. Pelton.

15. Interview with Jan Ereth, May 24, 1995.

16. Armstrong, 315.

17. Armstrong, 51.

18. Bernadine Dorhn, "In the Best Interests of the Child" [presentation] (panel of Chicago Humanities Festival, Chicago Art Institute, Nov. 12, 1994).

19. Ereth interview.

20. Ereth interview.

21. Ereth interview.

22. Ereth interview.

23. Interview with Jacqueline Smith, Feb. 6, 1995.

24. Interview with Richard Cozzola, Feb. 15, 1995.

25. Ibid.

26. Ereth interview.

27. Ereth interview.

28. Ben Wolf, qtd. in Richard Wexler, "The Children's Crusade," *The Reader* (Chicago, Mar. 14, 1995), 13.

29. Ibid.

30. "Citizen Review: The Case for Accountability," *The Review of the National Association for Foster Care Reviewers* (Fall 1994).

31. Ibid.

32. Ibid.

33. Penny Johnson, Carol Yoken, and Ron Voss, "Foster Care Placement: The Child's Perspective," *Chapin Hall Center for Children University of Chicago Study* (Chicago: 1990), 7–11, 17–30.

34. Wexler, 13.

35. Nancy Gibbs, "The Vicious Cycle," *Time* (June 20, 1994), 26–27.

36. Ibid.

37. *State of America's Children Yearbook 1995,* 86.

38. Ibid.

39. Ibid.

40. Ibid., 84.

41. Armstrong, 14.

42. Linda Gordon, *Heroes in Their Own Lives* (New York: Viking, 1988), 4, 252.

43. Mike Males, "In Defense of Teen-aged Mothers," *The Progressive* (Aug. 22, 1994), 22.

44. Ibid.

45. Interview with "Angelica," September 1995.

46. Interview with "Donna," September 1995.

47. Interview with "Melinda," October 1995.

2

❀

Poverty's Child

There is [a] hateful attack on programs that benefit youth, brought about by cuts in government spending and the refusal to invest in education, employment programs for underrepresented youth…the assault on youth is happening without the benefit of adequate rights, fair representation, or even public outcry.[1]

HENRY GIROUX

It is not that Washington has done too much, but that it has done too much of the wrong thing.[2]

MICHAEL HARRINGTON

The heat in the South West Youth Center was damp and oppressive where I waited. Hanaan entered with a flowing traditional dress that reached the floor, and her grey chador veiled all but her face. Her son Samir carried a tablecloth and basket packed with a Palestinian meal. "Please eat," she said in Arabic, laying out humus, falafel, pita bread, a salad of cucumber and mint, and kifta. In spite of her years of case work interviews and the ordeal of tense, frightening, and guarded interactions, she has come as a Palestinian to share a meal. After this, she will tell her story. The interview will be on her terms—the terms of hospitality.

Everyone got in on the act. The youth director, a Palestinian who'd helped the family when the DCFS (Department of Children and Family Services) took Hanaan's son Samir and her babies who were $1\frac{1}{2}$ and $2\frac{1}{2}$, translated. An Arab psychologist, who was eventually contracted by DCFS after the kids were taken, came to explain the cultural illiteracy that led to Hanaan's losing her children. The youth director was more direct: "DCFS's treatment is racist." Another Palestinian said that if the Palestinian Youth Agency hadn't supported the family, defended Samir, and fought for his release, the family would have been destroyed: "There's no way Hanaan would have her kids back."

Hanaan's husband, who was a dental technician in Jordan and now works as a bellhop, left her with five children. She lived in a foreign culture, spoke no English, had no job skills, had debts, and had a twelve-year-old son who ran the streets and hung around gang members. He was also a bright kid who was sad that his father had left. Desperate to control him, and close to the breaking point, she gave him an ultimatum about staying in the house after a certain hour. When he defied her, she burned him with a kitchen knife. They took him to the doctor, who reported Hanaan for child abuse.

Perhaps DCFS called the home first. But Hanaan didn't understand English. Samir or his brothers said, "Please, we are OK. Don't come here." As it was, three police officers came to the door. Samir hid. "I won't go," Samir said over and over, until the officers grew tired of it.

> **Samir:** The cops came into my room and beat me up. Then they took me to the station and said I assaulted them even though I had bruises on my arm and neck.

> **Youth Director:** The DCFS investigator who accompanied the police never told the mother why the children were being taken.

> **Hanaan:** I was terrified. I didn't know in this country they could take someone's children away. They put my babies in a shelter for six weeks. I don't have a car or phone, but my friends here at the Youth Center drove me to the appointments.
>
> Once I saw my Fedwa had a bruise from a fall. I told the worker if Fedwa fell in my care she would be taken away. But none of this happens to you.
>
> My little boy was chafed raw because they didn't change him enough.

> **Samir:** I was sent to a foster home, but I ran away twice. It was because I wanted to see my family. My caseworker never would arrange it. Some-

times I'd run home for two or three days. Then they'd come for me.
First my worker would come. Then if I wouldn't go with him, he'd
call the cops.

When I was real mad, I'd run away from Maryville, too. I was at six
places. I was doing good at Maryville, but when I graduated they sent
me to Child Serve, a group home with six kids—I didn't like it. It
took a month to be allowed to go outside for ten minutes.

Youth Director: Hanaan had to take four buses to see Samir at Maryville. It was a five-hour ride. She knows no English. We offered to
drive her. DCFS never provided her with transportation.

Psychologist: At Maryville, Samir was doing well, so in their "wisdom"
instead of sending him to a place like Independent Living with more
independence, they sent him to Child Serve, a place more restrictive
than Maryville.

Hanaan: Nothing could convince them to return Samir. But they said
they'd place my babies with a relative. So we saved money to bring my
sister from Palestine. In the meantime I found distant relatives to take
the children. I went to see them as much as I could. But it was so far
away.

Psychologist: She was so stressed out when she came to see me. No
provisions had been made for her to travel. If she didn't make visits,
DCFS implied she wasn't a good mother.

Hanaan: When I did visit my children, the DCFS worker arrived and
followed me from room to room, saying I couldn't even give the children water to drink. If I brought food, the worker said I was trying to
bribe them to love me.

Psychologist: Both babies were examined in a hospital and showed no
signs of abuse. Still, she could not have them.

Samir: At Maryville, staff punched me if I tried to go out. One guy
busted my lip because I went off on him. Security guards handcuffed
me, and then the cops came. He pressed charges. But I couldn't.
Who'd believe me?

Psychologist: They exaggerated his acting out behavior. This kid is
bright and willing to challenge. They weren't culturally sensitive. His
Arabic was becoming rusty; he was supposed to pray five times a day,
and he wasn't. He was becoming Americanized, and his family didn't
know him.

Youth Director: He wasn't accepted by American culture, and pretty
soon he wouldn't be accepted by Arab culture. That's another reason
we intervened. His worker wanted Samir to adapt to American culture. When he came to visit the family in the neighborhood, all the
neighbors came over. "These people are gypsies," he said.

That started it. We went to Ben Weinberg at Legal Aid to help us get
these kids back. The worker said we were culturally prejudiced. Samir

needed to learn to respect authority, and we were encouraging him to rebel. Actually, we told Samir to do whatever DCFS asked, no matter how ridiculous, in order to get home. He tried. He said he learned in counseling sessions at Child Serve what he "should" say to the therapist.

If he'd stayed there much longer, he would have busted someone or something. He was under a lot of pressure. He missed his mother.

Psychologist: DCFS promised me, as the family psychotherapist, that there would be a family session with all members. The family came. DCFS never showed up for appointments. My goals and DCFS's goals were totally different. I needed to stay objective. DCFS victimized this mother. They constantly said, "If you don't do this, you won't get your kids back."

She went to two different Arabic psychiatrists. Both said she should have her kids back. DCFS wouldn't return them because they said the agency didn't appoint psychiatrists. I *was* appointed by DCFS. She still couldn't get her children back.

Samir: The workers didn't like my family.

Psychologist: When I defended Hanaan, a DCFS worker accused me of being prejudiced because I was an Arab. In court I insisted DCFS was overruling my professional opinion. The DCFS worker said Hanaan was manipulative.

Samir: Those workers lied in court. They said my mother did things she didn't.... Every time I went to court it was my worker's word against me and my family.

Youth Director: Once at a hearing, when it appeared the caseworker was lying, we petitioned the worker to be removed. We had to be diplomatic because if we lost the request, the consequences for Samir were terrible. He'd pay. It's like if you have a dog and tell him to sit, and if he doesn't, you hit him to train him. Samir was like a dog.

Two years ago when he was thinner, you could look at his eyes and see the sorrow. He's so different now.

Psychologist: I'd send reports, but Samir's worker would go to court without having read them and give inaccurate information to the judge. He'd say Samir was behaving negatively and therefore should not be returned home. I explained that as long as he was kept from his home, he'd react negatively. Of course he was negative. When his mother asked if he could be home for the holiday El Eid (when the Ramadan fast is broken), they refused.

Samir: I figured if they wouldn't let me go home I was being punished. So, fuck it, I'm not going to cooperate. I used to smoke when I got nervous. But now I quit. I was so damned frustrated.

I never had one visit without a staff person present. It was half a year before I could visit my mother for one hour. I felt like a victim of DCFS.

I'm OK now. I'm graduating June 15.

Youth Director: This mother did abuse her kid, but it was because she was trying to protect him (from defiantly hanging out with gangs). She overdisciplined a rebellious kid, without the father in the house. They had financial problems, and she just cracked. She also did everything possible to connect with her boy and was thwarted at every step.

Judge Sophia Hall actually listened to counsel when we asked the worker to be removed. We considered it a big victory.

Psychologist: Hanaan lost her babies for a year. When DCFS brought the children back, they told the father, who had returned home, he'd have to leave. Now get this. When they first removed the children, they were going to give them to the father! (He could have them, they said, if he had an adequate place to live.) Later he had to leave. Somebody had to be out of the house no matter what.

Samir: Yeah, then they wanted my older brother to leave because he was over eighteen. You're eighteen—go!

Hanaan: We felt so lost. They never helped us. They'd say go here, go there—this isn't the right report. Your husband has to leave. We paid $1,600 for a flight to get my sister here [to be the relative foster caretaker], but then DCFS said no.

I don't know why we were treated so bad.[3]

Could Samir possibly have been safer with the child protective services than with his family? This is a story about child abuse and abuse of power. It is also a narrative about the power of the state and the power of community solidarity. The Arab community organization (the Youth Center) and the psychologist who advocated for the family's reunification identify the cultural bias of DCFS as the cause of the family's breakup. But there is more. The narrative indirectly reveals the class and gender presumptions that child protection services embody. Would the police and DCFS drag a twelve-year-old out of a white, middle-class home if the father, a professional worker, were home and the neighborhood were watching?

Hanaan appears without power in facing the monolith of caseworkers, lawyers, and judges. Yet she marshals her own rescue team to get her children back. Her son uses good behavior (*I learned what to tell the therapist*) or bad behavior (*I'd just run away*) to exert some control over his life when he seemingly was powerless.

Although both Hanaan and Samir identify the worker who was "a liar and mean" as their nemesis, the community workers and psychologist see the family's treatment as the result of institutional racism. Samir's story, which is representative of a whole sector of families and children in the child welfare system, points to a number of system-induced actions and reactions. First, the state has the power to take children away, especially from families without class power (the legal, political, or economic means to fight back), from immigrant families without cultural or linguistic literacy, and from families headed by women. From the perspective of the privileged, who have the relative assurance that the state will not take their children as long as they have the economic power to buy legal help or to call upon political influence, child welfare protection is about defense of abused children. From the perspective of those without class or racial status, child protection service is about the state's power to take your child away.

In order to keep her child, the mother must marshal forces *outside of the system* because within the system she is virtually powerless. When the community is organized, as in the case of immigrant communities, resources, moral support, and collective power can be marshalled to keep families together.

PROTECTING WOMEN AND CHILDREN
FROM THEMSELVES

No analysis of child protection is precise without identifying the link among poverty, social welfare, and child abuse. Although some argue that child abuse crosses class and race lines, the people whose children the state removes from their homes are almost always the poor.

Why is it, then, that the media links horrifying examples of child abuse to the lives of poor people, immigrants, and people of color as if an "underclass" were distinctively different from the rest of us, somehow more brutal, pathological, and violent? Why is the link a psychological indictment of inadequate mothers rather than an indictment of a system that fosters poverty and stress?

Child abuse has been called an "epidemic." Yet child abuse has been as politically explosive and ideologically useful (as in Newt Gingrich's orphanage solution) today as it was in the 1800s. The history of family violence, as historian Linda Gordon has shown, is as American as apple pie and as politically constructed as motherhood: "Anxieties about family life...have usually expressed socially conservative fears about the increasing power and autonomy of women and children, and the corresponding decline in male, sometimes rendered as fatherly, control of family members...these anxieties have been particularly projected unto lower-class families."[4]

The backlash against women and youth has gained momentum throughout the 1980s and 1990s. Perhaps never before in America's history has a fear of youthful violence and reports of violence against children been such a national preoccupation.

Our children are in danger, and sometimes the very agency assigned to protect children from danger colludes in their abuse. For example, Erik Greene's family did all they could to save a two-year-old from a life-threatening beating, but their constant calls to the Illinois Child Protective Services Hotline of DCFS were considered a nuisance.

When Erik Greene saw the bruises on his four-year-old son during a weekend visitation, he immediately took his son for a medical exam, hired a lawyer, and got an order of protection from a Cook County judge against the boy's mother's boyfriend. That accomplished, the Greenes turned their attention to their son's two-year-old half sister, who, they believed, was also in danger. They inundated the crisis hotline with calls for several months. Their "allegations" were still pending when the two-year-old was shaken so violently that she had bleeding behind her eyes, seizures, and brain swelling:[5]

> "If she gets out, she will probably have to be institutionalized," said Deanna Greene. "From her waist to her ankles, she was covered with bruises.... Our cries to the [Illinois Department of Children and Family Services] were not being heeded. Two families plus friends were trying to call. It wasn't bad enough: 'A few bruises.'"[6]

When the two-year-old's great-aunt Carrie Simpson called for the sixth time in a year, she was told that she would be charged with harassment if she didn't stop making reports.[7] Such a horrifying story evokes a simple but misleading response—find the incompetent crisis worker and fire him, if not bring charges against him. But it wasn't just one worker—several workers received these calls. The calls must "fit" very specific guidelines for abuse and neglect. Sixty hotline social workers with college degrees, two years' experience, and only forty hours of training must field and make judgments on 1,400 calls per day! Imagine the fragmentation of such a process. Imagine the likelihood that cross-referencing would not take place, that children would become "cases." Is the problem hotline caseworkers or a dysfunctional system that fails both children and troubled families? What is it about the work and organizational structure of child welfare systems that produces these tragedies?

Even if we indict this bureaucracy, we can't hold child welfare systems responsible for the social conditions and social permissions that spark intrafamily violence. However, we can hold child welfare responsible for its punitive practices that concentrate on managing family violence rather than preventing it.

CONFRONTING THE CAUSES
OF SOCIAL VIOLENCE

Two keys to transforming violence against children are empowered communities and empowered families. The last two chapters of this book offer examples of organized community and youth development projects that transform conditions which give rise to despair and violence. These self-determining community initiatives do not make the news, nor are they debated on the Congressional floor; rather, the media focus on *consequential* reactions to powerlessness. The media misidentify effects—social chaos, despair, and family violence—as *causal*. For example, the "family values" proponents identify the two "key" causes of violence as predatory African American and, to a lesser extent, Latino males and teen mothers who bear infants out of wedlock. The lack of job opportunities, decent housing, health care, and good education that *causes* social and economic powerlessness is never targeted.

All this is not to deny the real dangers children and youth face as a result of obliteration of communal networks of care and the damage wrought by "reforms," such as those focusing on social welfare, immigration, education, and health care. In each case, the "reform" has reduced government assistance to the poor and dispossessed. As a result of "reforms" that left poor neighborhoods without housing or adequate social services, along with the concurrent loss of manufacturing jobs, the social cohesion of poor neighborhoods has been shattered.

We need to locate an analysis of child welfare within the larger context of a process of technological revolution that is radically altering economic opportunities, social cohesiveness, and the social safety net. The data in the box below illustrate the social dangers children faced in 1994 as globalization of the economy, with its ensuing joblessness, ratcheted the violence level higher and higher.

The international human rights organization Oxfam has called the plight of the world's poor children a silent holocaust.[8] It is in the context of this unacknowledged world and national crisis for children that the exponential increase of maltreatment reports and the flawed response of protective services must be examined. For the maltreated children of destitute families in the United States, the crisis is not only "a silent holocaust"; it is also invisible because most Americans do not see the abject poverty in their midst.

Maltreated children are visible when the six o'clock news reports a baby found in a dumpster or a five-year-old is scalded to death or a two-year-old is so violently shaken that she will have to be institutionalized because of the severity of the damage. We are forced to look. We do not see what happened to the brothers and sisters of the murdered children. Child welfare protective services have them. We want to believe they are safe at last. But are they?

The U.S. Advisory Board on Child Abuse and Neglect found that "the system the nation has devised to respond to child abuse and neglect is failing; there is chronic and multiple organ failure. Indeed, the system itself can at

---

How Dangerous Is America for Poor Children?

Here are the dangers American children face in one twenty-four-hour period:

- 3 children die from child abuse
- 9 children are murdered
- 13 children die from guns
- 30 children are wounded by guns
- 63 babies die before they are one month old
- 101 babies die before their first birthday
- 145 babies are born at a very low birth weight (less than 3.25 pounds)

- 100,000 children are homeless
- 2,868 babies are born into poverty

The U.S. infant mortality rate ranks twenty-second worldwide. The black U.S. infant mortality rate ranks fortieth worldwide below poor nations such as Sri Lanka, Malaysia, Jamaica, and Portugal.

Children's Defense Fund and UNICEF[9]

times be abusive to children…. Not only is child abuse wrong, but the nation's lack of an effective response to it is also wrong. Neither can be tolerated. Together they constitute a moral disaster."[10]

The advisory board does not simply wring its hands, blame violent, pathological parents, and then absolve government and the rest of us. The board addresses fundamental causes of maltreatment and in so doing implicitly link maltreatment to poverty: "When parents and caretakers have the psychological capacity to care for their children adequately but lack the economic resources to do so, society itself is derelict when it fails to provide assistance."[11]

Increased Reports of Abuse
or Increased Reports of Neglect?

Most reports of child abuse and neglect appear to be about beaten or raped children because of the media notoriety given to abuse cases. However, the majority of reports are about neglect. According to a national incidence study on abuse and neglect, the rate of abuse for families with incomes below $15,000 was 4.5 times higher than the norm, and the rate of neglect was nine times greater. Neglect is a finding linked to poverty.[12] For example, failure to get proper immunizations for one's child and inadequate hygiene, nutrition, or clothing are listed as criteria for neglect charges and subsequent loss of one's children. Only the parent who has never lacked bus fare, insurance, or money for healthy food can assume that any parent would choose such helplessness and the resulting deprivation for the child. Denise Plunkett, a social worker in charge of infants who are state wards at Chicago's Columbus–Maryville Children's Reception Center, says, "The finding *neglect* on a mother's part is just another word for impoverished. Amongst the other terrors a poor family faces, the state could take your kid."[13]

Increased reports, though primarily neglect complaints, do serve more than a class and cultural bias. These growing numbers justify child welfare's bureaucratic existence.

PUBLIC BUREAUCRACY: HOW TO SUCCEED
BY SYSTEMATICALLY FAILING

John Hagedorn, who spent $2\frac{1}{2}$ years attempting to reform Milwaukee's child welfare system, claims that a system as dysfunctional as child welfare would not have survived without having created a powerful bureaucracy capable of fending off attacks from critics and guaranteeing its survival in spite of scandalous failures:

> The expansion of social services in the 1970s had little correlation to improved services to children and their families. Rather the chief beneficiaries of increased social service spending have been urban social service

bureaucracies, who have used the funds to adapt to a punitive climate, expanding their capacity to investigate poor families and to remove children from their homes.[14]

Child welfare's role as regulator of the poor has not been uncontested. In the insurgent 1960s, welfare reform activists and community organizers developed community-based programs that provided support to families in depressed urban communities. However, the community-based model did not survive. This situation was not due simply to child welfare's political and institutional access to public funds as opposed to a local community's access. Child welfare's bureaucratic solidity, growing since the 1930s, had created an institution whose primary mission became its own survival. The centralized institutional model triumphed over the decentralized model of community-based initiatives. Community and family needs did not, and would not, supersede the bureaucracy's existence.[15]

The old retort that "if we don't survive, there will be no institution to continue doing good work" justified strategies that expanded child welfare bureaucracies. According to Hagedorn, "It's simply too risky for bureaucrats to admit that their agency may not be 'doing good.' The erosion of that myth may lead someone to investigate them or even propose cutting their budgets."[16]

Hagedorn explains child welfare's ability to survive while consistently failing at its stated policy of family support by examining the system's organizational work structure over time. From its inception in the Progressive era, child welfare mirrored the industrial work structure that was hierarchal in command and job segmented in terms of labor. By the 1930s, the organization of social work in both child welfare and social welfare followed the scientific management principles of Taylorism, further dividing caseworkers' jobs into specialized investigative and service tasks. The result was not the anticipated efficiency but fragmentation of services and expanded management (supervisory jobs). Although in the 1980s corporations' drive for profits in a globalized market would adopt new, team-managed organizational forms to match the complex and fluid tasks required by the technological revolution, child welfare bureaucracies remained centralized, hierarchal organizations: "These structures were not functional for preserving families but were well suited to carry out specialized court related tasks to punish the 'undeserving poor.'"[17]

The Numbers Game

Data can be used to justify increased organizational expansion. One key to analyzing the prevalence of child abuse and neglect is to distinguish between reports of abuse and neglect and *substantiated* reports. There's a big difference. But even that difference does not clarify the high incidence of substantiated "neglect." A finding of neglect, as cited earlier, is determined through the class and race lens of a public bureaucracy.

The National Committee for the Prevention of Child Abuse indicates that 3.1 million cases of child abuse and neglect were reported in 1994.[18] Between 1976 and 1987, reports increased by over 200 percent[19] and some researchers estimate the increase since 1987 as being up to 300 percent. Disagreement about the extent of child abuse continues among child welfare scholars. The Family Research Council claims that only 60 percent of the reports are substantiated and that child protective services have a hair-trigger response.[20] But David Finklehor, co-director of the Family Research Laboratory at the University of New Hampshire, cites the National Incidence Study of Child Abuse, which showed a 53 percent increase in substantiation of reports in 1986. Moreover, even where reports are unsubstantiated, 25 percent will become substantiated within a four-year period.[21]

This issue is not simply a debate about numbers. It is politically complex. A critique of inflated statistics was applied to women's claims of increased incidences of rape and domestic violence in the 1970s. These "increases," researchers claimed, resulted from heightened public awareness due to the "discovery" of a hidden social problem. Such a conclusion carried the fatalistic and cynical implication that society need not be alarmed, because women had always been raped or physically abused.

According to Richard Wexler, however, increased reports of child abuse and neglect have the opposite effect, of deflating social response to a problem. The child abuse "epidemic" is a continuation of the nineteenth-century child saver campaign, which targeted the impoverished as the morally damaged social element that needed to be saved. The socially manufactured crisis of child neglect and abuse permits state intervention into the lives of the poor and legitimates child welfare at a time of increased scrutiny of child and family welfare systems.[22]

What Needs "Fixing"?

Child savers (liberals) want to "fix" poor families, conservatives want to punish families (in order to "fix" America's moral decline), radical reformers within public agencies (a distinct but authoritative voice) want to "fix" child welfare, and social transformers want to rebuild poor communities (to "fix" the social and economic conditions that spawn poverty and powerlessness). Models of community and youth development (described in Chapters 10 and 11) depend on help from social services in order to move families toward community programs that lead to self-determination and social autonomy. If that is to happen, child welfare reform efforts initiated from within child welfare bureaucracies are critical—both those that are effective and those that fail. The latter, perhaps, is a more important focus than the former because failed reforms are often the ones that risk structural change—the key in revamping, or even just altering, entrenched public agencies.

It is for this reason that the reform lessons learned by sociologist and criminologist John Hagedorn and his team of reformers are so critical. Hagedorn is sure that his $2\frac{1}{2}$-year leadership of the Milwaukee County Youth Initiative "ended in failure...Milwaukee's public remained more concerned with punishing abusive parents than restructuring social services.... The punitive national mood continued to push bureaucrats to emphasize investigating the

poor and taking their children away. It would be a stretch to say that we suc-
ceeded in 'making a difference' to the children of Milwaukee."[23] But the lessons
learned are valuable maps that chart a labyrinth few have navigated so far before the gates of the bureaucracy slammed down. Whereas independent private agencies have piloted community-based family preservation programs,
structural reform of public child welfare systems leading to those outcomes has
rarely even been tried. "Reforms," as we shall see, are not only common; they
are also part of bureaucratic strategies to fend off scrutiny, allay public criticism, and secure increased legislative funding.

Hagedorn identifies two strategic needs for real—not symbolic—reform
of social services to take place: change in the core work of front-line workers
and support for decentralized community-based and community-controlled
family support service systems. To accomplish this, the Youth Initiative de-
signers created collaborative child welfare teams trained in all aspects of service provision—generalists rather than specialists—who worked closely with
community councils to support and preserve families in need. Two urban areas
were selected for the pilot projects. In addition to strengthening the social service centers in these poor neighborhoods, the child welfare teams invited other
public agencies—health care and schools—to collaborate in a team approach
to the community.

The costs of family preservation, based on an adaptation of the highly successful Homebuilders model of Seattle, are cheaper than either foster care or
costly residential treatment. Community-based initiatives meant that money
would be diverted from the pricey traditional child welfare service provision
budgets to community service providers. The liberal director of Milwaukee's
Human Services was willing to divert $1.6 million earmarked for the "war on
drugs" to these pilots, but he was unwilling to tap the $50 million budget for
traditional service provisions. Beyond that, the Youth Initiative was opposed
by "old boy" bureaucrats who felt that the pilots drew staff away from needed
investigatory and court work, as well as by the union representing social workers and middle managers.

The bureaucrats' instinctive resistance to the community-based family preservation teams was an intuitive reaction to what would have become a restructured child welfare social service system. It is one thing to "allow" a family
preservation unit or, more often, a philosophy of family preservation, but it is
quite another to link family preservation teams to daily collaborative work in
neighborhoods. Community-based family preservation teams subvert centralization, hierarchal decision making, job segmentation, service fragmentation,
and child removal policies. Moving teams of workers into "outstations"—
with the intention of using collective wisdom and creativity to collaboratively
provide integrated services—would reorder agency work structures. Shifting
to community-based family preservation significantly alters the core tasks of
caseworkers, thus reorganizing job structure and agency culture.

This *action* strategy turns most organizational theory—which is focused on
goals—on its head. Hagedorn's intent was to subvert bureaucracy's ability to
co-opt reform initiatives by absorbing energy in endless planning, proposal

writing, and internal struggles over goals, language, and budgets before an action plan is even tried. When the "compromise" plan is finally applied, it is invariably an "add-on" program that leaves core work assignments and hierarchal, centralized structures unaffected. However, the "reform" presents to critics and disaffected staff the illusion of change.

More critical than learning that bureaucrats (predictably) blocked the Youth Initiative is to learn about the mistakes made by Hagedorn's reform team. For example, although the community representative councils included local residents, too often social service families were not members of the councils. Nor was it clear that the councils had actual, rather than advisory, decision-making power. And perhaps most critically, Hagedorn says that "one of our major weaknesses was that while we had support from both the community and many social workers and administrators, we never figured out how to involve youth or clients. The Youth Initiative was more of a 'bureaucratic insurgency'... our reforms were mainly fought out behind office walls as struggles between various managers."[24]

Although Hagedorn continues to promote the need to struggle for structural change from within public social service systems, he identifies community decision-making control as a key outcome with which to measure reform effectiveness. This is a demanding standard, but without it, reforms, even daring internal reforms like Milwaukee's Youth Initiative, remain symbolic. Hagedorn is rigorous in identifying a series of "symbolic reforms" that function to divert criticism, quell dissent, and garner more funding. Public agencies are always involved in reforms, never more vigorously than when demanding more funds. "The demand for more resources," says Hagedorn, "is the holy sacrament of public bureaucracy, the quintessel symbol of reform."[25]

Questionable Child Welfare Reforms

Hiring new caseworkers to expand protective service investigative work increases the number of children removed from their homes and perhaps reduces caseloads slightly, but it does not lead to structural change. Even periodic reorganization reforms become diversions if they fail to change front-line workers' job assignments from investigation to family preservation.

Even by 1995–96, for instance, the Milwaukee Department for Human Services still *espoused* family preservation. The problem, according to Jan Ereth, the Milwaukee County director of Juvenile Court, is that "the Department of Human Services upholds Family Preservation but they don't offer families any support services. There is no supervision, no accountability, no adequate staff training, no rewards or incentives to workers and their caseloads are enormous."[26]

Finally, Hagedorn identified the process lessons that the Youth Initiative Team taught themselves. A key lesson was that "the plan may not be as important as the act...what success we had was always the result of action, even when we weren't exactly sure of what all the outcomes would be...our experience shows that even fundamental goals are often discovered through action and may differ from those in the initial plan."[27]

I have described the Youth Initiative's attempt to reform Milwaukee's child welfare system at length, because such studies are rarely found in the research literature on child welfare reforms and because the experiment put into action organizational theories about structural change. In spite of the fact that Hagedorn considered the effort a failure (this is because he held his efforts to the same evaluative standards as he demanded of the Department of Social Services—that is, by outcomes, not by programmatic input), the "lessons" learned teach us the future path of actual reform. The Youth Initiative's strategic aim was true, although its tactics or methods need retooling. The Youth Initiative's goal was to fix (structurally change) child welfare bureaucracies, not to fix families. At the same time, the team sought to collaborate with communities in providing services for families in need. Community-based family preservation work was not "new," but installing family support as the primary task of public social service caseworkers was radical.

A CHANGING FOCUS

In 1980 child development scholar Urie Bronfenbrenner shifted the focus from fixing the family to fixing the surrounding (ecological) conditions that lead to family violence.[28] But during the Reagan years, "family values" traditionalists were able to move the argument, once again, away from social or ecological causes.

Bronfenbrenner's ecological focus showed that class position in the United States was a more predictive factor in determining a child's development potential than in poor nations, where, for instance, infant mortality should be higher than in a more technologically advanced nation such as the United States. Yet Singapore, Greece, and Ireland have lower infant mortality rates than that of the United States.[29] These poor nations' policies of social support and prenatal health care lowered the infant death rate well below levels in poor communities in the United States. Our high infant mortality is related to poverty.

Infant deaths and the current unprecedented removal of children from their homes are social issues also connected to poverty. In 1993, 15.7 million children lived in poverty, representing the highest incidence of child poverty since 1964.[30] In 1996, at an apex of child pauperization, Congress was poised to end social welfare "as we know it" by eliminating AFDC payments to an estimated five to six million children.[31]

America's social welfare payments in the form of public assistance lag behind those of every developed nation. Yet we have "reformed" that system, casting into desperation, pauperization, and imploding rage or despair millions more Americans. The resulting pressure on already overburdened child protection services is predictable. Although most Americans agree that "welfare" (as public assistance has come to be named) does not lift anyone out of poverty, will cutting it solve anything? The reasons given for cutting public assistance are multiple: the system is in crisis, increased payments are draining the budget, welfare rewards mothers who have illegitimate children, welfare keeps people dependent and encourages joblessness, welfare subsidizes the black lower class.

Welfare Reform: Fact and Fiction

In 1996 President Clinton endorsed a welfare reform plan that eliminates AFDC assistance to families whose breadwinner has not found work within two years. This bill cancels the states' obligation to provide education, job training, or child care to those on welfare or to provide transitional child care and health care to women moving off welfare and into employment.

This reform was made in spite of the fact that the United States, unlike the majority of western European nations, offered no state or federally supported day-care programs that might allow mothers to work outside their home without spending much of their salary to pay for child care. Public policy analysts predict that households will be pauperized and vulnerable to removal of their children because of neglect charges or because they "refuse" state workfare mandates.

The proposed "reforms" shift fiscal responsibility from the federal government to individual states through block grants. Of twenty-five states surveyed on child maltreatment, 96 percent "feared [the legislation] would have a negative impact on social service delivery" to families "at risk."[32] Under the proposed block grant the states, which currently contribute 45 percent of welfare payments, would not be required to pay anything. According to Diana Pearce, "Lawmakers in Maryland, California, New Mexico, Rhode Island, Connecticut and Hawaii proposed cuts ranging from 10 to 30 percent" in 1995.[33] Clinton's welfare reform bill allows states to cut benefits as much as they need. Senator Daniel Moynihan criticized the welfare reform plan, which he said "would be the most regressive event in social policy of the 20th century."[34] The passage of the welfare plan caused Clinton's top welfare advisor, Mary Jo Bane, and the head of planning for the Department of Health and Human Services, Peter Edelman, to resign their jobs in protest.

When Senator Moynihan learned that a Department of Health and Human Services report estimating the human cost of the Senate welfare reform plan was blocked from release by the Clinton administration, he railed that "those involved will take this disgrace to their graves."[35] According to the report, the $65 billion in welfare cuts to immigrants, disabled children, substance abusers, and poor single mothers and their children, over seven years, would harm 4.8 million children.[36]

Congressional "reformers" identify unwed teenage mothers, in particular African Americans, as those who leech away tax dollars, undermine family values, and bear illegitimate children subject to neglect and abuse. Such targeting distracts public attention from the actual causes of poverty and offers masses of frightened middle-income people a scapegoat for America's economic crisis. The following box indicates the myths and the facts about welfare.

Fiction and Facts About Welfare

- The social welfare system is in crisis.

There is a poverty and job crisis, not a welfare crisis. Welfare benefits have dropped steadily since 1970—a 40 percent loss in value. *Five million children and youth have been added to welfare rolls since 1975.* According to Evelyn Brodkin, "Looking at these data one could argue that a crisis is developing because welfare has become less effective and reliable in protecting families against destitution. It needs to be strengthened, not dismantled."[37]

- Increased welfare payments are draining the budget.

AFDC accounts for 1.5 percent of the budget.[38] Actually, it is social programs that have been drained. Here is the breakdown of cuts between 1980 and 1995: housing—$390 billion, job training—$101 billion, aid to cities—$117 billion, anti-poverty—$49 billion, community development—$53 billion, and education—$39 billion. During the same fifteen-year period, the military received from the government $1,116 billion and prisons and corrections received $59 billion.[39]

- Welfare causes and rewards illegitimacy.

States with the highest welfare payments have the lowest unwed birthrates, and states with the lowest welfare payments have the highest unwed birthrates.[40]

- Welfare recipients receive a decent income.

In Illinois, a mother of two has $12.50 a day in cash assistance to support a family. The welfare recipient's dollar is worth 52 percent less than it was in 1970.[41] More children and families were living in destitution in 1992 (an annual income for a family with three children of $5,593, which is half the Bureau of Census poverty threshold) than in any year since 1975.[42]

- Welfare prevents recipients from getting jobs.

According to Edelman, "Poor children's families earn twice as much money from work as they receive from welfare."[43]

- Welfare is a way of life that discourages people from getting off the rolls.

Seventy percent of welfare recipients leave the program within a two-year period.[44]

- Welfare causes children to have children.

According to Mike Males, "the most recent National Center for Health Statistics data show that only one-third of births among teenage mothers involved teenage fathers. Most were caused by adult men over the age of twenty."[45]

- Welfare creates dependency.

According to Brodkin, "If ever there were a program designed to discourage dependency, it is welfare. It is one of the least attractive government subsidies you can get. In most states, the support is minimal—$370 per month for a family of three. And the administrative ordeals to which welfare recipients are routinely subjected would simply not be tolerated by beneficiaries of other government programs."[46]

- Welfare subsidizes the black underclass.

There are more whites than blacks on welfare.[47]

- In spite of its drawbacks, the U.S. welfare system is better than other models.

European social welfare programs offer income, health care, housing, parental leave support, and generous pension and unemployment benefits aimed at equalizing income so that families can be drawn back into the work force. Sweden, France, Germany, the Netherlands, and the United Kingdom "lifted" from 66 to 75 percent of their poor out of poverty between 1984 and 1987. The United States rate was 8.5 percent.[48]

CHILD POVERTY: A CASE
OF ABUSE AND NEGLECT

Never before has one generation of children been less healthy, less cared for or less prepared for life than their parents were at the same age.

1990 COMMISSION OF THE NATIONAL ASSOCIATION OF STATE BOARDS
OF EDUCATION AND THE AMERICAN MEDICAL ASSOCIATION[49]

Advocates for welfare reform successfully separate the causal links between poverty and underemployment. Presenting child poverty as a problem separate from the lowered opportunity of poor children's parents keeps Americans from indicting an economy that benefits the wealthy and penalizes the poor. Additionally, the myth of a classless society masks the levels of poverty, especially child poverty, that persist in one of the world's most technologically advanced nations. The successful isolation of poverty as an individual family problem masks its structural character and masks the transfer of wealth upward. For example, in 1979, 35 percent of black children lived in households with adjusted incomes of less than $10,000 per year. Ten years later, 44 percent of black children's families had incomes below $10,000. At the same time, the top one half of 1 percent of the population increased its aggregate wealth 4.5 percent, or 28.8 percent of the total U.S. wealth of $15.1 trillion.[50] The "Child Poverty" feature below illustrates some of these discrepancies.

Child Poverty in the United States

- Three million more children were poor in 1994 than in 1980, bringing the number to 14 million.[51]
- Every fifth child in the United States is poor. One in every eight is hungry. A study by Tufts University Center on hunger, poverty, and nutrition found that there are approximately twelve million hungry children in the United States.[52]
- Child poverty has increased 50 percent since 1969, even though our gross national product has increased by 50 percent.[53]
- A black baby born in the shadow of the White House is now more likely to die in the first year of life than a child born in Jamaica or Trinidad.[54]
- According to a United Nations Children's Fund report, the United States has the highest child poverty rate of any rich nation in the world.[55]

- One in seven poor children had no health insurance in 1993.[56]
- Poor children are five times more likely to die from disease and illness, three times more likely to die during childhood, three times more likely to be hospitalized, and two times more likely to have physical or mental disabilities.[57]
- Just over half all of U.S. children were fully immunized against preventable childhood diseases in 1992.[58]
- Poor children have a four to twenty times greater chance of being born with mental retardation.[59]
- Many more children in the United States live below the poverty line than in Great Britain, France, Sweden, and Canada. These countries each spend two or three times what the United States spends on children and families.[60]

(continued)

Child Poverty in the United States (continued)

- Of those who receive food stamps, 51.4 percent are children. Children receiving food stamps increased by an unprecedented 51 percent between 1989 and 1993.[61]
- Over half of the families of poor children have incomes $5,700 *below* the official poverty line.[62]
- One out of four reported homeless persons is a child.[63]
- One fourth of poor families pay 75 percent of their income for rent.[64]
- Of children in single parent households (87 percent of which are women), 73 percent experience poverty at some time during their lives.[65]
- Almost 40 percent of black teens are poor, 30 percent of Latino teens are poor, and 50 percent of pregnant teens do not receive prenatal health care.[66]
- Poor youth between the ages of sixteen and twenty-four are two times more likely to drop out of high school and half as likely to finish college.[67]
- Seventy-five percent of black students and 46 percent of Latino students attend schools ranked in the lowest socioeconomic status.[68]
- A 1993 United Nation Children's Fund Report which measured each nation according to the social health and welfare performance it should have achieved based on its wealth found that "Vietnam had a plus rating of 116 while the United States had a minus rating of 3."[69]

CONCLUSION

According to the U.S. Advisory Board on Abuse and Neglect, child protection services in the United States have failed. The majority of reports about child maltreatment are about neglect, and neglect is linked to poverty. Why isn't there a national focus on the causes and extent of poverty rather than on the symptoms of desperation? The link among child welfare, social welfare, and poverty is critical to understanding child abuse and neglect for two reasons: (1) the majority of families served by child welfare are also on public assistance, and (2) both systems hold mothers responsible for family breakdown and maltreatment of children, regardless of male culpability.

Despair, family chaos, and violence are products of a social order that produces powerlessness for some and privilege for others. These social responses are not causes but reactions. Yet media and politicians identify African American male youth and teen mothers as the causes of violence and moral breakdown rather than lack of opportunity, lack of decent housing, lack of health care access, and lack of adequate education, which produce social and economic powerlessness. In spite of the fact that the U.S. Advisory Board on Abuse and Neglect links maltreatment of children to conditions of poverty for which failure society bears responsibility, these myths persist. Portraying the poor as violent and pathological in their treatment of children serves the interests of both the powerful elements of society and the child welfare bureaucracies.

Sociologist John Hagedorn shows that increased expansion of social services is justified by exploding reports of abuse and neglect. (The fact that the majority of the reports are for neglect resulting from the dissembling effects of poverty is not publicly understood.) However, the expansion of services has not led to support for children and families. Instead, the beneficiaries have been social service bureaucracies that use increased funding to investigate families and remove children from their homes.

Although private agencies and even some state public agencies have adopted family preservation initiatives, not all those efforts have also been community based, and if community based, the initiatives still remain under the direction of professionals. The Milwaukee Youth Initiative was an internal reform effort aimed at changing Milwaukee's child welfare system from a regulatory, investigative child removal system to a family preservation system by creating pilot teams of caseworkers who worked with community councils and community agencies to support families in need.

Today's child welfare reformers focus on impoverished communities called "the underclass." Ecological child development experts such as Urie Bronfenbrenner focus on fixing the environmental conditions that surround and affect poor families. Such a shift in perspective targets the class, race, and gender benefits or penalties experienced by families living in particular neighborhoods or regions.

It makes all the difference in the world for child welfare policies if we believe we have to fix families "at risk" (which is the code for state intervention) or we have to fix the conditions that *cause* "risk." The first strategy targets poor families for change. The second strategy targets the conditions that create poverty.

Personal Narrative

Desiree Maurer

Desiree Maurer works in the Cook County Assessor's Office, and she is planning on entering a college program. This is the remarkable story of her journey from homelessness to a job where she is well respected not only for her skills but also for her unfailing kindness. She works as a volunteer organizer with the Coalition for the Homeless, especially advocating for mothers and children who are homeless.

An Abusive Childhood

My mom and dad were abusers. Drugs or alcohol was always available. My father died of alcoholism. That was the cause of almost everyone in my family who died, alcoholism. I come from a very abusive background and even now…I was abused. I was kind of a throwaway. My mom always tried to hold me back. They had such a lack of

self-esteem that they didn't want their kids to go out and try to do things, so they made them feel like you can't do it.

I didn't start really using [drugs] until after I was married—at fifteen. I left my mom's house. I lived in the streets. I was really homeless as a teenager. I had to leave home because it was killing me; I felt it. On the other hand, there was guilt because I had to leave my brothers and sisters. I helped my mom raise them. There was no adult living in the house. I mean they tried to make me the little adult caring for a family. You just can't do it. It all catches up to you.

Here I go out into the world thinking and doing what I thought were adult things like paying bills, doing all this stuff, and inside I was totally empty. So when it does catch up to you, it's like an explosion. I mean I went rock bottom so fast and I never could get out of it because I never saw anyone get out of it. My dad is still in it. My mom is finally dealing through it. She's never come to grips with our past, so it's very hard. I mean it's not hard for me to talk to her anymore, but it was. You get older, you put the past behind you and go on. Because you know you got to raise your kids.

After I got married, I hit the bottom. My husband was on methadone, but I didn't know it. But I wouldn't have cared because it all seemed normal to me. You've got your father dealing out of the house, you've got your mother out doing one thing or the other, never home, so you don't really think that it's a bad thing. You're raised with Mom and Dad's set of rules as they made up according to their convenience.

I really just kind of lost ten years and did terrible things. I think guilt held me back, because I figured even if I did make it how was I going to deal with that? My family had totally abandoned me.

My husband went to jail, and then I ended up homeless because they had cut off my public aid and the landlord… actually, I was being evicted because I couldn't pay my rent anymore. I just told the landlord I would leave because we had already ruined our reputation, so I didn't want to cause any more problems, and really I was in a vulnerable situation because now I was alone.

So I ended up in a city shelter. No services, no anything. It was just a warming center. It wasn't a place where you could start a new life. Then I went to St. Sylvester's, and things started happening for the better for me almost right away.

What happened is I went back to my old neighborhood. I was scared, and I was alone, and it was a rainy day. The only time you have friends in that neighborhood is when you have money. If you don't have any money, forget it. So I'm walking down the street—I didn't

have that much money—I was getting ready to get a bag of dope, and I was waiting by the bus stop, and the kids were crying. I had Tory in my arms, and this feeling just came over me. To this day I will never forget it. It was a feeling of loneliness all the way to my soul. I said to myself if you keep on doing this you're going to be alone for the rest of your life and you'll always feel this feeling. It totally overwhelmed my whole body, and I started crying. I was on Division and Pulaski. Finally it was like I came back, because I didn't see anybody around me or anything; I didn't even see my kids. I looked down Division, the bus was coming, and I made up my mind: that was it. And I went back to the shelter. I haven't used since that day.

When I became homeless, my son Tory—he was the baby who was nine months at the time—was taken out of my care. What happened before that was I had a warrant out for my arrest because I had been dodging DCFS because my son Tory was born drug addicted. I would go to the hospital every day, and the nurse that was in charge made a mistake and had me take the baby home. After I left the hospital the DCFS caseworker put a warrant out for me because I was supposed to give my baby to the worker so that he could take Tory to the shelter, but I prevented that from happening for about nine months. By then I was in a shelter with the kids. They found out I was getting my public aid check at the shelter, and that's where they caught up with me. My caseworker from DCFS came to visit me, and he told me that I had a court date. Actually he could have arrested me right then and there, but he knew I wasn't going anywhere.

So, when I went to court, it was for substance abuse. I had a public defender who knew absolutely nothing of my case. Every time I went to court I had a different one [defender] until I found out how I could obtain a lawyer while I was in the shelter. I was railroaded all the way through. I had nobody to stick up for me.

It was really a terrible experience in the shelter because I really hadn't even told anyone that I had a drug problem because I had just started admitting it to myself. I was afraid if I told someone I'd be thrown out of the shelter. When you're there, you don't trust anybody. But I knew I was going to have to tell the nun who was head of the shelter. When I told her, that's when people started reaching out to me and telling me what I could have done to prevent trouble or what I could have done at the courthouse.

Fighting DCFS to Protect Her Baby

Tory came down with chicken pox. It happened like the next day when they were supposed to come and pick him up. My DCFS worker said there was no facility where Tory could be put with chicken pox. So we had to go to a hospital so that the worker would have a paper saying that Tory had chicken pox, and it had to be a hospital that was under DCFS rules. We drove around all day, then stopped at this hospital, and we waited about two hours just so they could have it on paper that Tory had the chicken pox. Then we went back to the shelter.

When they took Tory from me, I asked my worker if I could go see him that night and he told me, "Sure you can." After he left, it was very emotional at the shelter. We were all standing there, everybody looking on as they were taking my baby from me.

I left that night to go see if I could find Tory. Since the hospital, we had never been separated. It was snowing really bad. We got all the way to Maryville/Columbus on Montrose, and they told me that Tory was not there. I called my DCFS worker up, who was not available. It was late at night, and I was getting frantic. Yet I just knew he was there. I just thought that they weren't

telling me. Sure enough, the next day I came back, and he was there. Before I left the shelter I called my DCFS worker and told him what happened the previous night, and he said he must have forgot to tell them to let me see him.

When I went back the next day, Governor Jim Edgar was there. It was the most ironic thing I ever saw in my whole life. I went to go get my son, and he had a rash from his thighs all the way up to the middle of his stomach. When I went onto the infant floor to see where they had him, he was isolated. He was in a corner all by himself, no T-shirt on, with a pair of shorts. It was cold in there, and he was crying and had a fever of 102. No nurse had come by to look at him, because I asked. I just walked out of there. I grabbed him; I took him. I went to find a nurse. Then I went to get some medicine she was supposed to have brought to Tory, and there was Governor Edgar talking about how good this whole center was. I just wanted to shout—I couldn't get near him because of security, but I wanted to say, it was a damn lie; I have a proven case here.

I told the Director, "Look, he is being abused right here. He was not in that condition when I was taking care of him at the shelter. So, if you're saying that taking him away from me because this situation is better than the shelter, I don't believe it." Tory was completely over the chicken pox when they took him. He had no fever; he was dressed warm. To come and see him scantily dressed with a 102 fever, a rash—I mean I was just crying and mad at the same time, and here was my other kids following me because they don't know what's happening. Now they think they're going to be taken away. They're crying 'cause that's their brother. And he's a baby who can't even talk yet.

So I had to calm down. After I realized there was nothing else I could do, I left.

I always felt that every time I went to court—while I was in the shelter and because I didn't have a lawyer—that I was being shafted. Because as soon as I got an attorney, things started changing. I just could not believe it. I became involved with Della from the Coalition for the Homeless and poured my whole story out because I was so frustrated. Rene Heyback from Legal Assistance helped get me an attorney who helped me get Tory taken from that shelter, which was under DCFS, to Catholic Charities. Sister Jean provided me with names of people that could help me.

After that, it got a little better. The judge started listening to me—they put you through a lot. I'm not saying you don't deserve it or that you shouldn't go through that, because it helps you in every way.

Every time I would go back to court they had me thinking that I was going to get him back, but they would throw another hoop in there. I had to do one more thing! DCFS has the hardest time keeping track of things. They lost my records. My caseworker would be late for court, and one time he didn't even show up. I would have to go to his office and beg for services that were promised me. You know what I found out? While I was living at the shelter and he came to visit me, he was supposed to offer me—because all of my children were under DCFS at one time—he was supposed to offer me assistance to get me out of my situation. When I asked him about it, he said that there was no more funding available.

Every time I went to him he would send me a voucher for my bus pass a week later. You need the bus pass to get to treatment. If you get a voucher from DCFS and it's a week late, they will not cash it. There's only five Jewels in the whole city of Chicago that will cash these vouchers. One time I had to go to all five of them. One time I got so mad. I went there by myself, and this is after I had been with the Coalition for a while, so I kind of knew how to go in. I had a notebook and a pen like I was taking

notes of everything. I had a friend of mine waiting in the lobby, and after I got so mad and asked for his supervisor, he came and told me there was nothing he could do about the bus pass. He was sorry that it happened. My caseworker came and threw at me—threw them— five tokens! I said, "Well, you know what, I can't do anything with these because I need to get a transfer."

This was the kind of treatment I was getting. He acted like every time I called him up I was doing him a disservice—like I shouldn't be calling him for any reason. I was appalled. If I didn't have the Coalition for the Homeless support or Sister Jean, what would have happened to my children? If they hadn't arranged for me to get a bus pass through the Coalition so I could do all this, if I hadn't been introduced to them—excuse me, but if you don't kiss someone's butt [at DCFS and in court], you don't get anything.

I did everything. I did everything right, and I didn't get no help from them. It was almost like it was fixed for you to be set up to fail. The children were falling through the cracks. If people hadn't made me aware of what was happening, I wouldn't have done these things; my son's life would be theirs.

After I left the shelter and [got] in an apartment, I was having a very hard time getting the DCFS caseworker to visit me, and everything depended on his visits. As soon as he could say everything looked OK, I could have my son back. It took me one month to get him to my house. I could have had my son right away. But he thought I was pushing. I was upsetting his schedule. The judge would just laugh when she'd see this guy. Not at him. He was in no way reprimanded about anything. He was just accepted. That's rough. It's a no-win situation. I know they see a lot of kids going back and forth, but there is only that one who is your child.

None of them saw what happened while my baby was in foster care in a private home. I got three visits for three hours. He fell down the stairs. They said it was because he was learning how to walk. But his whole face was totally blue. Maybe this could have happened. But why weren't they watching him? I was scared he was abused. When my caseworker brought him to me, she would always tell me that I had to be careful about doing this and that, but when she saw him like that that time she didn't say nothing. She just gave him to me and left.

After that incident it seemed like things started to move. I think because of my involvement with the Coalition they thought I might start to raise a protest. When I told someone from the Department of Human Services I was involved with the Coalition for the Homeless, they said it was not a good organization to be involved with. Later on I found out why. When I would get someone from the Coalition to come to court with me, DCFS hated that. They knew they were being watched. They knew I had the support of other organizations. I think that was a big help—that was what made me get my son back. But what about someone who doesn't have this? It just makes you know why kids get lost.

NOTES

1. Henry Giroux, *Fugitive Cultures: Race, Violence, and Youth* (New York: Routledge, 1996), 118–19.

2. Michael Harrington, *The Other America: Poverty in the United States* (New York: Penguin, 1971), xxii.

3. Interview with Samir Hanaan, youth agency director, and psychologist, May 25, 1995.

4. Linda Gordon, *Heroes in Their Own Lives* (New York: Viking Penguin, 1988), 3.

5. Darlene Garvon Stevens, "Abuse Case Puts Hotline on Hot Seat," *Chicago Tribune* (Mar. 26, 1996), 5.

6. Ibid.

7. Ibid.

8. *Oxfam Report,* 1995.

9. *The State of America's Children Yearbook 1994* (Washington, DC: Children's Defense Fund, 1994), 14, 18, 108.

10. U.S. Advisory Board on Child Abuse and Neglect, qtd. in *Child Abuse: Opposing Viewpoints,* Ed. Karen de Koster (San Diego: Greenhaven Press, 1994), 35–36.

11. Ibid., 36.

12. Arloc Sherman, *Wasting America's Future: The Children's Defense Fund's Report on the Costs of Child Poverty* (Boston: Beacon, 1994), 35–36.

13. Interview with Denise Plunkett, May 20, 1995.

14. John Hagedorn, *Forsaking Our Children: Bureaucracy and Reform in the Child Welfare System* (Chicago: Lakeview Press, 1995), 37.

15. Ibid.

16. Ibid., 99.

17. Ibid., 114.

18. Deborah Daro and David Wiese, *Current Trends in Child Abuse Reporting and Fatalities: The Result of the 1994 Annual Fifty State Survey* (Chicago: National Committee for Prevention of Child Abuse), 18.

19. Brian McNeill, "Poverty Causes Child Abuse," in *Child Abuse: Opposing Viewpoints,* 92.

20. Family Research Council, "Threats to Children: A Generation Under Siege," in *Free to Be Family* (Washington, DC: Family Research Council, 1992).

21. David Finklehor, "The Extent of Child Abuse Is Not Exaggerated," in *Child Abuse: Opposing Viewpoints,* 27, 31.

22. Richard Wexler, *Wounded Innocents: The Real Victims of the War Against Child Abuse* (Buffalo: Prometheus Books, 1995).

23. Hagedorn, 137.

24. Ibid., 158.

25. Ibid., 146.

26. Interview with Jan Ereth, May 24, 1995.

27. Hagedorn, 155, 157.

28. Urie Bronfenbrenner, *The Ecology of Human Development: Experiments by Nature and Design* (Cambridge: Harvard University Press, 1979).

29. *State of America's Children 1994*, 14.

30. *The State of America's Children Yearbook 1995* (Washington, DC: Children's Defense Fund, 1995), 19.

31. Ibid., 17.

32. Daro and Wiese, 17.

33. Diana Pearce, *The Women's Committee of One Hundred Update* (March 1996), 1.

34. "Dismantling Welfare," *Bread,* 7:6 (1995), 6.

35. "U.S. Data Says Welfare Bill Could Harm Millions of Kids," *Chicago Tribune* (Oct. 28, 1995), 4.

36. Ibid.

37. Evelyn Brodkin, "A Tear in the Safety Net: Faculty Respond to Welfare Reform," *SSA Magazine,* 6:2 (1995), 2.

38. Ibid., 3.

39. Budget of the U.S. Government, OMB, 1980-1996; the National Low Income Housing Information Service, in *New Priorities Voice* (Spring 1995), 2.

40. Mike Males, "Poor Logic," *In These Times* (Jan. 9, 1995), 12.

41. *Public Welfare Coalition Study* (Chicago, Illinois, 1995), 1.

42. *The State of America's Children 1994,* 2.

43. Marian Wright Edelman, qtd. in *Wasting America's Future,* xxi.

44. Don Reeves, "The Welfare Policy Debate," Bread for the World Background Paper No. 133, *Bread* (May 1995), 6.

45. Mike Males, "In Defense of Teenage Mothers," *The Progressive* (Aug. 1994), 22.

46. Brodkin, 3.

47. National Association of State Budget Officers, "Welfare as We've Known It," *New York Times* (June 19, 1994), sec. 4, p. 4.

48. Timothy Smeeding, "Cross National Perspectives on Income Security Programs," testimony before the U.S. Congress Joint Economic Committee September 25, 1991, cited in *The State of America's Children 1994,* 7.

49. 1990 Commission of National Associations of State Boards of Education and American Mental Associations, qtd. in Noam Chomsky, "Rollback II: 'Civilization' Marches On," *Z* (Feb. 1995), 27.

50. U.S. Bureau of Labor Statistics, qtd. in Stephen Rose, *Social Stratification in the United States* (New York: New Press, 1992), 18, 22.

51. *Wasting America's Future,* 4.

52. "Poverty Amongst U.S. Children," Bread for the World Newsletter, *Bread,* (Mar. 1992), 3.

53. Edelman, *Wasting Our Future,* xvi, xx.

54. Sylvia Hewlett, *When the Bough Breaks: The High Cost of Neglecting Our Children* (New York: Basic Books, 1991), 12.

55. Ray Mosley, "Among Rich Nations, U.S. Has the Highest Child-poverty Rate," *Chicago Tribune* (Sept. 23, 1993), 4.

56. *State of America's Children 1995,* 27.

57. *Wasting America's Future,* xvii, 62.

58. *State of America's Children 1994,* 15.

59. *Wasting America's Future,* 71.

60. Hewlett, 14.

61. *State of America's Children 1995,* 46.

62. *Wasting Our Future,* 4.

63. *State of America's Children 1995,* 63.

64. Jack Nelson Palmeyer, "Brave New World Order," *Sojourners,* 21:1 (1992), 15.

65. National Research Council Commission on Behavioral and Social Sciences and Education, *Losing Generations: Adolescents in High Risk Settings* (Washington, DC: National Academy Press, 1993), 44.

66. Chicago Legal Assistance Foundation Children's Rights Project, *Adolescent Service Initiative Packet,* 1995.

67. *Wasting Our Future,* 62.

68. National Research Council, 69.

69. Mosley, 4.

3

❀

An American Tragedy

Disposable Children

Dull conscience, irresponsibility and ruthless self interest
already appear.... The test of our progress is not whether we add
more to the abundance of those who have much; it is whether
we provide for those who have little.[1]

FRANKLIN DELANO ROOSEVELT, SECOND INAUGURAL ADDRESS

The Third World War has already started—it is a silent war,
not for that reason any less sinister. This war is tearing down practically
all the Third World. Instead of soldiers dying, there are children
dying; instead of millions wounded, there are millions unemployed;
instead of destruction of bridges, there is a tearing down
of factories, schools, hospitals and entire economies.[2]

LUIS IGNACIO SILVA ("LULA"), BRAZILIAN WORKERS' PARTY

Emmett lives in a two-and-a-half room apartment off Roosevelt Road on Chicago's west side. The Jane Addams project's dirt courtyard is lined with men when we visit. Two old men sit impassively beneath the only tree, and guys with Nikes, blue bandannas, and baseball caps cocked to the side form huddles. Inside Emmett's apartment, a muslin curtain separates the bedroom from the living room, where a TV and stained couch face each other from cinder block walls. A crucifix and a photo of a sleek Black Lexus sedan sitting on a California beach hang on the wall. Emmett, who had been a state ward throughout his childhood after his mother died of a drug overdose when he was four months old, has finally made it on his own. He is a twenty-two-year-old who tends to forget things when under pressure. He has spent his educational life in special programs for the learning disabled and is grateful to a high school teacher who became his advocate.

"A lot of people helped me," Emmett says. It's easy to see why. Emmett is the one of the sweetest, most guileless people I've ever met. My companion, Cindy Clark, from the Public Guardian's Office, calls Emmett "a black Forrest Gump, but with no luck."[3]

Here's what she meant. Emmett was working temporary part-time security at O'Hare Airport, had two children and a fiancée, Daphne, who was trying to finish her GED in order to get off welfare, when his deadbeat addict father used his Social Security number to get credit cards for which Emmett was held responsible: "I can't get the kids the clothes they need, but Daphne's mother helps us." If that isn't enough, "Security took $75 out of my check to pay for a security guard uniform. It's a setback."[4]

If Emmett's "luck" is not good, his instincts are. One night when he saw turf tension heat up between the New Breeds and the Gangster Disciples, he made Daphne and the kids leave with him: "When we got home I said, 'Damn! There's a bullet on the floor.' I'm looking at the walls, and there's a bullet hole. I was scared. I thought one of us could have gotten hit.… I want to leave here, but I can't afford it."

Bad luck or poverty? "I need glasses…and I have asthma but don't get Medicare to pay for glasses. If I'm having an asthma attack, I have to walk all the way to Cook County [hospital]." Emmett has been trying to learn to drive so that he can get to O'Hare in less than an hour and not have to be walking to the el late at night. But he has no relative to teach him. He saved $130 for driving instructions but had to use the money to pay for a bill his cousin incurred.

He and Daphne, a teen mother, have been "engaged" for years. She'd lose welfare if they married.

Emmett admits he's thought of selling drugs when he feels desperate. But "I'm too scared, and I've got kids."

Perhaps Emmett's "slowness" accounts for his innocence, kindness, and forbearance. If quicker, he'd have rage or despair. Joining the Gangster Disciples might give him something to belong to and a sense of power, but this is not Emmett's way.

Emmett's family is one trapped not by bad luck but by poverty. What they need and want are jobs. They hold out desperate hope that they, unlike their parents, can get out of the projects.

But even if Emmett had not become involved with DCFS, he, Daphne, and their two children would be confronted with their most fundamental problem: finding a job. Without decent paying work, they are trapped. Their children are trapped. They'll remain dependent on the state and dependent on services.

Even if child welfare bureaucracies were to initiate reforms that produced better services, the economic transformation that is eliminating blue-collar jobs would still continue to produce desperate, broken people like Emmett's drug-addicted mother and hustler father. This is not to suggest that Emmett's parents had no choice or were such victims of circumstance that they bear no responsibility for failing their son or each other. Poor people, most often, make noble choices to keep struggling even when the "deck" is stacked against them. Emmett and Daphne are a case in point. But if Emmett's parents "gave up" or "gave in" twenty years ago, before globalization of the economy erased labor-intensive work, then what are poor young blacks facing today?

POSTINDUSTRIAL SOCIETY

According to historian Michael Katz, postindustrial society is shaped by (1) globalization of the economy; (2) depopulation and the change of the faces of the poor from whites of European ancestry to African Americans, Latinos, and new immigrants; and (3) transformation of space: suburbanization, gentrification of urban areas, concentration of the poor in segregated, decaying neighborhoods, and the revitalization of downtown areas. These interrelated changes constitute an urban reality never before encountered in history.[5]

In an attempt to explain the reality of the ghetto, scholars have referred to the very poor as the "underclass." The term seeks to explain drug use, crime, and teen pregnancy among "minorities" and to distinguish their reactions to poverty as more pathological and incomprehensible than those of any previous era: "*Underclass* conjured a mysterious wilderness in the heart of America's cities: a terrain of violence and despair; a collectivity outside politics and social structure, beyond the usual language of class and stratum, unable to protest or revolt."[6]

However, Katz argues that *underclass* is simply the new metaphor that has replaced the "unworthy poor" of the late nineteenth century and the "culture of poverty" of the mid-twentieth. The language is new; the reality is old. Urban poverty has changed in three ways, however. It is more visible, more concentrated, and more expanded: "Arguments for a new underclass represent the resurgence of old images of the undeserving poor, an attempt to mask the recurrent, grinding poverty generated by the working of the economy and social system with an argument that blames the victim and justifies harsh, punitive responses."[7]

The transformation of the economy, of demographics, and of space does explain a new historical phenomenon affecting the lives of the poor at the end of the twentieth century. Urban poor youth are facing a future in which public welfare benefits have been cut, part-time and summer jobs have been cut, health care and services have been cut, schools have become battlegrounds, homelessness is on the rise, there are no more traditional manufacturing jobs, and incarceration has tripled as a response to the "violence of the underclass." Their neighborhoods are isolated, crumbling slums. Chronic joblessness among the poorest of urban African Americans is structural rather than episodic: "The connection between race, urban poverty and disassociation from the labor market is new in American history…. Poverty now exists within a context of hopelessness."[8]

The War on Poverty Became the War on Poor Children

By examining the social transformations of the economy, the race and ethnic composition of the poor, and urban geographic shifts, it is possible to identify the need to change *environments,* not *people,* as underclass proponents implicitly urge. But changing the conditions surrounding people's lives cannot be a government initiative in which the residents are passive recipients of services and programs. Those earlier programs, from urban renewal to the War on Poverty, were ineffective because they failed to create an inclusive process that tapped the creativity, energy, and capacity of local residents who were affected by the programs. The programs simply did not lead communities to self-determination. However, local initiatives that rebuild fragmented communities through a process carried forth by the residents can transform the demobilizing effects of economic and demographic structural changes. Also, the term *underclass* targets the poor as one sector that has been profoundly changed by deindustrialization, ignoring the fact that globalization of the economy has restructured all of American life.

What follows is an analysis of globalization that reveals dynamic changes in social life. Developing a context to understand the international forces that are radically altering daily life, especially for the poor, seems imperative in a study of child welfare and for understanding the chasm that separates the adult world from a youth culture that is the front line engaging these cataclysmic changes. This chapter shows how the technological revolution is producing surplus unemployed who are the primary candidates for family crisis, "at-risk" children, and, too often, state intervention.

WORK, WELFARE, WEALTH, AND THE WALL OF SILENCE

America has the most unequal distribution of income in any industrialized nation in the world.

ROBERT REICH, LABOR SECRETARY OF THE UNITED STATES

The jobs are gone, and they are not coming back. This is not just in the deindustrialized Midwest, where Emmett lives. It's global. What Emmett is facing, French working-class youth are facing, and so are Peruvians, Zimbabweans, and Mexicans. Whole populations are no longer needed in the global economy, even as cheap labor. Business management analyst Peter Drucker calls this quantitative and qualitative change in work and the work force "far more than a social change...it is a change in the human condition.... It is the first society in which ordinary people—and that means most people—do not earn their daily bread by the sweat of their brow."[9] Drucker calls the computerized technological revolution, which has replaced human labor with machines programmed by elite knowledge professionals, a social transformation. For the nonprofessional majority, it represents social devastation.

Corporations eliminate two million jobs each year.[10] This change in both the nature of work and who works is not only different from the work tradition of this century, but also from what has existed at any other time in history. Drucker admits that the loss of industrial work that offered health benefits and pensions has affected African Americans, Emmett's people, the most. According to Drucker, "for the overwhelming majority—whites, but also Latinos and Asians—the fall of the industrial worker has caused amazingly little disruption and nothing that could be called an upheaval."[11] Amazingly little disruption? What about the Los Angeles riots involving Latinos and Asians? The Oklahoma bombings by (allegedly) dispossessed farmers who blamed government for giving benefits and jobs to blacks and immigrants? Inner cities that have become "unmanageable"? The highest imprisonment rate in the world yet soaring violence, with the United States leading the world in homicides? What about the 14.6 million full-time workers whose salary is below the poverty level for a family of four, the 7.9 million officially unemployed, the 4.9 million part-time workers seeking a full-time job, or the 7.3 million people who want work but are not counted in the official unemployment statistics because they are too discouraged to actively seek jobs? All of these total 34.7 million unemployed or underemployed. Is this a small disruption?[12]

Or is Drucker referring to the quiet destruction of poor children and their families? For these communities, lack of jobs is not a new phenomenon. Hardscrabble subsistence is a way of life. It is and has always been the way of life for Emmett and Daphne, the New Breeds, and the Gangster Disciples. Now, however, a new desperation and rage fills the streets of the poor. One out of two adult African Americans is unemployed.[13] Perhaps Drucker is correct that white America has accepted that disruption without "upheaval," but it is catastrophic for poor black and Latino communities.

The pauperization of masses of Americans has become normative. A wall of silence keeps us from linking the elimination of jobs with the fact that 40 percent of America's children live below the poverty line. But it is a wall of silence constructed by a barrage of words that blames the poor and successfully confuses Americans about the true source of the nation's (and globe's) crisis.

Another source of confusion is that the official unemployment rate is decreasing in many states and America's manufacturing productive capacity has increased by 35 percent while all this worker downsizing has occurred.[14] What's happening? The new jobs are in the service sector and offer low wages— 25 percent of the American work force is concentrated in such jobs as janitor and domestic servant, along with minimum-wage, no-benefits service sector jobs.[15] Technological advances are so rapid that the service sector is about to go the route of farming and manufacturing. Yet productivity is up because automation and computer technology can perform the jobs that were eliminated: "In the coming century, employment as we have come to know it, is likely to be phased out in most of the industrialized nations of the world."[16]

So who does this Information Age benefit? According to the Federal Reserve Survey of Economic Finances, in 1992 the top 1 percent of American households were worth more than the bottom 90 percent of American households.[17] Not since the Census Bureau began in 1947 has the gap between the rich and the poor been more exaggerated. The richest 20 percent of the nation receives over 48 percent of the national income, and the poorest 20 percent receives 3.6 percent.[18]

One measure of what it means for a fifth of the nation to receive under 4 percent of the national budget is hunger. In New York City, where one out of every four New Yorkers are poor (in the Bronx, 40 percent are poor), a study "by the Food and Hunger Hotline shows that in 1979 there were 30 emergency soup kitchens and food pantries in New York City serving about a million meals per year. In 1991 there were 730, serving almost 30 million meals."[19] According to a Tufts University Center on Hunger, Poverty and Nutrition study, hunger has increased 50 percent in America since the 1980s— from twenty million hungry people and children in 1985 to thirty million in 1995.[20] "I think we're in great danger of becoming two nations, one of first-world privilege and another of third-world deprivation," says Children's Defense Fund President Marian Wright Edelman. "We've had a whole generation of children, white and black, grow up in an era where they've been told by our political leaders that government is useless, that blacks and the poor are to blame for their own condition."[21]

Poor, reviled, feared by white Americans, and trapped in deteriorating housing projects, in schools that have all but given up, and in neighborhoods that resemble refugee camps or war zones, black and many Latino children live so separately from mainstream culture that they are, as Edelman suggests, in another nation—Michael Harrington's "other America." Statistics cannot measure the pain and humiliation these children live with. Nor can statistics reveal the despair of their young mothers held accountable for the social problems that befall communities that are racially excluded and economically dispensable.

Yet the statistics address the facts of poverty in America: "that the number of African Americans below the poverty line has increased in the last 20 years from 7.5 million in 1970 to 10.9 million in 1993...nearly half of all black children under the age of 18 are being raised in families below the poverty line, as compared to 16 percent of whites."[22] And, according to U.S. Bureau of Census data for 1992, 40 percent of Latino children live below the poverty line.[23]

Heritage scholar Patrick Fagan explains the increase in poverty and welfare dependence as resulting from a breakdown of the family: "In the debate over welfare reform...it is now a widely accepted premise that children born into single parent families are much more likely than children born into intact families to fall into poverty and welfare dependency."[24] Once again, single mothers are seen as responsible for poverty and welfare dependence. However, Frances Fox Piven states that "birth rates are higher in states where [welfare] benefits are low, and lower in states where benefits are high."[25]

In spite of the fact that twenty-five years of welfare-to-work "reforms" have produced faint results, politicians of both parties agree that mothers receiving AFDC payments must be forced into another rendition of these programs. Just as children are silenced in child welfare processes, mothers are silenced in welfare policy debates. "No one invites the mothers," says Fox Piven, "who suffer the indignity of being hustled from one foolish work preparedness scheme to another, and who are sanctioned with slashed benefits if they do not cooperate."[26]

Although thirty years of research on welfare reform has led Frances Fox Piven to agree that reform has failed, it is for precisely the opposite reason than the one that conservatives offer: "Our welfare policies have gone wrong not because they have coddled the poor, but because they have punished the poor. American welfare practices denigrate people on welfare keeping them so miserably poor that they are outside the mainstream of American life, by endlessly investigating and disciplining them, investigating their rights, and even going so far as to criminalize impoverished women with procedures such as fingerprinting."[27]

While politicians focus national attention on cutting AFDC—a federal program that accounts for approximately 1 percent of the federal budget—the richest $1\frac{1}{2}$ percent of Americans have amassed nearly half (48 percent) of the nation's financial wealth.[28] The upward transfer of wealth has created a global class more politically and economically powerful than any elite sector in history: "The world's richest 101 individuals and families now control wealth valued at some $452 billion. This is more than the total yearly income of the entire population of India, Bangladesh, Nigeria and Indonesia put together: one-and-a-half billion people in all."[29]

Corporate Welfare

Although the poor are held accountable for their dependency on the state through welfare, no public attention is paid to government assistance to corporations. If the explosive budget deficit is not a result of government spending on welfare benefits for the poor and immigrants, then who or what is responsible? In the 1980s government sought to "divert" the huge research infrastructure of the Cold War era to U.S. corporations. The purpose of the research subsidies was to stimulate job creation and support American industry. To that end, $6 billion of American tax monies were given for research projects to such corporations as General Motors and International Business Machines. Although IBM received $58 million for research to aid in the creation of jobs, it cut its own research budget by a third, laid off workers, and made a $3 billion profit in 1994.[30]

According to the Cato Institute, Congress pays $35 billion in subsidized program aid to business; with tax breaks the cost exceeds $100 billion—"half the annual federal deficit."[31] Additionally, the military spends in two weeks what AFDC costs taxpayers for a whole year.[32]

According to conservative political analyst Kevin Phillips, "The 1980s were the triumph of upper America—an ostentatious celebration of wealth, the political ascendancy of the richest third of the population and a glorification of...free markets and capitalism."[33] In 1987, when jobs were being cut and media focused fears on the "underclass," the typical CEO's salary, after taxes, was $1.8 million and climbing. The next year it was $2.02 million.[34] This concentration is in a nation with aggregates of poverty such as in Harlem, where, according to the United Nations development index, a black man in 1992 had a lower life expectancy rate than the average male in the Sudan.[35]

Global corporations' growth results from subsidies, acquisitions, mergers, and takeovers. In addition, through control of the knowledge industry (corporations control 90 percent of research and development resources), multinationals manage the world economy. Megacorporations are no longer tied to the interests of individual nations. In fact, MIT professor and political analyst Noam Chomsky considers transnational corporations a world government unto themselves. But they are anything but democratic. Corporate profits drive global policies that shape the fate of the world. These policies, whether related to the environment, social welfare, schools, health care, or workers' rights, are made by organizations that are inherently undemocratic. Decisions are top-down, noninclusive, and hidden from public view.[36]

Why the Public Is Not Protesting Corporate Control

American officials, confronted with the massive transfer of wealth upward, have been unable to brake or discipline global power brokers. While citizens decry the impotence of political leadership confronted with social chaos, violence, homelessness, rising crack cocaine use, and the elimination of jobs, international corporations amass the greatest accumulation of wealth and power in the world's history. But the public is misguided, because in a democracy the political institutions are what people identify as having power. The definitive power of the corporate sector is hidden because citizens are taught that democracy is stronger than special interest groups, who represent the corporate interests.

Another way in which corporate power is hidden is media's identification of the interests of global profit with the interests of Americans. Americans are invited to be consumers as a way of belonging. In a culture that has seen the decimation of community, the only sense of participation people have is through their ability to purchase. Mall culture has turned suburbia into a teenage wasteland. Inner-city kids will get things any way they can in order to be somebody. Social success and social identity are tied to patterns of consumption—I am because of what I have.

According to Richard Barnett, "The rage and fury found ... in this country is directed almost exclusively at government because mainstream media virtually never target the global corporations as major contributors to the nation's socio-economic woes.... Neither [the Democratic nor the Republican] party is prepared to take on the core issue that is transforming American life, because both depend on corporate money and connections to win votes...."[37] Ironically, Patrick Buchanan gained some popular support in 1996 precisely because he campaigned against corporate greed, but his championing of the middle-class "working stiff" focused on a working man of European ancestry. Other working men (women weren't considered) were generally ignored by him.

GLOBALIZATION AND DEMOCRACY

The world is getting smaller, as people like to say, but it is not coming together. Indeed, as economies are drawn closer, nations, cities, and neighborhoods are being pulled apart. The processes of global economic integration are stimulating political and social disintegration. Family ties are severed, established authority is undermined, and the bonds of local community are strained.[38]

RICHARD BARNETT AND JOHN CAVANAUGH

The 1992 United Nations Human Development Report revealed that the richest 20 percent of the world owns 83 percent of the globe's wealth and that the poorest 60 percent survives on 6 percent of the world's wealth.[39] One year later, the report looked at the globalization of political power. The 1993 report said that 90 percent of the citizens of the globe have no control over institutions that directly affect their lives. The researcher for the report, Mahbub ul Haq, the former Pakistan Director of Finance, said that "exclusion rather than inclusion is the prevailing reality."[40] Rather than holding women, the poor, and "minorities" responsible for their own powerlessness, the report says that they are excluded from power: "It is clear that certain groups, whether they are poor, women, minorities or rural dwellers, just do not participate, do not have access to power and do not share in the benefits of the economy in most countries of the world."[41]

Antidemocratic forces in less developed nations are clearly identifiable. But in the United States the *ideal* of democracy masks an electoral process that is not democratic. The way election campaigns are financed—by corporate interests—subverts a democratic process by awarding political power to those who can buy it:

> Only 1 percent of all Americans give $200 or more to a congressional candidate. [Yet] the residents of one zip code on New York's Upper East Side contributed more money to congressional races in 1994 than did the residents of each of 24 states. At least...28 percent of the U.S. senators are millionaires.[42]

Although the U.S. House of Representatives has fewer millionaires than the Senate (only 17 percent), nevertheless, to win a seat in the House costs an average of a half million dollars.[43] Candidates arrive in office with political "debts" to pay to their fiscal backers. Those who balk or who stand in opposition to the "business as usual" monied interests don't get reelected. Low voter turnout indicates the public's fading hope in a legislative process far removed from their lives. Even when voters don't vote, their "interests" are covered. According to Sheila Collins, "Corporations are spending hundreds of millions on advertising, lobbying, and 'fake' grassroots campaigns organized to support their interests."[44] If the working class "grassroots" interests are contrived, then the interests of the poor are ignored.

Government has become the servant of transnational corporate power blocs. Global corporations have "achieved a degree of global integration never before achieved by any world empire or nation-state...whatever flag they fly, [multinationals] can use overseas subsidiaries, joint ventures, licensing agreements, and strategic alliances to assume foreign identities when it suits their purposes—either to help them slip under tariff walls or to take advantage of some law of another country."[45] The attraction of the global market has made U.S. corporations less loyal to America and more aligned with their international corporate cartels. Global corporate interests supersede what is left of the calculated loyalty to an American work force or national welfare. Corporations escape responsibility for the harmful effects of globalization of the economy. According to Richard Barnett and John Cavanaugh, "The direct and indirect costs of deindustrialization—in unemployment and welfare benefits, added strain on the health, police and penal systems in stressed out communities across America—add up to a catastrophic loss."[46]

Surplus People

Civic responsibility for the poor is becoming as extinct as the buffalo or pristine forests. Like the buffalo and the native people who hunted them, populations are expendable in the new world order of the corporations. Economist Xavier Gorostiaga believes that the transnational corporate cartels, no longer dependent on cheap labor to amass wealth, are creating surplus populations: "There is no niche in such markets for the poor and excluded. They cannot fit in as workers because economic growth, under this model, is fast becoming jobless growth; they cannot contribute as consumers either."[47]

The poorest nations of the third and fourth worlds, as well as the poor in the core city and former farming areas, have been written off. Is it any wonder that people turn to drugs? Is it any wonder that the ensuing internal wars over the only capital (drug profits) to reach depressed inner-city areas are permitted? For example, the average imprisonment time for violent crime (the majority of which was related to drugs) tripled between 1975 and 1985. Yet, if the "get tough on crime" solution were effective, we should have seen a decrease in violent crime.[48] Instead, the U.S. prison population tripled. One in three black males are in jail, prison, or on probation. In Minneapolis during the 1980s, drug arrests for African Americans increased by 500 percent as opposed to only 22 percent for whites, according to Debra Dailey, director of the Minnesota Sentencing Guidelines Commission.[49] And according to the Brookings Institute, if current incarceration rates continue, by the year 2054 half the population of the U.S. will be incarcerated.[50]

To eliminate a large percentage of the violence that bleeds away the life of America's children and youth, we would have to challenge the corporate policy that shapes politics. The Government Accounting Office and the National Medicine Institute have documented the effectiveness of drug treatment programs to reduce drug use and related crimes, yet the waiting lists for drug rehab programs in inner-city areas are so long that many people drift back to using. Prison rehabilitative programs are virtually nonexistent. And there are few jobs for former inmates in any case. These are expendable populations.

In 1970, Sidney Willhelm identified the African American population in America as no longer needed even as a cheap labor base. Black workers were disposable once machines could replicate their industrial labor:

> With the onset of automation the Negro moves out of his historical state of oppression into one of uselessness. Increasingly, he is not so much economically exploited as he is irrelevant.... The dominant whites no longer need to exploit the black minority...the Negro transforms from an exploited force to an outcast.[51]

Blaming unemployed African Americans for lacking a work ethic masks the reality that jobs are gone as well as deflects political criticism from government's failure to defend social equality. The ideology that castigates poor blacks for the *results* of economic strategies that have stripped them and left a wake of wreckage—underfunded schools, hospitals, and housing—turns attention away from the cause of their poverty. A wall of silence not only separates most Americans from the lives of the dispossessed but also from understanding the transformation of social life that has put all but the very rich in jeopardy.

INCREASED POVERTY
AND "AT-RISK" CHILDREN

Addicts, gangs, single mothers on AFDC, and poor children are abstractions to most Americans. We hear reports of their deaths within miles of our homes, yet it is as if their situation is a distant war. We have no part in it except to avoid the danger zones. According to Geoffrey Canada,

> It is because most people in this country don't have to think about their personal safety every day that our society is still complacent about the violence that is engulfing our cities. What if I were to tell you that we are approaching one of the most dangerous periods in our history since the Civil War? Rising unemployment, shifting economic priorities, hundreds of thousands of people growing up poor and with no chance of employment, never having held a legal job. A whole generation who serve no useful role in America now and see no hope of a future role for themselves. A new generation, the handgun generation. War as a child, war as an adolescent, war as an adult.[52]

When the "war against poverty" failed, the other war began—the war against poor children. In the 1960s, 27 percent of children under the age of eighteen lived below the poverty line, but the war on poverty reduced that figure to 14 percent—a percentage still higher than that of other industrialized nations.[53] By the 1970s, child poverty rates began to climb as deindustrialization obliterated blue-collar jobs. Job flight resulted in disintegration of neighborhoods or rural counties. When community cohesion is demolished, social fragmentation and chaos set up conditions that isolate families.

The children of these families are referred to as being "at risk"—not at risk of poverty, but at risk of social failure: dropping out, being abused, becoming homeless. They become part of the disposable population no longer needed in the economy. According to the U.S. Census Bureau, in 1991, 21.8 percent of the nation's children lived below the poverty line.[54] That's at risk. In the words of historian and political analyst Lerone Bennett, "the black poor are a given, relegated to the scrap heap of human inevitabilities like 'death or taxes.'"[55]

Where are the studies of poverty that represent the poor without judgment, condescension, or paternalism? According to Dan Pence and Richard Ropers, "If to be poor in this society is everywhere represented…as synonymous with being nothing, then it is understandable that the poor learn to be nihilistic. Society is telling them that poverty and nihilism are one and the same. If they cannot escape poverty then they have no choice but to drown in the image of a life that is valueless."[56]

Increased Unemployment
and Increased Child Maltreatment

Increased unemployment affects child maltreatment rates. A study of two poor neighborhoods in Spokane, Washington, found that the neighborhood with the highest unemployment rate (three times higher than the norm) had a two times higher rate of child abuse reports than the poor neighborhood less devastated by unemployment.[57]

Being poor and desperate is depressing. Feelings of powerlessness and frustration result from lack of control over one's life. A study of 241 single African American mothers with an average of three children showed that job loss or job interruption led to "depressive symptomology [and] predicted more frequent maternal punishment of adolescents…and mothers' negative perception of their maternal role…. Adolescents who perceived their families as experiencing more severe economic hardship reported higher anxiety, more cognitive distress and lower self esteem."[58]

Intensified disciplining of teenagers by parents under stress is hardly maltreatment. But even the Spokane study shouldn't be construed as indicating that poor families are more likely to maltreat their children. The vast majority do not. Rather, conditions of poverty are abusive, and some families break under the pressure. According to Marian Edelman,

> No child is physically, economically or morally safe in 1995's America.…
> While 15.7 million children live in poverty, 9 million lack health care,

preschool vaccinations lag behind some Third-World countries, and millions of children begin life and school not ready to succeed, the top 20 percent of Americans increased their share of our national income by over $116 billion between 1967 and 1992—about equal to the total gross national product of Saudi Arabia.[59]

The World's Children Summit points out that children can be protected. Addressing the nations of the world, a declaration reminded all that "the Convention on the Rights of the Child provides a new opportunity to make respect for children's rights and welfare truly universal.... The lives of tens of thousands of boys and girls can be saved every day, because the causes of their deaths are readily preventable."[60]

CONCLUSION

To understand maltreatment of children, we need to understand the precise dangers that children face. This is not to absolve abusive parents but to point out the need to reinterpret a hidden source of social violence and to locate the recipients of child welfare policies in a context of social expendability. An analysis of global restructuring's impact on child welfare services to "expendable" families is essential to understanding the current crisis in both child and social welfare.

The poor are not a stratum of society more prone to pathology, violence, or despair, although they endure transformed conditions that have given rise to a new undercurrent of hopelessness as jobs and public welfare are eliminated. It is essential to examine three transformations that have affected the poor: the economy, demographics, and the social environment. Such a focus allows us to see the way these dynamic and interconnected realities explain the social problems confronting America and the problems faced by the families of poor children. The term *underclass* reduces these dynamic changes to a focus on the poor as the cause of their own problems.

The globalization of the economy has transferred wealth upwards while creating ever more expansive levels of poverty in the world. A technological revolution has replaced human labor with automation programmed by elite knowledge producers. Deindustrialization and downsizing have produced structural unemployment because the manufacturing and lower-level management jobs that were eliminated by restructuring are not replaceable. Large pools of unemployed workers cannot be reintegrated into the economy because manufacturing jobs are gone and because retraining in the knowledge industry is not offered to traditional blue-collar workers. This growing corps of the unemployed is a surplus population. The new dynamic is creating two nations within the United States—one for the wealthy and one for the poor and the working class.

The traditional American working class has been dislocated by this social transformation. Black and Latino workers who had achieved skilled and semi-skilled jobs in manufacturing are left without livelihoods. Families in core cities have been confronted with job loss, the dismantling of public health care, lack of housing subsidies, schools that have become more dangerous than educational, and neighborhoods riddled with drugs and despair. The link between loss of jobs and increased poverty, especially concerning children, has been masked by intensive attacks on unwed teenage mothers and AFDC mothers who are held responsible for America's social problems. Communities hit with unemployment report increased maltreatment of children. But rather than connect mistreatment of children with environmental pressures, child welfare has focused on the family, especially poor mothers, as the "problem" that needs "fixing."

The rise of multinational economic dominance has been accompanied by a weakening of the power of individual nations. Government has little power to corral global corporations. According to a 1993 United Nations study, 90 percent of the citizens of the globe have no control over the political institutions that affect their lives. In the United States, the democratic electoral process has been subverted by corporations' ability to maneuver outcomes through fiscal backing of candidates.

Personal Narrative
Jackie and Paul

What follows are the testimonies of Jackie Rivet-River and her foster son, Winifred Paul Dennis. (Unlike all the other boxed narratives following the first five chapters, I have summarized Jackie's story except excerpts in which she speaks in her own words. Paul's narrative is all in his own words.)

This is a story of crosscultural "adoption," where the child and family pick each other without the intervention of the state. How these two artists, one from the white upper-class lakeshore set and the other from a black impoverished ghetto, chose each other remains a mystery.

Paul is currently attending Columbia College, where he is studying art and majoring in computer art. He held a job as an art research assistant at an educational publishing house until he completed his GED, scoring in the 95th percentile range, and entered Columbia College.

Jackie's narrative focuses on the struggles both with Paul's family and with DCFS.

Jackie Rivet-River
Jackie is not your average foster mother. She's made award-winning documentary films. Her husband, Lewis, is a neurosurgeon.

I still tell his caseworkers I'm Paul's foster mother, but we never did get licensed, *Jackie says.*

Paul is eighteen now. He was nine years old when they met. He was playing in the park with her son, Beau. Paul was a street kid pretty much on his own. But he was miles from the streets on the Southside where his mother, an addict, lived with his brother, Terry. Paul's streets ran along the Lincoln Park lagoon in an upscale lakeshore neighborhood sprinkled with some low-income senior citizen high-rises. One such apartment is where Paul lived with his great-grandmother, who was stoned a lot and who lived with Jimmy. Jimmy was very special to Paul—the best parent he knew. Great-grandma Prezilla, who was frequently in pain, did her best. At 7:30 each morning Paul left, because kids weren't allowed in the building. He couldn't return until 10:30 at night. But he managed. He went to school most of the time, played after school in the park, and hung out until he could slip back into the building. The tough part was meals.

Paul was playing with Jackie's son, Beau, when they met. Maybe it was hunger, but Jackie thinks it was something else that impelled Paul to admit he was hungry. He was a proud boy and wary, but at nine he still expected something from the world, in spite of everything he'd been through.

It was such an incredible act of trust on his part, but he came home with us to eat. And that began a lifetime relationship.

This trust came from a child who stood wild-eyed when his other grandmother, who lived in Las Vegas, was stabbed to death in front of him. Terrified, he and his brother Terry ran away. They slept in abandoned cars for two weeks before a social worker found them. Paul was four years old.

By the age of nine he was watching his back. But he wasn't closed off like his brother, Terry, who was older and took on more of their mother's pain and abandonment.

Terry turned into a raging bull as a result of all this, but not Paul. Paul was gentle, a compassionate human being. Who knows why? Paul tells stories of constantly moving because they couldn't make rent, of physical abuse. He told me he was hit with an iron skillet and a belt. He talked about "those guys" who were always around—maybe his mother's boyfriends. I don't know… but they were batterers.

Paul could hardly have imagined the world he was entering. Jackie and Lewis's apartment overlooks Lake Michigan, high above the city's squalor and danger. Three glass walls catch a flood of light that washes over porcelain, mahogany, sculpture, crystal, a flare of poinsettias, and a Louis XIV desk. At the end of a long entrance hallway a blue

veiled Madonna holding a child gazes from a gold-framed Raphael painting.

The painting was in Lewis's family for generations. His mother wanted us to have it.

For months, Paul hung out with Beau and his family, having dinner, sometimes staying overnight. Only when Paul had missed school too many times and the teacher called Jackie did they learn that Paul's great-grandma Prezilla was in the hospital and Paul had been living alone. That was when the school called DCFS.

That's when we became involved with Paul's mother, Taronda [pseudonym]. She had two girls five and six, each child by a different father. Taronda is such a victim of institutionalized racism. Her grandmother and mother worked in bars to survive. They were always seen as niggers. This is a long line of strong women.

Pretty soon Taronda agreed that Paul should stay with Beau's family. But it wasn't legal. So Jackie went to court.

Here's where it gets murky. We go before a judge and Taronda has to say, "Yes, I'll let Paul become a ward on the promise that he can live with the River family." We become temporary foster parents on our way to becoming certified foster parents. The FBI did a background check and fingerprinted us. We're upper-middle class. We live an orderly, comfortable life. My husband is one of the finest surgeons in the city. Still, we had to have an FBI check. We were fingerprinted, photographed. We told our life story. What a joke! Then a DCFS worker came to measure the bedroom Paul would sleep in. Most of these kids don't have a mattress to sleep on, but they came in here with tape measures! It was an invasion…. What they should have been measuring was our ability to be caring parents.

It had only begun.

We were temporary foster parents for a year. I called constantly to check on our status. It's like getting through to the *Pentagon*—it's impossible. Here we are with the means to support a child, and we can't get licensed. Then the DCFS worker finally called to say they'd lost our records and we'd have to come in for another FBI check. We were back to square one. We refiled and got fingerprinted. In the meantime my husband was hospitalized, and they wanted copies of his hospital records. It was so invasive.

DCFS never did get the paperwork done. But Paul had a home. At Christmas he went to the Southside to be with his mom. On Christmas day Taronda had enough. She tried to kill herself with an overdose of pills. Before she fell in front of her frightened daughters, she told Paul he'd better get prepared to take care of his sisters. Paul saw his mother taken away in handcuffs because she refused to go in an ambulance.

Paul called me. I called for help. I reached a neighbor who would stay with the children. I know I should have gone down. But I was burned out with my own family illness. I couldn't take it all on. By then Taronda had a new baby she named Lewis, after my husband. Taronda named the baby after Lewis because he was able to get her medical help with the infant at a critical time of her pregnancy. A welfare mother can't get into drug rehab programs on their own. They must be triaged in. Cook County will triage you if you're wigged out, bleeding, fainting, etc. Lewis was able to triage Taronda so that she was able to go to a drug rehab program.

The drug rehab worked. Baby Lewis was born drug free, and Taronda's intelligence so impressed program workers that she was asked to stay on as a substance abuse counselor. But she left. By the time baby Lewis was six months old, she was using again. That Christmas was when she attempted suicide.

Paul has been in twenty-eight schools, fourteen foster homes. He lived with us from the age of nine to fifteen. At fifteen I worked hard to get him into Lakeview Academy. He's a gifted artist. He was thriving. My uneducated psychological view was that he couldn't handle the structure, the discipline. He couldn't run the streets, be out all night. He had to come home, do homework, have dinner, go to bed. This was foreign to him—it was either too good or too much.

Paul was in his own bedroom. He always slept under the bed with a lamp on his face. He would take the drawers out of his dresser and dump everything out, stack the drawers up, then take clothes from his closet and throw them on the drawers. He created this chaos in order to reconstruct a familiar, comfortable lifestyle.

One can only imagine Paul's efforts to reconstruct his life. At fifteen, when he had the chance to make it in the white privileged world, he balked. Jackie came home one afternoon to listen to a phone message from Paul's counselor: "Paul doesn't want to live with you anymore."

When I see Paul he is crying, telling me he wants to live with a black family. That was true. That was his quest. He went to live with a foster mother and daughter on the Southside. But putting Paul with a black mother figure was explosive. Then a caseworker came to our house. He was arrogant. He took Paul into his room, threw him on the bed, and said, "You want out of this place? You leave here and I'll see to it you'll never get back. You don't know what's out there. You ain't never seen the other side of midnight."

But it was midnight Paul was seeking— the black world where he could know himself. Jackie says she didn't understand the depth of Paul's struggle for cultural identity.

Paul was seeking Malcolm X's notion of psychic conversion. I hadn't done my homework enough to know this. He needed to see himself as a black kid. He was an "oreo."

After that, Paul lived in a series of group homes or with foster parents who had a houseful of teenage wards. Jackie calls them kid factories, where kids were not allowed to use the phone or wash their clothes in the house. One day he brought a girlfriend who he'd met in a group home to meet Jackie.

I told him how much I missed him and that I wondered what he was doing with his life, his art, his schooling. His girlfriend turned to him and said, "You're an ungrateful asshole. You've got somebody who cares about you, and you don't even call or keep in touch. I've never had anybody in my life who felt that way about me."

But Paul was searching. When TV talk show hostess Bertrice Berry flew Taronda to Chicago for a show reuniting welfare families, Paul's caseworker refused to let him go. Besides, Paul wanted nothing to do with his mother. But his father's name came up for the first time in his life. Paul and his brother, Terry, began a journey to find their father in Rockford, Illinois.

Terry Sr. was a drug dealer with an arrest record as long as your arm. Whether it was Terry's macho hyperbole or a fact, Paul claimed Terry Sr. had forty-three kids living in the Rockford area. At last Paul had a family. What a family—he had half-brothers and sisters in half of Rockford. Only later would he learn Terry Sr. was not his father but his brother Terry's father instead.

Terry went to work for his father, but Paul refused. With the help of a family that befriended him, he started a small sign-painting business in their laundromat. But he couldn't make it. Terry offered help. What Paul had to do was be a courier for his father for a week, and he'd have money to carry him. Within two days the crack house was raided.

The police beat him. They held him out a window by his feet until he "confessed" that he was a crack dealer. Then they put on him assault charges, possession of a deadly weapon, and possession of cocaine. Class X felonies—three counts. It was his first offense.

The artistic kid who could survive on his own at nine years old peered into the tough other side of midnight for three months before Terry called Jackie and asked if she could raise $5,000 bail. She drove to Rockford to find Paul's public defender. If it weren't for him, Paul would be in Stateville Prison. The public defender told Jackie, "Racism is so pervasive here in Rockford that for blacks to make it requires guerilla survival. I will try to get the assault and gun charges dropped." The lawyer knew that planting guns and charging assault after police had beaten up black men was common, and he felt he had leverage to get the charges dropped.

It worked. After fourteen months of litigation and seventeen trips to court, the charges were in the process of being reduced to Class 4, with 24–30 months' probation.

Meanwhile we've taken on DCFS, who promised Paul room and board at Columbia College. We've sued them through Patrick Murphy's office. But no one from DCFS came to court to honor their subpoenas. When they were summoned a second time with criminal contempt, they came. Each DCFS employee (three of them) brought a DCFS lawyer saying, "They hadn't received their mail." There were nine DCFS workers and three lawyers. They have finally agreed to place him in Lawrence Hall, where 80 percent of his room and board will be paid. One wonders why it took all that effort just to get them to give him what they promised.

Winifred Paul Dennis

My memory blocked out a lot. At the age of three I was in foster care with my aunt. My mother was into drugs and prostitution. She had me in the street as a baby while she was prostituting. My brother was two or three. That's when we were taken away and placed with my aunt while my mother went to drug rehab. Then I stayed with her until I was five and I was sent to my grandma's in Las Vegas. My brother and I had fun. But when I was six my grandma got stabbed to death in a bar fight in the Brown Derby.

Then I came back to stay with my aunt. But my brother was taken by [child welfare]. They couldn't find me to take me away. It took my mother two years to get my brother back from Las Vegas.

I lived with another aunt, Bubbles, before I moved into an apartment with my great-grandma [in Chicago]. Aunt Bubbles liked me, unlike my mother, who favored my brother. Aunt Bubbles took me everywhere, and she brought me to pick greens with her on the farm.

My brother's bigger, and he's high yellow and better looking. I was a straight-A student who never got in trouble, but he'd steal from my mother's purse and blame me. She believed him. I got it. She called it "whuppins," but I called it beatings. She used extension cords, ropes. I decided I didn't want anything to do with either one of them.

From age seven to nine, I was with my great-grandma. I also liked my great-grandpa, Jimmy, as well as my great-grandma. She was my heart. She brought me through a lot. We lived on Circle Pine Grove in a senior citizen home when I first met the Rivers and their son, Beau.

Every once in a while it got bad at Grandma's when my uncles, who were worse than my mother, showed up. One was a professional pickpocket, and the other was in and out of jail all the time. My grandpa was a lamb, but my grandma, who was part Indian, would take a broomstick and go after you. She was almost ninety, but you didn't play with her or you got a beating. Then Grandma got sick. She was in and out of the hospital. Every time she went into the hospital my uncles would come

home drunk, rowdy, etc. She told me if those uncles kept coming and causing trouble she'd be kicked out of the apartment. Once when they were messing with me, my grandma came in and kicked them out. When she was gone, my uncles made me sleep in a closet.

Then my grandpa died of cirrhosis of the liver, my grandma was in the hospital, and I was living alone. The janitor let me work for $15.00 a day sweeping the stairwell and later shoveling snow. Then somebody called DCFS, but I hid.

In the meantime Jackie offered me a home to stay in if my mother would give written permission.

Then DCFS found me and said, "You can't stay here. This is a white family, you're a black kid, and it's against the regulations. Also, the Rivers are not [licensed] foster parents."

Jackie said, "OK, we'll become licensed."

The DCFS worker said, "He can't stay with you until that takes place; he'll have to go to a shelter." I said, "I'll run away. I'm not staying in a stinking shelter." They screwed me. They put me with the H family for a few months before I ran away. Then I went back with the Rivers. Then DCFS sent me to Lawrence Hall. I was there for a semester before I was kicked out.

While I was there I had a girlfriend. She was my "baby cakes." I loved her. If she didn't take her pills, she'd pass out. We ran away three times a week. I was a terror blossom.

My brother was also in Lawrence Hall. He was depressed. He'd been in mental institutions. He'd been beaten by my mom. He still goes through it. My brother is intelligent, but socially he's a vegetable. Thug-wise, he's Einstein. He's making $500 a week selling dope.

In Lawrence Hall, I ruled the staff. My brother was a six-foot giant on my side. He ruled the kids. We both ruled

Lawrence Hall. I knew how to get around the rules. I should be a lawyer, but they're crooks. We were rumbling at Lawrence Hall, man. They couldn't catch us. My brother and I and [my] girlfriend ran away all the time. I took her pills with us. But she'd go out on her own, forget her pills, and the police would bring her back. Then she was sent to a mental hospital. I showed her the ropes of Houdini. Maybe it was my fault.

The day they put her in an institution I was walking around depressed. Then her old boyfriend jumped me. The fight got so bad—I demolished him—that I got arrested. It was bloody. I was having a ball taking all the anger [out on him] I had at myself for putting her in that situation. She was my heart.

I broke open his door, I broke a chair, I hit a staff person. I was like a wild child. Let them file charges, I thought.

I was sent to the Audi Home [juvenile detention center] for three days. The Lawrence Hall staff said, "This boy is not coming back here." So I got sent back to the Rivers. Yeah, I was in eighth grade. Caseworker says it's mandatory I go to counseling because of my attitude. It's called attitude adjustment—but it's brainwashing. But the counselor was OK; I called him "Doc." We'd sit and chill—he didn't give too much advice. My stories were about fighting, and he tried to help me cool out. He encouraged me to draw to express my anger. I was in fights a lot. I was about to be kicked out of school. I transferred before they kicked me out.

They were gonna kick me out of Blaine, so I transferred to Alcate. When Alcate wanted to kick me out, I transferred again. This went on during high school also, all because of fighting.

My caseworker said, "If you don't straighten up I'll send you to Allendale [residential treatment center]. It's a lock-down facility where the train comes once a day. It's like a penitentiary for youth." Caseworker said, "You think you're a bad dude, but you go to a sissy high school. Allendale is a gladiator school. They want a young boy like you to be a woman. We'll just see how tough you are there."

I figured if I was sent there I'd just get myself kicked out. I was getting kicked out of high schools for fighting and cutting class. Then the Rivers put me in Lakeview High School with twenty students. I had a ball. I could whup everybody except Donna; she weighed 250 lbs. We became best friends. I stayed a year. I had only 2.5 credits, but I stayed in the art classes. During the school year I happened to tell the counselor I wished I didn't have a [white] family. Jackie learned about this and was upset. I told her I wanted to leave. She cried. I cried.

I'd lived with the Rivers six years on and off, but I wasn't around blacks, my people. So I was gonna leave. After I got in trouble and was sent to the Audi Home, my caseworker came over. He glares at me, but I couldn't look anybody directly in the eyes because of everything [shameful] that had happened to me. He slapped some paper out of my hand and said, "Look at me!" The guy's a power freak, a militarist. He's a racist toward whites. He hated Jackie because she made him do his job—get me clothing vouchers, look into my case, etc. He hated her because he had to do paperwork.

I said to him, "You don't own me. You can't come in here and talk this crap to me. You need to leave."

He upset me. If I was 88 ft. taller, I'd have whupped him, but he was 6 feet, 200 lbs., with big muscles. I couldn't twist or turn him. He hated me; I couldn't do nothin' to him.

He put me in Teen Living; then they put me with Miss Smith, who just happens to be an Illinois State Sheriff who weighs 250 lbs. She was a big horse.

The incident that got me sent to the Audi Home was that some guys I know robbed the Rivers of a TV and computer, but I was implicated because I came up to these guys when the cops came. Anyway, Jackie believed me, but my caseworker didn't. I was sent to Foundation House, an emergency shelter. It was my lowest point. I was a little dog. Cold. Boys on one side, girls on another. I was there four months even though you're supposed to be there two weeks.

But after a while, I thought I was king with the girls. I was dressed to "the nines." I had my fingernails done, my hair done. I was kickin'. I was always on the girls' side. I had five earrings and one in my nose. I thought I was the "Bomb."

Then I went back to a Southside foster home. I was living in a basement; it was cold. She didn't give me my allowance, so I walked around with empty pockets. She never used the DCFS food allotment money for me. Instead, she fed her family off it.

So I moved to another foster mother, but she locked the refrigerator on us and we couldn't use the washing machines. Our bedrooms were like walk-in closets. She wouldn't take us out to use our clothing vouchers. I hated her.

I was at Austin High School by then. But I got into another fight and couldn't go back to school. I wasn't drawing. No art classes. I had nothing going. I was fifteen and a half.

I ran away to Aunt Bubbles's daughter's home, whom I hadn't seen in ten years. Then DCFS gave me to my cousins to be my foster parents. Then I moved in with a guy I knew and his girlfriend. At Christmas I went to my cousins, and when I returned they gutted the place—my portfolio with my drawings, my clothes, money—everything was gone.

Then I went to the homeless shelter. I didn't want to go back to DCFS. I went to Unity Shelter at 79th and Es-canaba. And who's the director of Unity House but my old caseworker. My heart was in my stomach. Then I found out my brother Terry was there. Great. The caseworker was afraid of Terry because of his fierce temper. I hadn't seen my brother since Lawrence Hall. I was happy.

Then the caseworker says, "Oh no, I'm not going to have two of you!" But his supervisor says to let us stay. One guy said something about our mother, and Terry blasted the guy ugly. We beat up everybody. I got the mouth, Terry the fists.

Then our mother called from California. She says, "Do you want to see your father?" We say, "Yeah, for eighteen years." We wanted to get on a bus that night and go beat up this guy.

The guy [was in Rockford]. He was a big guy, looked exactly like Terry. His chest and thighs were huge. We decided to stay cool. We hung out with him. One time my father jumped out of the car and says, "Pay me!" Then he slaps this guy around. The guy's crying. Then my father pulls out a .22 and aims for the guy's kneecaps. My heart is jumping. Then he takes the guy's wallet and shoes and leaves him in the snow.

I think, "Who is this guy? My father? I couldn't do this to anyone."

But I decide to go live with this father of mine. He has a nice house. He has fathered forty-three kids! I would have been forty-four, but I found I wasn't his. I talked to my mother for the first time in five years. I said, "How come I'm the only dark one?" Then they told me about another guy who looked like me who lived in Rockford. My mother admitted he was my father.

Terry's father said he was my father, too, because he wanted me to sell dope for him. When I wouldn't, he kicked my brother and I out.

I had a small art business, painting signs, but after eleven signs the business folded. My brother said he would not lend me any money. He would give me

$400 if I would transfer dope from spot A to place B. Cool. I was waiting for my brother for the pick-up, but he called the police (that's the word that's out but I still don't know). But I do know I was set up.

I had charges of attempt to deliver, battery, carrying a weapon (it was Terry's)—thirty-seven years, seventeen with good time. It broke my heart. I fought with my brother, but I put his life before mine.

NOTES

1. Qtd. in Kenneth Davis, *FDR: Into the Storm 1937-1940* (New York: Random House, 1993), 42.

2. Qtd. in *Challenge: A Journal of Faith and Action in Central America* (Fall, 1992), 4.

3. Interview with Cindy Clark, public guardian investigator, June 7, 1995.

4. Interview with Emmett Johnson, June 7, 1995.

5. Michael Katz, *Improving Poor People: The Welfare State, the "Underclass," the Urban Schools as History* (New Jersey: Princeton University Press, 1995), 79.

6. Ibid., 64.

7. Ibid., 65, 66.

8. Ibid., 79.

9. Peter Drucker, "The Age of Social Transformation," *Atlantic Monthly* (Nov. 1994), 64.

10. Jeremy Rifkin, "Work: A Blueprint for Social Harmony in a World Without Jobs," *Utne Reader* (May–June 1995), 53.

11. Drucker, (part 1), 62.

12. Sheila Collins, Helen Lachs Goldberg, and Gertrude Schaffner, *Jobs for All: A Plan for Revitalization of America* (New York: Apex, 1994), 40–48, 59–61, and Jobs For All National Coalition fact sheet (Spring 1995).

13. Holly Sklar, "Imagine a Country," *Z* (Nov. 1992), 23.

14. Rifkin, 54.

15. Celine-Marie Pascale, "Normalizing Poverty," *Z* (June 1995), 38.

16. Rifkin, 53.

17. "U.S. Richest Got Richer in '80s Boom," *Chicago Tribune* (Apr. 21, 1992), 3.

18. Staughton Lynd, "A Jobs Program for the Nineties," citing the *BNA Labor Relations Reporter* in *Social Policy* (Fall 1994), 25.

19. Alexander Cockburn, "Tomorrow's City Today," *The Nation* (Jan. 23, 1995), 83.

20. Dan Pence and Richard Ropers, *American Prejudice: With Liberty and Justice for Some* (New York: Plenum Press, 1995), 104.

21. Marian Wright Edelman, "The Child's Defender," *Teaching Tolerance* (Spring 1993), 12.

22. Stephen Steinberg, *Turning Back: The Retreat from Racial Justice in American Thought and Policy* (Boston: Beacon, 1995), 212–13.

23. Althea Huston, Vonnie McLoyd, and Cynthia Garcia Coll, "Children and Poverty: Issues in Contemporary Research," *Child Development,* 65:2 (1994), 275–76.

24. Patrick Fagan, "The Real Root Cause of Violent Crime: The Breakdown of the Family," *Imprimis,* 24:10 (Oct. 1995), 1.

25. Frances Fox Piven, "Poorhouse Politics," *The Progressive* (Feb. 1995), 23.

26. Ibid., 24.

27. Ibid.

28. *New Internationalist,* quoted in *Too Much: A Quarterly Commentary on Capping Excessive Wealth* (Spring 1995), 8.

29. Ibid., 4.

30. An investigative study by the *Philadelphia Inquirer,* qtd. in "Federal Subsidies Not Creating Jobs, Newspaper Finds," *Chicago Tribune* (June 5, 1995), 3.

31. Stephen Moor, "How to Slash Corporate Welfare," *New York Times* (April 5, 1995), A25.

32. "Where Your Income Tax Really Goes," *War Resisters League Pamphlet* (1995).

33. Holly Sklar, "American Dreams, American Nightmares," *Z* (Nov. 1990), 42.

34. Pascale, 39.

35. "UN Data Offers Disturbing View of U.S.," *Chicago Tribune* (Apr. 24, 1992), 16.

36. Noam Chomsky, "Democracy's Slow Death," *In These Times* (Nov. 28, 1994), 28.

37. Richard Barnett, "Lords of the Global Economy," *The Nation* (Dec. 14, 1994), 756.

38. Richard Barnett and John Cavanaugh, *Global Dreams: Imperial Corporations and the New World Order* (New York: Simon and Schuster, 1994), 13.

39. Xavier Gorostiaga, "World Has Become a 'Champagne Glass,'" *National Catholic Reporter* (Jan. 27, 1995), 11.

40. "UN: Access to Power a Myth for Most," *Chicago Tribune* (May 20, 1993), 3.

41. Ibid.

42. Ellen Miller, "Paying to Play," *Sojourners* (Nov.–Dec. 1995), 22.

43. Ibid.

44. Sheila Collins, *Let Them Eat Ketchup! The Politics of Poverty and Inequality* (New York: Monthly Review Press, 1995), 29.

45. Barnett and Cavanaugh, 15, 280.

46. Ibid., 292.

47. Gorostiaga, 12.

48. Michael Tonry, *Malign Neglect: Race, Crime and Punishment in America* (New York: Oxford University Press, 1995), 121.

49. Ibid., 113.

50. "America's New Enemy," *The Progressive* (Oct. 1994), 8.

51. Sidney Willhelm, quoted in Jeremy Rifkin, *The End of Work* (New York: Putnam, 1995), 79.

52. Geoffrey Canada, *Fist, Stick, Knife, Gun* (Boston: Beacon, 1995), x.

53. Huston et al., 275–76.

54. Ibid.

55. Lerone Bennett, "There's Been a Misunderstanding About the Sixties," in Daniela Gioseffi, *On Prejudice: A Global Perspective* (New York: Doubleday, 1993), 587.

56. Pence and Ropers, 165–69.

57. James Garabino and Kathleen Kostelny, "Family Support and Community Development," in *Putting Families First,* Eds. Sharon Kagan and Bernice Weissbourd (San Francisco: Jossey-Bass, 1994).

58. Vonnie McLoyd, Toby Jayaratne, Rosario Ceballo, and Julio Borquez, "Unemployment and Work Interruptions Among African American Single Mothers: Effects on Parenting and Adolescent Socioemotional Functioning," *Child Development,* 65:2 (1994), 563.

59. Marian Wright Edelman, qtd. in *State of America's Children 1995* (Washington, DC: Children's Defense Fund), 3.

60. Sklar, "American Dreams, American Nightmares," 41.

4

⊛

Stubborn Children
and Vagabonds

Family is a farce among the propertyless and disenfranchised.
Too many families are wrenched apart, as even children are forced
to supplement meagre incomes. Family can only exist among those
who can afford to have one....At a home for troubled youth on
Chicago's South Side, for example, I met a 13 year old boy
who was removed from his parents after police found him selling
chewing gum at bars and restaurants without a peddler's license.[1]

LUIS RODRIGUEZ

Chuck Golbert turns from an office window that overlooks Juvenile Court, the Detention Center, and two alleys on Chicago's near west side. The office he shares with three other Cook County Public Guardian lawyers is lined with teetering stacks of briefs, coffee mugs, boxes, and open file drawers. Chuck sits erectly at his desk. He appears the antithesis of his maverick boss, Patrick Murphy. Although he's been up half the night preparing to do battle with the Illinois Department of Children and Family Services, his suit and starched white shirt are immaculately presented. He taps a sheaf of legal papers confidently. He wants me to understand his legal argument, which he explains in staccato legalese. When I slow him down, he painstakingly restates the law. Unlike the media's favorite renegade official, Patrick Murphy, Golbert lays the issues out in a—well—lawyerly way. There is no swearing, no pillorying of DCFS, no colorful metaphors that caricature ineptness, no one-liners that make you gasp or laugh. Chuck Golbert gazes steadily from behind round professorial spectacles.

Style aside, Golbert and Murphy are on the same mission. Chuck's eyes narrow when he talks about the current case. He's going to beat DCFS. "We've done it before," he says as he rattles off cases, "and we'll do it again."

When asked if he wants to eliminate DCFS, he says he does not, conceding that the state child welfare system is compromised by its herculean task. "It's not the specific director that's at fault," he says, referring to the current director's reform efforts. "DCFS hurts kids. In that, it's historically consistent. Let me tell you about Latoya," he says. "It's a story that spans 25 years." Then begins the story of one of his clients, Latoya, who is in college today.

"It was 1958 or 1959," Chuck begins. The papers read "Imprisoned and Enslaved Girl Rescued." Chicago papers blared the story of June, a young girl whose foster mother locked her in a room, where she was forced to lick envelopes seven days a week. Her only food, oatmeal, was withheld if she failed to complete her quota. She was fifteen years old, and the foster mother would not permit her to attend school. She could bathe once a week.

When the teenager's story hit the papers, she was removed from the home and her foster mother's license was revoked. But in the 1970s the same woman was again licensed as a foster mother. Was this an unfortunate but understandable mistake of a large bureaucracy, perhaps one worker's failure to check files? Possibly. But listen to Latoya's story.

In the early 1980s, Latoya and three younger children were assigned to this woman's foster home. Latoya never had it as bad as her younger friend. That child was made responsible for total care of the household, as well as the other children. One burned meal, broken vase, or pair of lost mittens evoked punishment, the threat of an electric cattle prod. It was too much for the teenager. She attempted suicide. She wasn't successful. Or maybe she was, because DCFS removed her from the home.

But they left Latoya, a five-year-old boy, and a seven-year-old girl. Within a year the state agency placed a baby with fetal alcohol syndrome in the home even after Latoya's friend's suicide attempt. All duties fell to Latoya. She was close to breaking down but tried to keep up for the little kids' sake. She wasn't allowed to give the baby nutritious food. As a result, the infant was starving.

Alarmed, a DCFS worker came to remove the baby from the home. The foster mother "nurturing" this infant, by the way, was eighty-one years of age. She still had the energy to belligerently confront DCFS. She refused to let the worker remove the infant. "I'll set dogs on you," she warned. "They'll kill you if you come in."

The Police Canine Unit was called. The infant was removed. The officers reported smears of dog feces and human feces in the house. Nevertheless, Latoya and the two younger children were not removed from the home—only the infant.

During the ordeal, a police dispatcher heard the emergency call for backup. The dispatcher caught her breath when she heard an address that had remained indelible in her mind for over twenty years. It couldn't be, she thought. She checked the name of the foster mother. My God! Then she called DCFS. Revoke this license, she told DCFS. She's crazy, vicious, dangerous. I know. I was the child she tortured twenty years ago. My name is June.

Three months later DCFS placed three more children in the house.

In 1984 a telephone repair man reported the foster mother for smacking the kids, calling them "stupid retards." The dinner that the children were served, he said, was spoiled food. They ate it anyway.

Later in 1984, Chuck Golbert says, DCFS *warned* the foster mother to improve conditions. Still, they did not remove Latoya or the five children. By 1985, DCFS contracted with a private agency to send a social worker to handle the home situation. The private agency worker called the foster mother crazy and said the house was infested and covered in filth.

Not even the social worker who showed sympathy for the children's plight knew the whole truth. He didn't know she had used electric cattle prods to discipline the children. They said nothing. Who'd believe them? What good would it have done to tell, knowing they'd face recriminations? Nothing had convinced the state to act before.

Latoya attempted suicide.

Once again, DCFS "rescued" a child. Once again, the agency removed the child from the home but did not revoke the license of the foster care provider. This time the remaining children were without any protectors. Not until 1986 would they be removed from the home. By that time their childhood had all but hemorrhaged away.

This tragic story is not without traces of beauty or light. Today, Latoya is a college student preparing to take up the struggle to defend the rights of the defenseless. Some would call her a successful state ward. However, the credit is solely Latoya's. It is a miracle that her mind and spirit are still unbroken.

Chuck has reams of these cases. He slaps two of the latest on his desk. He doesn't care about the DCFS overload, the inevitable oversights resulting from a glut of abuse and neglect reports that spins the bureaucracy toward chaos: "The state is obliged to protect these children from harm." Forgetting to do procedural check-ups can cost children's lives: "Look at the Helena H case." PSI is an organization contracted by DCFS and required by law to run a criminal background check on any family before it is licensed as a foster care provider: "In Helena's case they didn't bother running a check on the foster

father, who was sentenced for rape and drug dealing. I mean, a known convicted rapist and drug dealer. He rapes Helena regularly for three months. She
was eleven years old."

Chuck is just warming up. "Read this case—the story of the Banks Home."[2]

FAILURE BY FRAGMENTATION

Although Chuck would hold DCFS administrators culpable for such horren-
dous abuses of children, along with the caseworkers who continued to place
children in the home of a known abusive foster parent, the systemic abuse of
children results more from child welfare organizational structure than from individual negligence. A child or family has no one caseworker who knows them
in any continuous manner. One worker doesn't know what another worker
knows except through the case record. Records on children and families are
rarely complete, accurate, or positive. Instead, the records are an account of
family weaknesses, not strengths. In the case of foster parents, caseworkers
may hesitate to put negative assessments in the record because the need for
"beds," particularly homes that will take hard-to-place children, is desperate.

Let's examine the way Illinois' Department of Children and Family Services works to protect children (DCFS is more or less a functional model of
national child welfare protective services except for a few states, such as Vermont, Washington, and Alaska, which have changed from a protective service
removal model to more of a family support system):

- First, there is a **report of abuse to the DCFS Hotline,** in which an
  operator decides whether the complaint has merit.
- Next, a written complaint **report is sent to the DCFS investigative
  office,** and investigators have twenty-four hours to contact the family.
- If the child is judged to be not safe, **he/she is taken from the home
  and placed in a shelter or temporary foster home** to await a
  custody hearing.
- **A court hearing to decide if removal was warranted** is held within
  forty-eight hours.
- If the court rules for DCFS, the **child is placed in a foster home,
  with a relative, in a group home, or in an institution.**
- A DCFS **administrative case review** to decide where the child will
  eventually be placed begins within forty-five days.
- A **civil trial to determine if the parents have abused or neglected**
  the child must take place within ninety days after the child is in custody.
- A **dispositional hearing to determine if the child would be safe at
  home** takes place within 120 days.
- A **permanency plan that plans the child's future** must take place
  within eighteen months.

- Then there are three possibilities for "closing the case": (1) parental **rights are terminated and the child is adopted,** (2) the child is **returned home** with monitoring by DCFS, or (3) the child **stays in placement until he/she reaches emancipation age** and is then transitioned to live on his/her own.

Notice that the entire system is based on crisis response to family breakdown. And note the fragmentation of responses to both the child and family. For example, after the hotline worker's task is completed, the "case" goes to an investigator. The investigator's work on the "case" ends when he or she substantiates or invalidates the complaint. The investigator must do extensive paperwork and then pass the "case" to an ongoing caseworker who will meet with the family and child and take another family narrative. If the court places the child in a foster home, another foster care worker from a private agency with which DCFS contracts will work with the family and take yet another narrative. If the child has special needs (medical or psychological), two other caseworkers from mental health and health care may require the family and/or child to tell them their story once again. If an adoption takes place, an adoption worker will handle the case.

In time, the case record of the child in placement will come to represent his or her life. In this way a silencing takes place because dialogue has been obliterated by the fragmentation of service responses. The case record becomes the most accessible and efficient way to deal with the family and child. Diagnosis, treatment, and placement will be made on the basis of that record.

As to whether DCFS complies with its own guidelines, it is instructive to look at the permanency plan that federal law mandates must be in place within eighteen months. Caseworkers have reported to me that the average time for a permanency plan to be put together in Illinois is three years and, at times, four years! Milwaukee County is even worse.

THE INVENTION OF CHILD WELFARE:
A HISTORY

Fragmentation of services is a legacy of Taylorism's scientific management principles, which were appropriated from business in the 1930s by public welfare systems seeking to become more efficient. But, as John Hagedorn points out, increased, differentiated social service functions also offered a way to ensure child welfare survival by expansion of services. Even before expansion and multiple service provision, child welfare ensured its survival by implementing the regulatory practices that the dominant culture ideologically upheld. The history of child welfare reveals an America whose approach to the children of the vagabond or "dangerous" classes has been either paternalistic or punitive. The social ideas and conditions that account for child welfare's conflicted policies—of both support and control—are reflected in its history from colonial times to the present.

Child welfare policy is a social construction. Neither child abuse or neglect, nor the child welfare policies that would respond to maltreatment, are phenomena that are determined or inevitable. Instead, family violence and social policies of reaction to abuse are responses that change with shifts in economic opportunity and changing ideas about children and families.[3]

Regulating Poor Mothers

Social efforts to control family violence directed at women and children have been led by women's rights advocates, although the policy makers and administrators of those policies have more often been men. According to Linda Gordon, "In some periods the experts confronted wife-beating and sexual assault, male crimes, while in others they avoided or soft-pedaled these crimes and emphasized child neglect, which they made by definition a female crime."[4] If anti-family violence activists directed public attention to child and woman abuse, "family values" traditionalists used periods of economic hardship to scrutinize and penalize the unworthy poor. At such times the pathology and danger of "underclass" families, especially single mothers, was—and is—used to impose stringent standards. "Epidemics" of child abuse, though not wife abuse, flourish in such periods.

Regulating the Unemployed

In addition to restricting women to their traditional place, the need to control the insurgence of the underemployed and unemployed has also shaped child welfare policies. For example, when laborers were needed on the frontier, thousands of children "rescued" from urban slums were sent west on orphan trains to be adopted by pioneer farmers who needed their labor. It is imprecise to assume that social crusader Charles Loring, who was one of the founders of this practice, was motivated to use surplus immigrant labor to expand the nation and defuse rising militance. Rather, the shifting moral and political ideas that saw children as reformable rather than depraved, as Calvinist forefathers believed, inspired his campaigns. It is the convergence of cultural, economic, and political forces and ideas, as well as resistance to those forces, that has shaped and determined changing child welfare policies throughout history.

The "Stubborn Child" of the 1600s

The New England colonists considered the child a sinner who could be saved if born again into obedience, discipline, and respect for the authority of religion, parents, and state. Woe to the child who questioned those powers. In 1646 the *Body of Liberties,* as stipulated by the Massachusetts General Court, stated that if a "stubborn" sixteen-year-old refused to obey his mother or father, the youth should be brought before court magistrates, where following testimony "such a son shall be put to death." The *Body of Liberties* bleakly acknowledged the possibility of child abuse. It stipulated that if a "sixteen year old shall CURSE or SMITE their natural FATHER or MOTHER, he or she shall be put to death unless it can be sufficiently testified that the Parents...so provoked them by extreme and cruel correction, that they have been forced thereunto, to preserve themselves from death or maiming."[5]

However, the law was rarely needed because family life was so embedded in collective village and religious life that neighbors could and would broker rising family tensions. Furthermore, the patriarchal rule of fathers was so uncontested as to forestall challenge.[6] What the Puritans gave to the history of family and child welfare was a law that defined child, parent, and state relationships.

The *Body of Liberties* codified from the beginning the state's role as *parens patriae*. American law considered children to be the property of their parents, and if children became wards of the state they became state property. Rebellion against authority could result in death. But the legal code was also the first in history to recognize illicit parental authority and to grant children legal redress. If parents were wickedly severe, a child might bring the grievance to authorities. The problem, then as now, is how the party without power (children) could use the law against the parties whom the law favors, parents and the state.

America's moral code toward children was fundamentally shaped by New England Puritans, who promoted the work ethic as a sacred obligation that the state must enforce. Families that permitted their children the sin of idleness had their children removed from their homes. In 1737, selectmen in Watertown, Massachusetts, placed children older than seven out of the homes of "negligent and indulgent" parents in order to work for other families.[7] Foster care was an imposed solution for families or children who deviated from social or moral expectations.

The Protestant work ethic, so psychically and morally tied to the nation's spirit, has never acknowledged the structural barriers that thwart opportunity for some citizens. Those with blocked opportunity for employment are invariably, as social psychologist William Ryan[8] showed, blamed for their own unemployment. In effect, the victims, not the social conditions that create poverty, are blamed for their plight.

For the moral reformers of the 1800s, it was the culpable poor and their reformable children who were the focus of social concern.

Rescuing Street Children of the 1800s

In the nineteenth century, the "tenement classes" were composed primarily of immigrants who crowded into urban centers where sporadic employment kept families in desperate poverty. In the mid-1800s Irish families lived ten people to a one-room basement apartment with one window, sooted ceilings, walls splotched with muckworms, tubercular children, and a father able to work a few months of the year digging or carrying. Abandonment of the family by fathers who drank or simply never returned from a work contract was frequent. Their ragged children sold papers, took in laundry, shined shoes, and peddled flowers. Children worked and played in the streets late into the night.

In another example, through a *padrone* system Italian families sent children to the United States as indentured laborers to stay with families, which would return some of the children's earnings to their impoverished families in Sicily.[9]

These organ grinder children with their dancing, begging monkeys were found on the street corners of the urban slums. Newspapers "exposed" the musicians as nothing more than filthy beggars with a gimmick. They were, in the racist jargon of the day, "street Arabs" who needed to be saved from the evils and brutality of the vice-infested cities. Alcoholism, prostitution, and thievery flourished in the enclaves of the destitute. The respectable middle class and upper classes didn't venture into the streets of the "dangerous classes."

The same streets that offered immigrant parents pittance incomes from their children's ingenuity also became, as the children entered adolescence, a source of family contention and, at times, abuse. Bilingual, bicultural youth grew independent of their parents and chose the culture of the streets, with its emancipated sexual allure and risky petty-thievery opportunities. Young women who snuck out to forbidden, unchaperoned dances were often beaten by fathers attempting to "protect" and control them. Boys caught pilfering and brought before judges were subject to beatings by frustrated immigrant fathers confronted with the overreaching seduction of the new world and the loss of family and cultural life as they had known it.

Women and children were abused and abandoned in the harsh life of the immigrant and urban poor. The *padrone* system exploited children. Dejected Irish fathers beat their wives and punched and throttled adolescents they couldn't control. But child experts who would discipline families in order to save the children imposed a class standard of family life that the poor could not meet. What immigrant families needed—decent jobs, housing, health care, and cultural respect—was not what they received. The moral reformers assumed that these families should emulate accepted standards of family life regardless of the cultural and economic disruptions that made it impossible, if even desirable.

The child reformers were impelled by two concerns: compassion for children and a fear of the exploding immigrant class. Catholics especially needed "assistance" in learning American standards of family life. Catholic immigrants offered the most resistance to these standards, drawing much of their social support from a religiosity considered by mainstream America to be superstitious and ignorant. In spite of their resistance, immigrant families from peasant communities—separated from village kin, illiterate, and unaware of their social rights—had little power against the Yankee reformers, who had the legal and social power to remove their children in order to protect them from maltreatment.

The rough and sometimes violent discipline of slum dwellers conflicted with both women's rights advocates and moral reformers' campaigns against corporal punishment. Immigrant families' strategies for keeping their children from the lure of the streets of Boston or New York, where danger or pregnancy threatened their children, did not match the child-rearing ideals of family gentility that the middle class and elite class espoused. Parents confronted with malnutrition, illness, and social disregard demanded children's compliance through physical punishment. What middle-class reformers labeled as child cruelty was, for exhausted mothers and demoralized fathers, an attempt to keep their children from the brutality of the streets and the reach of both child welfare agents and the police.[10]

Child abuse resulted from family power conflicts over one's "place." Fathers, losing power and respect in a culture that held unskilled immigrants in low regard, also lacked the generational resources of land and inheritance of tools to protect their children's future. Physical fights with belligerent sons or beatings of daughters (or mothers who defended them) who rebelled against "old-fashioned" courtship rules ensued.[11]

Yankee Reformers Versus Street Urchins

In 1825, New York State legalized the incarceration of neglected and dependent children in houses of refuge. Although the constitutionality of virtually imprisoning children without due process was questioned, child protectors insisted that such intervention was necessary to prevent criminal or delinquent behavior.

Charles Loring, a critic of the houses of refuge movement, argued for deinstitutionalization of children. Although Loring rejected the criminalizing of children, he saw his task as rescuing the children of the "dangerous" class from the corruption of urban life. Hard work with farm families on the frontier would be the salvation of street urchins as well as orphans. To learn initiative and proper discipline, children should be *placed out* (the euphemism used to describe removing children from their homes for more suitable surroundings).

Thousands of children rode the orphan trains. In its almost eighty-year existence, Charles Loring's Children's Aid Society placed out 100,000 children.[12] The Boston Children's Mission and the Juvenile Asylum placed out thousands more. Many of the children were rescued from the streets by agency workers. But other "orphans" were brought to the humane organizations by single mothers desperate to save their children from urban danger or the family's deepening poverty.

Groups of children as young as three, as well as teenagers dressed in their one woolen suit or organdy dress, rode the orphan trains headed for Illinois, Indiana, or Wisconsin, then farther west. When the train arrived in a small farming town, the children were gathered in the train depot, town hall, or church and arranged upon a stage while the farm families indicated to chaperons which child they wanted. Occasionally, brothers and sisters were chosen together, but usually not. A boy sent to Benton County, Arkansas, described the feelings of children not initially chosen:

> We were taken from the train to the Methodist Church. Speeches were made and folks were asked to take an orphan home for dinner. Later that afternoon we were brought back for the selection process....I felt sorry for the others because some of them were not chosen. I know how much it must have hurt them to feel that no one wanted them.[13]

The New York Children's Aid Society, founded in 1853, placed out the abused, neglected, vagrant, runaway, and delinquent children of the immigrant working class. The society sought to save the sector of impoverished children that New York Chief of Police Matsell called "idle and vicious children" from whom flows "a ceaseless stream to our lowest brothels—[and from there] to the Penitentiary and State Prison."[14]

Although the Children's Aid Society sought to reform the army of "street Arabs," it left unquestioned a system of class, culture, and gender privilege that produced a ceaseless stream of poverty for some families and a stream of comfort for others.

The Cruelty Police

By 1875, reformers had focused on the abusive or neglectful parents of the poor classes: "Public officials and reformers…faced a delicate question: how to force a family to surrender its children."[15] A zealous cadre of humane reformers answered the challenge. The founders of the Society for the Prevention of Cruelty to Animals (SPCA) used the irony of legal redress for abused animals to foment social support for abused children, who had no such mandated advocates on their behalf. The Society for the Prevention of Cruelty to Children (SPCC), founded in 1875, was the charitable project of some of New York's wealthiest men—Cornelius Vanderbilt, Peter Cooper, and August Belmont.[16]

The SPCC's charter asserted that children had some rights, a legal and moral concept that limited but did not subvert familial patriarchal authority. Although the SPCC would expose cruelty to children regardless of the status of the family, those who were the recipients of their intervention were invariably pauper families. The state of New York granted SPCC agents legal and enforcement powers to investigate abusive and neglectful families. According to Michael Katz, "They encouraged neighbors to spy on one another, investigated cases referred to them by other agencies, initiated prosecutions, and, at least in New York, incarcerated children awaiting trial. In Philadelphia, when the SPCC asked courts to remove children from their families, they also requested jail terms for their parents to prevent them from interfering with their children's placement."[17] The SPCC earned a reputation as the "cruelty" police for patrolling urban slums and seeking young vagrants to be sent to orphan asylums. If parents fought back, the SPCC invariably won legal custody.

When a father attempted to challenge his daughter's placement in a house of refuge in 1835, the Pennsylvania Supreme Court unambiguously reaffirmed *parens patriae*. The court declared in *Ex parte Crouse* that "the basic right of a child is not to liberty but to custody."[18]

By 1870, the Illinois Supreme Court, in a unique break with precedent, upheld the petition of a parent, Michael O'Connell, who won the release of his fourteen-year-old son, Daniel, from the Chicago Reform School. Daniel had been incarcerated as a "predelinquent" who was sent to reform school for his own good and for the "good of society." However, Justice Thornton ruled that a child could not be incarcerated without a conviction for a crime: "If, without crime, without the conviction of any offense, the children of the state are thus to be confined 'for the good of society,' then…free government [should be] acknowledged a failure."[19] Thornton's ruling was a startling departure from the state interventionist policies that supported and amplified the work of the child rescuers.

Although SPCC policies differed—with Boston and Chicago emphasizing family rehabilitation and New York administering a punitive model—the SPCC's linking of charity with investigation and enforcement is a legacy that still informs child welfare practice. In Chicago, for instance, Cleo Terry, the executive deputy director of the Department of Children and Family Services (DCFS), resigned following a week that she spent at a DCFS shelter watching families of children removed from abusive homes broken apart and sent to various foster or residential group homes. She described a seven-year-old referring to DCFS as the police. In spite of her resignation, Terry refused to blame her agency, which she sees as an institution heaped with the burden of thousands of children who society has turned its back on.[20] Cleo Terry's former agency grapples today with the legacy of the child-saving movement that achieved its institutional mooring in Illinois at the turn of the century.

The Practice of Child Removal

Because the recipients of intervention have been families of the lower classes, whose cheap labor was used to build the nation, critical historians have interpreted child and family welfare policies as attempts to discipline worker militance or a restive worker surplus. Historian Linda Gordon shows that such a perspective fails to account for intrafamily conflict resulting from changing social conditions, especially challenges to the privileges of fathers that were encountered by immigrants in the new world. Child and family welfare policy is, and was, as much determined by gender standards of family life as by class and cultural standards.[21]

The history of child welfare is embedded in the history of government assistance to poor people, most often mothers. In fact, state child welfare agencies were administered within state welfare agencies until the 1970s, when "they became separate agencies under a policy of separation of social services from income maintenance programs."[22] A multilayered lens is needed to focus on the correlation of histories that have shaped the child protection movement. Three histories, at least, intersect: the history of government public assistance (welfare), the history of child welfare, and the history of changing cultural standards toward women, children, and poor families.

Child welfare practice, as opposed to policy, is a history of removal of children from lower-class parents who have been deemed unfit: "The major service of child welfare agencies traditionally has been foster care placement."[23] What has been the response of the poor to the removal of their children? Of the children sent to almshouses, farm homes, industrial schools, and orphanages? What about resistance?

Too often, children's defiance through running away, rage, theft, or withdrawal has been interpreted as pathological, deviant, or immoral. What if it were, as anthropologist James Welch has shown, a weapon of the weak?[24] A response to their powerlessness that seeks to exert some shred of control over their lives, perhaps even offering some small triumphs?

There were some success stories, however. What Linda Gordon's research reveals is that for each tragedy of abuse of children, or often wives, another account of mothers' and children's ingenuity in using agency assistance for survival is also indicative of social and child welfare in America. That account of how recipients fought, manipulated, suffered, circumvented, redefined, and survived state incursion is a mostly untold story. It is the narrative of people with little political or economic power who both resisted and used these policies to improve their desperate lives. Mothers and children who dealt most directly with child welfare reformers and the courts were sometimes able to use these resources, as well as the kindness of social workers when help was offered without binding constraints.

Child welfare is also the story of certain social workers, allied with their clients, who challenged regulations in order to benefit families. These advocates subverted the practice of child removal by funneling whatever meager fiscal resources they could to fend off family catastrophe and the loss of children. This is not to say that advocates did not at times support parents' insistence on relinquishing their children because the parents did not believe they could give them a "decent" life or because their children had become unmanageable. At times, removal of children was and is a defense of life. However, the voices of these advocates, like those of the clients they served, have been virtually silenced by a child welfare narrative that treats the issue of child abuse and neglect as if it were a history beyond the contentious realm of power relations.

Regardless of the advocacy of nonconformist social workers, America's policy of removal of children from the homes of the poor and the culturally different has remained a constant policy in spite of ideological insistence on keeping families intact: "Theoretically, there may have been much opposition to the idea that poverty alone should not be grounds for breaking up families, or to the premise that parents of 'worthy character' who are 'efficient and deserving' should keep their children. It was just that poverty was thought to coincide with faulty parenthood and unworthiness of character."[25] "Faulty parenthood" is both a class and a gender construction of child welfare reformers. A charge of neglect invariably implicated the mother, and a charge of physical cruelty usually, though not always, implicated the father.

The history of child welfare uncovers both its anti-family practices, framed in a rhetoric of family preservation, as well as the unacknowledged resistance of children and their parents, most specifically poor mothers.

CONCLUSION

The history of family violence and child welfare reveals shifting policies shaped by expanding and contracting economic opportunities for the lower class and immigrant class. Another factor is the changing patterns of intrafamily conflict resulting from challenges to the patriarchal privilege of fathers.

American ideas about childhood underwent a profound shift from the seventeenth-century notion of the stubborn child to the nineteenth-century notion of the reformable child. Child welfare reformers did not address the causes of the pauperism that ghettoized immigrant families and unskilled "native" workers in the 1800s. Instead, reformers of this era rescued destitute children from "unfit" parents. Their objective was moral uplift. Thus, the child welfare policy of removal of poor children from their homes was set in motion.

Three intertwined histories are evident: (a) the history of child welfare, (b) the history of government assistance to poor families, and (c) the history of changing cultural standards regarding women, children, and families. Child welfare policy is as determined by gender standards as by cultural and class standards.

Just as the urban poor of the nineteenth century were scapegoated as the "dangerous classes," the urban poor of the twentieth century, who are labeled the "underclass," are seen as the source of social violence. The perception of child welfare as punitive and having the power to take children away has its roots in the 1800s, when SPCC agents were called the "cruelty police."

Personal Narrative

Tammy and Johnny Daniels

The trailer park where Tammy and Johnny Daniels live lies on the outskirts of Tolono, Illinois, a town of 2,400. Driving into Tolono from the flat stretch of lush bean and corn fields, you pass along the railroad tracks on one side and a granary silo, Tastee Freeze, and Judy's Tavern on the other.

Tammy greeted me with her eighteen-month-old daughter, Autumn. Later, Johnny returned from his weekend job as a painter. Their small trailer is attractive. Photographs of their sons, Justin and Jacob, are the main attraction on the wall separating the living room and kitchen from the back bedrooms. The boys are silver blondes, like their mother, and their smiles are angelic. They are four and five now, but they were two and three when the state took them.

Here is their story. It is a story that locates in flesh and blood many of the themes of this book: a court and child welfare system that punishes mothers for their husbands' behavior; the power of judges and caseworkers to "save" or destroy a family; the assumption of parental guilt; the destruction of children's sense of trust or self-esteem; the healing process that began for the parents and boys

(though their healing will take years) when a caseworker became an advocate rather than an adversary; and, finally, the evolving grit and determination of a mother who had initially, in the words of her husband, "let the authorities run over her." It is a tragic story, but one with hope.

Tammy Daniels

It was 1991 when they took the boys. My husband is an alcoholic. I'd start fights because I was angry he was drunk. There were shouting matches, and neighbors called the cops. [The second time the police were called] they took my kids. It was our fault. We needed to get our lives together. My husband needed to get help. We both came from dysfunctional families.

My husband's father was an alcoholic. Alcohol stood between us. But my husband was good with kids. It was my fault I'd get angry at his drinking. It wasn't my fault that he drank. I blame ourselves for the cops being called. But we didn't know any better. We were putting the kids through this, and our relationship wasn't healthy. In a way I'm grateful for what happened because we had no money for counseling, nor did we even know there were services. But I'm not grateful they took my kids. Oh, I miss my kids. It has been a nightmare. In a way it helped our family and it destroyed our family.

The foster mother where my boys were sent went to court and told the judge she'd been a foster parent for six years and she'd never seen children so bonded to their parents. "Send these boys home," she said. She even told the judge my oldest boy would stand at the window for hours and cry. She told the judge that he got up at night and climbed into the crib with his brother.

We thought [what had happened to our boys then] was bad. But it was only the beginning.

Even though the foster mother testified for us, the judge gave discretion to DCFS. That foster mother told DCFS, "I can't bear these boys crying anymore." She told DCFS she was considering resigning as a foster parent if they didn't send my boys home. Two weeks later, the boys were returned. We had complied by going to domestic violence classes. My husband agreed to go to an alcoholic treatment center for four months. He was reluctant, but he wanted the kids back.

He came home in July 1992, and four months later they took my boys again. The DCFS worker said that if my husband was drinking I should take the boys and leave. If I didn't, they'd take the boys. As part of my husband's recovery he had to admit his wrongs to each person he'd hurt. He told me things I didn't want to hear. He was getting closer to me, but I became angry when he told me about his infidelity. We didn't argue because we were afraid they'd take the kids. We just didn't talk.

One evening he left because I wasn't responding. He couldn't deal with it, so he left. I assumed he was drinking, but I wasn't positive. So I took the kids and

went to a girlfriend's. DCFS had warned me, and I was scared. The next day I went to the counselor and told him what had happened. Then Johnny came to the counselor, and Johnny tried to reason with me, but I wouldn't listen. I asked the counselor if I should contact DCFS to let them know what happened. But he said, "No, don't jump into the fire. Come back in two days, and if you haven't worked things out we'll call DCFS."

But the counselor did tell DCFS, who told Johnny to move out or they'd take the boys. So the caseworker drove Johnny to his mother's. My husband wasn't actually drinking that night. I felt guilty for a long time. Johnny relapsed much later but only after they took the boys.

DCFS has a program called "Family Reunification." What a joke! My husband asked how he could see his boys because he was [at] a distance. The caseworker said he'd get him a bus ticket, but it didn't happen. My husband finally hitched a ride to see the boys.

Our "reunification" process was stalled because the caseworker said my husband wasn't concerned about the boys because he didn't visit them. Yet in the report to the judge the same caseworker listed my husband's repeated attempts to get bus money [including a call to the Springfield ombudsman]. Nevertheless, the judge and state's attorney called my husband a worthless and unconcerned parent. I was furious, but I had no way to prove the truth.

In addition to the judge's attitude, the state's attorney said she was surprised I could read or write. I confronted the court transcriber and insisted she include that remark in the transcript, but she got defensive and threw the transcript up in the air. I let it go, just like I let everything else go. But I'm not letting it go anymore.

The caseworker told me to get an "order of protection" if I wanted my kids back. I wasn't scared of Johnny. But I did what [I] was told. Two weeks later we had a court hearing, and the judge said, "Chaos!" That's all he said. And my kids have been gone ever since.

The Boys' Journey

By now, our boys had been in and out of foster care almost a year. Sometimes DCFS wouldn't show up with the boys for our visit. No phone call. Nothing. I'd sit and wait two hours. I remember one time when my kids were leaving, my oldest boy said, "Mommy, when I'm a good boy can I come home?" [Tears are streaming down Tammy's face as she talks.] I asked the caseworker how can anyone reply to that. He didn't answer. So I took my boy's face in my hands and said, "You were always a good boy. This is not your fault."

I felt that our family services caseworker had betrayed us more than once. I said I wanted a woman caseworker and that I didn't trust Family Services. So from May of 1993 until August of that year I didn't have a counselor. When I went to court, the judge went off— saying I didn't care because I wasn't in counseling.

Finally they assigned a woman caseworker who we called "our little angel." She told me to drop the "order of protection," and she got us into marital counseling and a domestic violence program. I even requested to take the domestic violence program a second time because I felt I didn't benefit the first time because I was too frightened and caught up about losing the kids to pay attention. Services that were also provided were parenting classes, individual counseling, and alcohol counseling.

We learned a lot in those classes. For example, that time our boys were returned, we gave them everything because we felt guilty and were afraid to set limits. We knew that was wrong. We completed all the classes except AA, which is lifelong. I'm still grateful to "our angel" for doing her job as a DCFS worker and for really helping a family in the process.

By now I had the boys for two hours on supervised visits on Sunday. I complained to the new caseworker that the boys had head lice and my youngest had huge bruises on his leg. Justin had told me, "Jenny whipped him with a fly swatter." But when I pulled off his pants, I saw huge bruises. After that, I repeated this to my caseworker, who told me to call the hotline. Two days later I again called a DCFS investigator, and he said he had not gone to see my kids. He said he talked to other kids in the foster home (there were at least seven kids) and that another kid did it. But I didn't believe it. That foster mother devalued my youngest. Now he thinks he's bad and stupid. Finally, a month later, they moved my boys [who had been there a year]. But they never admitted he'd been beaten.

My youngest son developed physical and behavioral problems. A psychologist determined he had chronic insomnia. They put him on drugs, which made me mad. But there was nothing I could do.

When they were sent to the next foster home, the foster mother called DCFS in frustration and suggested splitting up the boys. She wanted my youngest son to leave. I was furious. A week before Jacob was moved, Justin said the boys were whipped with a belt. I called the caseworker, who told me to call the hotline. I said, "Forget it, it doesn't work! But document this, please." Then the foster mother called the hotline (I think she knew we knew) and told them *we* were abusing our boys. So then the caseworker said we had to have supervised visits again. My husband had had it by now. That's when he left and relapsed to drinking. I didn't condone this, but I understood.

A month or two after Jacob was separated from his brother, he was sent to Carle Pavilion, a small psychiatric unit of a hospital. He was there for four months because the foster mother said he was hitting kids, biting dogs, sliding down steps—strange behavior.

The Pavilion was no better. When I went to see him, he had a bump on his head the size of a golf ball.

"What happened?" I asked.

"The Pink Room," he said.

It's a small room with concrete walls, two locked doors. When I asked why the room was so prison-like, they told me it was for the kids' protection from others and themselves.

"He must have banged his head" was their explanation.

Jacob admitted he banged his head against the wall because he hadn't earned his "tokens" for good behavior.

Jacob was there for four months. Then they sent him to two different homes. One placement during the day and a special treatment foster care program at night. Later he was in the special treatment foster home exclusively. Jacob started acting out again. He was almost four years [old] by then, and he'd been potty trained for a year, but he began to poop in his pants. He also began, at not yet four years old, to speak graphically about sex. So they took him to Dr. B, who said she wasn't sure if he'd been sexually molested anally. It was a possibility.

So the DCFS worker pointed a finger at us. An investigator came to interview us and interrogated my husband. It was our fault even though this child had been in seven different placements! I told the investigator my husband can be an asshole but he'd never molest his children. I asked for a polygraph test for both of us. They never contacted me for the polygraph, only my husband. He took it and passed.

He said, "If I take this polygraph, I want every foster parent [involved with my children] to take it." This was agreed until during John's polygraph. I was speaking to this investigator and

asked him when the others were scheduled to take the test, but he said it was too expensive. He implied that we might have allowed our boys to watch us have sex. After that, the whole incident was dropped.

Then Jacob began self-mutilation. He bit himself. He chewed on his socks. He ran out in front of a vehicle at a foster home. He said, "I'm just going to kill me."

Then they called [the public and private caseworkers] together. Catholic Social Services were, by now, the private contractors. I was informed, almost casually, at an appeal hearing. Jacob was put in the Riverside Medical Center psychiatric wing for two weeks. Riverside confirmed that Jacob had been sexually molested. Jacob had explained to his foster father how he'd been sexually abused in the previous foster parent's home. The foster father begged DCFS not to interrogate Jacob but to take his word for it—or allow him to be present with Jacob. Jacob had told him what had happened in the other foster home. In spite of his pleas not to put Jacob through an interrogation or to, at least, allow him to be by Jacob's side, they went ahead and interviewed him alone.

The investigator walked out of the interview and said, "Inconclusive."

That foster father followed up his first report and called DCFS again to tell them about sexual abuse Jacob had revealed. But again they said "Inconclusive." I still believe Jacob did reveal things during that interview. It's because in 1994 [this was March of 1995] a Central Baptist Transporter drove Jacob from one home to another. She took this same foster father aside on one occasion and told him that an older boy had molested my son in the previous home. They never told me what was happening to our son. It was then that Jacob first began acting out, and it was the first time he was sent to Carle Pavilion, the psychiatric facility. The foster father didn't say anything because he was told to keep quiet.

Finally, a meeting was called with my attorney (which I couldn't afford but I had to have some defense) and the Guardian ad litem for children. The foster father came and broke down and cried and told them he was informed that Jacob had been sexually abused. He said Jacob had been forced to have oral sex by an older boy. Jacob was only three years old then. My husband cried. But then everything clicked: the coverup, Jacob's deteriorating behavior, etc.

The Guardian said, "We're going to file a class action suit against DCFS on this child's behalf for not providing a safe and caring environment."

What my boys went through is a travesty. And before all this came out in 1994, the state's attorney filed a petition to have our parental rights terminated. They said my husband had relapsed, which he had, and while he was drinking and broke, he committed a forgery. For this crime he did three months in the county jail. Because of this we were unfit. When we went to court in 1995, we put our first caseworker on the stand, and he was caught in a number of lies. The judge saw this.

My husband questioned him because he couldn't afford a lawyer and so he was his own counsel. The judge supported some of my husband's interrogation. It was the beginning of freedom. Both my lawyer and the kids' Guardian ad litem lawyer showed how inept DCFS was during our three-day hearing. The judge said the caseworker hadn't provided services for the first $1\frac{1}{2}$ years after they took our boys, so we couldn't comply with the state's standards.

The judge said, "Isn't it an unusual coincidence that when Deanne Walk [the caseworker who was an "angel"] provided services that Tammy and John Daniels were in compliance? This case is a travesty. I do not believe that you [first caseworker] are a credible witness. But

John Daniels has been credible. I will not terminate the Daniels' parental rights." This is a summary, but the judge's ruling lasted a full forty-five minutes.

The Boys' Dilemma

Justin is very quiet, so I still don't know the extent of his abuse—or if he was sexually abused. Even if we get Jacob back, he must attend "Baby Fold" in Bloomington, Illinois—it's a treatment center for abused kids—for, at least, six months or a year. Personally, I think having a lot of love at home and going to an outpatient treatment clinic would be best. Our kids are well behaved if we can work with them. I think my kids are unusual in this. I'm not waiting another year. I'll accept that we must gradually bring the kids home. But it's all loopholes. You have to jump when they say "Jump." It's got nothing to do with care of families. I had to beg for a "Family Life Skills Phase II" class because I know I need it because of my dysfunctional family background. Here I am begging for them to pay $400 for a class.

What they've done to my kids is inhuman. I'm very concerned about Jacob. Will a molested kid molest? Am I going to have to sit in juvenile court trying to protect my son from jail? Yet it would be hard to blame him for anything. But what is his future? Where does it end? Does it end?

At first, my husband wanted to kill the older kid who sexually molested Jacob. But then he said that kid was probably sexually molested just like Jacob was. I'll have to pay for my kid's counseling all his life. I don't want him killing himself or hurting himself because of all the pain he's carrying.

Since we first talked, they have finally returned my son Justin. He's doing OK in school, and we've spoiled him. But we've learned that he has a disease—Perthes disease—as a result of that time I told you about when he "fell" (actually,

I believe he was pushed down the stairs). Apparently, they X-rayed the wrong bone at the time, and his condition went untreated. When Justin first came home, he cried almost every night from his legs hurting. He's supposed to wear a brace at night.

We've spent enormous money dealing with all this—$4,000—a lot of money for us. I asked my attorney why you never hear about suits against DCFS (we're filing against them). He said it's because people settle out of court. DCFS gets sued constantly. But I said I'm not going to settle—that would betray my sons. We bought these boys a $1,300 bedroom set because they can't sleep together, according to Babyfold. My kids were perfectly all right when they were taken. Now one comes home with physical damage and the other has mental and emotional damage.

I'll never give up. I'll never forget. I can't. Even if they terminated my rights, I wouldn't give up. I'd come to the courthouse and picket. I told my boys I'll fight for them—always. They are my life, the air that I breathe.

Johnny Daniels

I just felt total powerlessness before the [child welfare] system. Our boys would cry out, but we couldn't help them. Nothing DCFS can do will ever replace the harm that's been done. Not all the money in the world can make up for those two irreplaceable years. Those boys were violated, beaten, sexually abused, separated—they lost their bond with each other, and they had no bond with their sister.

It was constantly, "Jump this, jump that." Now they [the court and DCFS]

finally realize we weren't lying, but the hurt goes so deep. I'm an alcoholic… this would drive a person to drink. I don't know…I just want my boys back. Alcoholism is nothing to overcome compared to the torture they put me through. They say alcoholism is a life-long disease, but this is, too. How do I explain this to my son Jacob—that I allowed this to happen to him?

Justin is more passive. He doesn't look for answers. He is the quiet one. But our bond with the boys—what suffering they've [the court and DCFS] imposed on us. We won the termination [of parental rights], but we lost over two years of our lives. We did gain parenting skills, knowledge about domestic violence which we might not have had. But look at the cost our children had to pay. It all boils down to powerlessness. They have the power; all you have is [instructions] to hurry up and wait, hurry up and wait.

We're suing [DCFS]. It's not the money; it's to prove a point—that people don't have to take it. Too many let their kids be taken and adopted, or the families are such mental wrecks they can't handle their own kids. We knew in our hearts we were right and victims of a bureaucracy. The family gets lost in the system. It's a system of 9 to 5, where it is kids' lives at stake.

I've got a huge file only because I was representing myself in court. So I read their case testimony—the lies are in black and white. I do want his job [the first caseworker, who failed to give them services or believe them about their children's treatment in the foster home]. That guy received a promotion! It's not revenge; it's just justice that I want.

NOTES

1. Luis Rodriguez, *Always Running: La Vida Loca Gang Days in LA* (Willimantic, Connecticut: Curbstone Press, 1993), 251.

2. Interview with Chuck Golbert, May 31, 1995.

3. Linda Gordon, *Heroes in Their Own Lives* (New York: Viking, 1988), 3.

4. Ibid., 4.

5. Qtd. in Joseph Hawes, *The Children's Rights Movement* (Boston: Twayne, 1991), 4–5.

6. Ibid., 2.

7. Ibid., 7.

8. William Ryan, *Blaming the Victim* (New York: Pantheon, 1971).

9. Gordon, 41.

10. Ibid., 179.

11. Ibid., 202.

12. Richard Wexler, *Wounded Innocents* (Buffalo: Prometheus Books, 1995), 35.

13. Marilyn Irving Holt, *The Orphan Trains* (Nebraska: University of Nebraska Press, 1992), 49.

14. Hawes, 13.

15. Michael Katz, *Improving Poor People* (New Jersey: Princeton University Press, 1995), 40.

16. Hawes, 20.

17. Katz, 40.

18. Michael Grossberg, "Children's Legal Rights? A Historical Look at a Legal Paradox," in Roberta Wollons, Ed., *Children at Risk in America* (New York: State University of New York Press, 1993), 117.

19. Joan Gittens, *Poor Relations: The Children of the State of Illinois, 1818–1990* (Chicago: University of Illinois Press, 1994), 89.

20. Cleo Terry, "DCFS Battles Overwhelming Odds," *Chicago Tribune* (Oct. 23, 1994), "Voice of the People" Op. Ed.

21. Gordon.

22. Leroy Pelton, *For Reasons of Poverty* (New York: Praeger, 1989), 18.

23. Ibid., 19.

24. James Welch, *Weapons of the Weak* (New Haven: Yale University Press, 1985).

25. Pelton, 3.

5

❀

Child Saving
Institutionalized

Our current emphasis in child welfare…promotes an inclination
to blame parents…and a disinclination to appreciate the ways in
which circumstances of poverty might give rise to these problems.
Such an emphasis has sustained the dysfunctional dominance
of the investigatory/coercive role in public child welfare agencies,
to the detriment of its family preservation role.[1]

DR. LEROY PELTON

The power…to interfere with and control, not only the estate but
the persons and custody of all minors within the limits of its jurisdiction,
is of very ancient origin. This is a power that must somewhere exist
in every well regulated society.…It is a duty then, which the country
owes as well to itself, as to the infant, to see that he is not abused,
defrauded or neglected, and the infant has a right to this protection.[2]

ILLINOIS SUPREME COURT, 1846

CHILDHOOD REDEEMED: THE
PROGRESSIVE ERA, 1890–1920

Parens patriae, which awards the state "the power to interfere with and control...the custody of all minors...a power that must exist in every well regulated society," presumes children to be property—a property the state can take if parents are unfit. Without this legal power, society would be "unregulated."

The founding of the juvenile court in Chicago in 1899 extended the regulatory role of *parens patriae.* The trend of either criminalizing poor children or removing them from abusive homes was institutionalized in this court. While progressives hailed this reform, which guaranteed youth a trial, less attention was paid to the court's legal power to determine the fate of dependent, neglected, or abused children. Judges were given broad discretionary powers to define dependency and neglect. The child in need of protection was

> any child who is destitute or homeless or abandoned; or dependent on the public for support; or has not proper parental care or guardianship; or who habitually begs or receives alms;...or whose home by reason of neglect, cruelty, or depravity on the part of parents...is an unfit place for a child.[3]

The law also provided that any "respectable person" who knew of a child who

> appears to be either neglected, dependent or delinquent could complain to the court...and in all cases where it can properly be done the child placed in an improved family home and become a member of the family by legal adoption or otherwise.[4]

The tradition of acting in the child's *best interest* without consulting the child, and then remanding the child to centers of rehabilitation or foster care, is almost a hundred years old. This threatening power of the court was, and is, unquestioned because of the benevolent and paternal language that expresses its intentions.

Although incarceration would become a major product of the juvenile court's process, child welfare reformers of the Progressive era were less preoccupied with criminalizing youth than with having a legal means to discipline errant youth. They were confronted with America's poor—children who were dependent on the state either as orphans or because of physical or mental disabilities. Disavowing the moral judgments of earlier reformers, the child savers saw dependency as the result of structural poverty rather than depravity. When overcrowded, explosive, and violent urban centers, spawned by an expanding factory system, threatened Yankee America, the liberal child savers placed their hopes in redeeming pauper children and in idealizing their own children.

The gospel of the movement was that children are savable. This confidence was bolstered by both a belief in a child's natural innocence and enthusiasm for the new scientific study of children. The child savers had a romantic and sentimental view of childhood and had faith in the power of the new social sciences and psychiatry. They fought the incursion of industrial technology with a belief in the innocence of the past, the pastoral, and children. They also embraced John Dewey's democratic education philosophy. Dewey's child-centered pedagogy held that the key to educating was the child's experience. But he also encouraged literacy in the new industrial technologies as a door to the future without offering much analysis of the inequalities that limited participation in democracy.

Child savers introduced several reforms. They moved children from almshouses to institutions and then moved them from institutions to foster care; they constructed a juvenile court and probationary system; they introduced compulsory education; they advocated improved health care to reduce infant mortality; and they supported mothers' pensions. Illinois was a showcase for the reform movement's two dynamisms: rescuing and disciplining. The juvenile court symbolically and materially represented the state's legal right through *parens patriae* to incarcerate incorrigible children *as well as* maltreated children and dependent children. The court sent delinquents as young as eight to reformatories, and it remanded dependent youth to institutions whose distinction from poorhouses was that they were to serve as boarding schools or training schools.

Illinois' industrial schools were forerunners of juvenile court. The industrial school for girls was a combination of reform school and orphanage. The 1879 industrial school for girls "served" the homeless, the beggar, the prostitute, the girl in an almshouse, or the girl who consorted with thieves. Poor girls were to remain virtuous and to learn a skill for productivity in industry. If the industrial schools were an improvement on the poorhouse, they were also dangerously close to prisons. By 1882, Alexander Ferrier told the Supreme Court that the industrial schools were illegally placing girls whose only mistake was poverty or victimization by adults. The Supreme Court struck down the challenge, ruling that the industrial school "was not a prison but a school." After the Ferrier decision, industrial schools for girls expanded.[5]

While juvenile court advocates dealt with the classification, processing, and institutionalizing of children, social reform activists Jane Addams and Julia Lathrop challenged the movement to enter the context of the clients it served by living amidst the poor. Addams's settlement houses, which offered support to poor communities, inspired the child-saving movement and its offspring, the social work profession, with an ethic of respect and compassion. However, Addams also shared the missionary zeal to save youth from the corruption of Chicago's slums. The difference is that she lived amidst the dangers she inveighed against, not without compassion but also not without the child-saver moral assumptions of her educated class. It is notable that child welfare practice carries today the same dual purposes: social responsibility for troubled "underclass" families and coercive intervention in the lives of those deemed as unworthy poor.

The child savers imposed their moral ideals and respect for authority. When parents failed to instill these values, the courts acted as both a symbolic and material corrective. The reformers, both men and women, saved children in order to preserve a patriarchal family system. In spite of feminist challenges to the rule of fathers in family life, women in the child-saving movement valorized women's *natural* nurturance role, which charged women with exclusive responsibility for domestic and moral life. These women's rights advocates, emphasizing *maternalist* solutions, espoused women's superior moral and maternal capacity, and implicitly legitimated hierarchial family roles.[6]

Volatile adolescents, especially young toughs, were a national anxiety. Less visible was a policy focus on young women. An imperative to regulate the lives of single, childbearing-age girls usually surfaces when traditional family life (women and children's dependency on men) is threatened. The industrial school for girls founded in Illinois in 1876 by the Centennial Association sought to "prevent 'depraved' 'unprincipled' and 'unpure' girls from growing up to reproduce 'their kind three to five fold.'"[7]

The child savers of the Progressive era defined child neglect in accordance with their class and gender standards. According to Gordon, "They broadened the definition of cruelty to children in one way, including all sorts of passive neglect, and narrowed it in another way, focusing exclusively on abuse within the family and ignoring nonfamilial sources of child abuse such as child labor."[8] Neglect charges then, as now, were provoked by a family's struggle against or capitulation to poverty. Mothers, rarely fathers, were held responsible for such neglect.

The phenomenon of a mother becoming fatalistically despondent and virtually abandoning her children was never transformed by child welfare policies. Instead of addressing poor women's dependent and economically trapped position, their apathy was treated as moral or psychological failure. Bad mothering justified child removal by SPCC agents. Lower-class mothers were silenced by social standards that condemned them without recognizing the obstacles that made effort useless. The child savers lacked imagination. They did not see how the powerlessness of destitution led to maternal paralysis or despair. Motherhood was sacred. Nothing, not even the hemorrhaging of one's identity, could excuse that failure.

PRESERVING THE FAMILY:
THE FIRST WHITE HOUSE
CONFERENCE ON CHILDREN, 1909

Middle-class women, displaced from their socially valued preindustrial role in domestic life, found a useful civic project in child protection. These "charity workers" were the social body of the new field of social work. By 1920, both the juvenile court agents—probation officers—and child and family welfare workers prepared for their vocation through academic training. Sentiment and compassion, while still preeminent as virtues, were enlightened by child development and education experts Stanley Hall, John Dewey, and Edward Thorndike. Knowledge was professionalized and sentiment demoted.

The emerging field of child and family welfare pressed its cause for official, uniform national policy. In 1909, President Roosevelt called a White House Conference on Dependent Children that took up the debates that had been stirring among child welfare advocates. The established humane societies, led by male reformers, resisted the Progressive child-saver argument against removing children from families because of poverty alone. Nevertheless, the child savers won. It was a policy victory for family preservationists. The conference recommended that children should not be taken away from their homes by reason of poverty alone.[9] In spite of this watershed policy statement, the foster care population, which should have plummeted following this recommendation, increased. The practice of child removal continued in spite of a hard-won policy consensus for family preservation.

The 1909 conference also recommended the creation of a federally funded children's bureau that would report and investigate child welfare. This was an unprecedented achievement—the establishment of a government bureau devoted to international child welfare. In 1912, Julia Lathrop, a leading settlement house advocate, was appointed as the first chief of the U.S. Children's Bureau.

The family preservationists' victory was only on paper. Progressives had identified the structural roots of poverty, thereby shifting moral blame from impoverished parents. Yet blaming and penalizing poor parents, especially mothers, for moral failure is deeply embedded in the American psyche. Placing children in foster care has continued ever since the 1909 conference. Class standards of "good parenting" and a gendered, punitive family welfare policy undercut family preservation practice. The "good" parent, who is the subject of state scrutiny, is the mother. Failure to meet the class, race, and gender standards of good parenting is met with punishment.

An institutional achievement of the child savers, the founding of the juvenile court, reveals the conflicted nature of child welfare practice. On the one hand, the child rescuers sought to end the practice of remanding juveniles to adult jails and prisons. On the other hand, they sought legal authority to legitimate their double-edged purpose of both supporting distressed families *and* enforcing compliance with their standards. Leroy Pelton accounts for an increase in the foster care population following the 1909 conference recommendations as resulting from the ascendancy of the juvenile courts into the arena of child welfare protection. SPCCs, children's homes, and relief agencies became case investigators who brought their complaints before the courts. Although the courts' major duty was to adjudicate delinquency cases, dependency and neglect complaints became a significant burden of their caseload. The other investigative arm of the juvenile court was the police and the newly invented probation officer. The number of probation officers in Cook County, Illinois, tripled between 1911 and 1921.[10] An array of workers supplied the courts with cases: "Children had become a commodity."[11]

Between 1915 and 1919, more than 10,000 dependency cases were heard in Chicago's juvenile court, of which about 58 percent were placed in foster care. Half of the cases brought before the court were dependency and neglect cases or mother's aid cases, and the other half were delinquency cases.[12]

MOTHER'S PENSIONS:
PITY AND PUNISHMENT

A family, living upon the scale allowed for this estimate, must never spend a penny on a railway fare or omnibus. They must never go into the country unless they walk. They must never purchase a half-penny newspaper or spend a penny to buy a ticket for a popular concert. They must write no letters to absent children for they cannot afford to pay the postage.... The children have no pocket money for dolls, marbles or sweets. The father must smoke no tobacco and must drink no beer....[13]

B. SEEBOHM ROWNTREE, 1901

Mother's aid hearings resulted from the efforts of child savers to win government stipends for widows in order to support their children without having to work. The struggle for mother's pensions, backed by women's organizations, settlement workers, private welfare agencies, and Midwestern child welfare organizations, was met with resistance from the humane and charity organizational establishment of the East Coast. Some detractors feared a feminist welfare state that would break up the traditional family by allowing women economic independence. The Eastern child welfare establishment feared the demise of their funding base, as well as harbored an abhorrence of government incursion in the private realm of volunteerism. In addition to these oppositions, tensions existed within the mother's pension alliances. The feminist factions, including the child welfare sector (referred to as "maternalists" because of their emphasis on the maternal role), supported a sexual division of labor in which men were the breadwinners and wives were unpaid domestic family workers. This faction supported pensions as a wage paid to mothers for domestic labor and left unchallenged a hierarchical and discriminatory division of labor represented by this family wage argument.[14] A more radical faction challenged the family wage basis of the mother's pensions, arguing for an equal wage that would make pensions less of a necessity.

Through political compromise, the mother's pensions laws were passed in 1911. But the payments were a pittance. In this way the special interests of the established charities were not threatened and the child savers would have the professional task of determining which widows were deserving of the subsidies.[15]

Mother's pensions were one cornerstone of the welfare state. The subsidies were precursors of the Aid to Dependent Children provisions of the Economic Security Act of 1935 and the later Aid to Families with Dependent Children (AFDC). While noting their limitations, social welfare historian Michael Katz calls the mother's pensions "an important, if halting, first step on the road from charity to entitlement."[16] The pensions were also the first official step on the road to state intervention in the lives of families. Child and family welfare agents took on the task of scrutinizing parental fitness as a prerequisite for family income subsidy. Mothers who applied for pensions subjected themselves to investigation. If they received funds, they were stigmatized as *relief* recipients. If they didn't receive funds, they were thought to be unsuitable parents because they were refused aid.

By 1920, mother's pension laws were under the jurisdiction of the juvenile courts in twenty-one states.[17] Adding to the criterion for "good parenting" were the scientific insights offered by psychodynamic theories of healthy family life. Maltreating mothers were no longer evil; they were "sick" or mentally deficient. Social work's early influence by settlement house reformers who sought to alter the social conditions that affected families in distress now located the source of the distress within family psychodynamics. Social work would institutionalize, for the foreseeable future, the case study method based on psychoanalytic theory.

African American women were not included in the founding discourse of the American welfare state, nor (with few exceptions) were they recipients of mother's pensions. Unincluded, black women formed their own organizations, most notably the National Association of Colored Women in 1911. Although black women's social welfare organizations shared the maternalist philosophy (of women's exemplary moral role) that white women espoused, they approached the recipients of their help in very different ways.[18] White women gave charity and saw the poor as "other." Black middle-class leaders had no racial distance from the women they would "uplift," and their class distance was often only a generation removed. For blacks, "race issues were poverty issues, and women's issues were race issues."[19]

African American women responded to the needs of children and poor families by building alternative health, education, and child day-care institutions. They built 200 hospitals and nurse training schools between 1890 and 1930.[20] Less focused on impoverishment, since 90 percent of blacks shared that condition, they created social services for and among the poor. Because black women were three times more likely to be unemployed than were white women, welfare activists advocated better wages and working conditions. Black women's conception of social welfare was workers' rights and the construction of hospitals, schools, and day-care centers.[21]

THE CHILDREN'S BUREAU

If African American women had been included in social and child welfare's founding debates, as were Children's Bureau founding advocates Florence Kelly and Lillian Wald, perhaps the American social and child welfare system might have been different. This is not to suggest that Wald and Kelly's relationship to official (male) power was not subordinated, only that if concessions were made, they would be toward the interests of the white women of the Progressive era. Both Wald and the fiery Kelly, who'd worked in the settlement house movement, had been instrumental in organizing their extensive network of social activists to achieve the 1909 conference and to push for the establishment of the Children's Bureau.

The white feminist maternalists' goal focused on gaining government assistance for women and children. To develop political influence, these advocates lobbied state and federal legislative, philanthropic, and organizational committees. In building an institution to protect the rights and meet the needs of poor mothers and children, feminist welfare leaders were shifting from nongovernmental social work, where their women's networks were strong, to the building of a welfare bureaucracy that displaced those networks with professionalized standards of social work.

Three fateful separations of interests took place at this time that would affect the fate of social and child welfare. The interests of women and children were separated, welfare reform never joined with labor reform, and social reform and social work separated.[22]

Influenced by the legacy of the child rescuers of the 1800s, who set children's rights against parents' rights, as well as the campaign against child labor, which implicitly separated children's rights from those of their parents, the Children's Bureau separated the interests of mothers and children.

Constrained by bureaucracy and professionalism, the Children's Bureau never connected welfare reform with labor reform, thus relegating welfare to the realm of charity and dependency. In spite of women's increasing employment and militance in labor, Children's Bureau maternalists still accepted the traditional view that poor and working class mothers should be home with their children rather than in the work force. Thus, welfare reform would not be linked to an organized, militant base. Further, the connection among poverty, unemployment, and welfare would remain an intellectual discourse in America rather than be a visible, living embodiment.

With the professionalization of social work, epitomized by case work (with its culturally impositional method), social work no longer represented an oppositional practice. In giving child and social welfare an institutional base that could ensure governmental attention to poor women and children, the child savers abandoned their adversarial position regarding immigrants and the dispossessed.

THE NEW DEAL

"I don't believe in handouts." "I'd be embarrassed to take 'welfare.'" These are typical middle-class sentiments. Yet the 1935 Social Security Act ensured that all Americans could collect social welfare payments in the form of unemployment compensation or Social Security pension payments. This legislation, which excluded blacks and women from its original planning, had a two-tier focus. Social insurance mandated unemployment compensation, and Social Security (entitlements) mandated pensions for everyone, the primary beneficiaries being white males. The Social Security Act's other tier targeted the poor, who would receive public assistance through Aid to Dependent Children (ADC). What has come to be called "welfare" was not an entitlement offered to all Americans. One had to qualify for ADC through "means testing." Once again, the poor, not the middle class, were stigmatized by their acceptance of government assistance, and they were (and still are) subjected to state intervention in family life if they applied for assistance.[23]

Michael Katz calls Social Security an income transfer program that Americans accept as an entitlement while they deride AFDC (Aid to Families with Dependent Children) payments: "Social Security now lifts most elderly people out of poverty; AFDC almost never does for the single parents with children who are its primary clients. Between 1970 and 1985, the average Social Security benefit increased 400 percent; the average AFDC benefit rose only 50 percent."[24]

The passage of the Social Security Act was credited as an apparent change in child welfare policy. Between the mid-1930s and the 1950s, the foster care population dropped, presumably because public assistance lifted some families out of destitution. However, Pelton speculates that the Great Depression and World War II derailed funding to private charity organizations, and the whole enterprise of public assistance was in transition from private to publicly funded state agencies. Policy had not changed, but the opportunity to implement child welfare policy was altered. By 1947, federal money for foster care was made available, and government spending for child welfare services doubled between 1950 and 1960. In this period, foster placement expanded.[25] As Pelton explains, "Another factor that may have contributed to the rise in the foster care population from the 1950s on is the extension of child rescue activities to black children."[26]

THE DISCOVERY OF THE
BATTERED CHILD SYNDROME

Putting child abuse in an historical context does not deny the presence of pathology, but insists that such conditions are part of socially constructed reality.[27]

LINDA GORDON

Historian Tony Platt argues that the founding of the juvenile court necessitated the construction of the concept of delinquency. The children, drawn from the long-standing pool of the rescuable destitute, were not invented, but the category that would authorize and define who would fill the reformatories was an invention. Similarly, in the 1950s, a new cadre of reformers, in this case medical professionals—radiologists, pediatricians, and psychiatrists—codified another social problem: child abuse.[28]

The medical professionals of the 1950s differed from the first "discoverers" of child abuse, the Society for the Prevention of Cruelty to Children (SPCC). The SPCC considered an abusive parent a moral degenerate. Pediatricians and psychiatrists considered the abusive parent to be mentally sick. When, in 1874, the SPCC discovered child abuse in the torture of a child named Mary Ellen, the press broke the story of a child whose evil "mama" cut her with scissors and whipped her with rawhide straps that drew blood and bruises. This horror compelled the Society for the Prevention of Cruelty to Animals (SPCA) humanitarians to indict a misogynist mother and awaken the nation to the plight of the neglected children of the streets. The animal cruelty activists exploited the irony of children being treated more cruelly than animals. What was never reported in this seminal "case" is that the "mama" was a foster mother and that the New York City Department of Charity assigned to Mary Ellen's rescue never monitored her subsequent care.[29]

Beginning in the 1950s, radiologists used X-rays to detect such hidden injuries as abnormal bone healing, skull hematomas, and fractures in infants. A new diagnosis was born. In the 1960s pediatrician Henry Kempe linked the X-ray evidence to physical abuse and named the problem "the battered child syndrome." Kempe, relying on psychiatry, was able to "explain" parents who murdered their children. They were psychotic, sociopathic, alcoholic, of low intelligence, immature, impulsive, self-centered, aggressive, or a combination of these characteristics. What they needed was *treatment*.

An "epidemic" followed these discoveries. Child abuse was a disease whose infection was spread by "sick" parents. The germ theory of disease, states Dr. Bernard Ewigman of the Department of Medicine at the University of Missouri, "is at least a century old and I often say that we're at about the year 1930 in terms of our understanding of child maltreatment. We are still arguing about whether a case is maltreatment or not, just as we once argued is this an infectious disease or not."[30]

The media and their audience could not get enough of battered child syndrome stories. Each narrative of child abuse riveted a horrified public. The child welfare system followed the "syndrome" like a well-trained bird dog pointing again and again to fallen prey.

Social workers embraced the medicalization of child protection, even though medical authority would eclipse the position they had held uncontested for the first half of the century. Now the experts in charge of child abuse investigations were doctors. Child protection teams, consisting of doctors, social workers, and police, made physical, social, and criminal examinations of the child and parent following the child's admission to a hospital.

"Scientists and physicians," says child psychiatrist Peter Breggin, have a "technical inventiveness [which] seems capable of mastering the physical universe. In America we hold them as impartial, humane, and, above all objective....[Yet] scientific solutions are often laden with their own biases, such as insensitivity to the value of liberty, and a moral vacancy around the rights and needs of children and minorities."[31]

Gods and saviors die hard. The new scientific authority vested in child welfare ensured the medicalization of the field. Child abuse and neglect reporting systems were legally mandated in every state. According to Clifford Dorne, "These state statutes actually codified the medical diagnosis of child maltreatment, or battered child syndrome, into a legal framework."[32] Child maltreatment reporting laws required child protective service workers, doctors, and mental health professionals to report maltreatment to state child protection services.

The reporting movement, as it was called, had two sources of reporters: mandated professionals and concerned citizens: "It is interesting that the civic group [reporters] were generally rooted in the middle or upper middle class."[33] Was it because of class or race loyalty that few reporters emerged from the clients of child protective services?

By 1974, the reporting movement had amassed enough cases and controversy about the extent of child abuse and neglect to warrant scientific verification of the numbers. The Children's Bureau developed the National Center on Child Abuse and Neglect (NCCAN) to compile statistics on the incidences of child abuse and neglect.

The medical model encouraged intervention in families no longer considered malicious but, instead, psychologically unfit. The increase in placement of children outside their homes cannot be solely explained as resulting from a mandated reportage system or from the psychodynamic theories that shaped child maltreatment policies. Additionally, in 1961 an amendment to Title IV of the Social Security Act gave federal monies to states for court-ordered placement of children whose families received public assistance, and in 1962 states were awarded grants-in-aid for social services to families. As a result, state child welfare agencies expanded, and a boom in foster care reached a peak in 1977.

Although increased federal spending was intended to support families, the funds actually "served to provide the resources for a child abuse crusade whose thrust was to detect psychological defects in impoverished parents rather than to provide concrete services in the home. The crusade provided the reports to be investigated and the rationale for child removal; the amendments provided the resources for more case workers to be hired who could investigate more reports and remove more children."[34]

An energetic and confident child protective system backed by the authoritative expertise of medicine and psychiatry expanded its definition of abuse to include emotional neglect. Once again, parents who did not respond to treatment lost their children. Failure to show up for services—counseling sessions and parenting classes—was indicative of parents' lack of cooperation. Unfit parents resisted "help" and "improvement."[35]

Those who are labeled neglectful are usually low-income mothers and frequently nonwhite. In 1960 the Child Welfare League codified diagnostic categories of neglectful mothers. Child protection workers could use the questionnaire along with the "Maternal Characteristics Scale" to measure neglectful types: the depressed mother, the impulse-ridden mother, the apathetic–futile mother, the retarded mother, and the psychotic mother.

Holding mothers responsible for child neglect implies a class and gender assumption that the mother's full-time employment is child care while the father's "role" is as breadwinner. This standard, unreachable if even desirable for most poor families, assumes that families should be financially self-sustaining and that failure to be so is their fault. If adults are unemployed, homeless, and/or stressed to the point of neglect, it's their fault. More precisely, it's usually seen as the fault of an apathetic, depressed, impulsive, or psychotic mother. As Gordon illustrates, "The very concept of child neglect…arose from the establishment of this norm of male breadwinning and female domesticity. In fact, this pattern is not 'traditional,' as is often claimed today, but was new when child protection originated. Indeed, child protection was part of the efforts to enforce this arrangement."[36]

What the psychodynamic model overlooks are changes in both family and economic life, such as men's responsibility for childrearing, the fact that mothers are usually full- or part-time wage earners and often a sole source of family income, and that economic depression in African American and Latino communities has eliminated industrial work and job-retraining options.

Labeling abuse and neglect as psychological problems generally assigned to mothers, rather than as problems linked to poverty or male abuse, obscures the fact that thousands of children are removed from their homes because of poverty, not pathology. A Westat National Incidence study commissioned by the U.S. Department of Health and Human Services in 1981 found that "fully 82 percent of all victims [of child abuse and neglect] were from families with incomes below $15,000 in comparison with 45 percent of all US children. Only 6 percent of the victims were from families with incomes of $25,000 or more."[37]

Failure to acknowledge the concrete social problems that poor clients face is not a result of ignorance or oversight. It is a constructed point of view and one all the more stigmatizing because both social workers and often clients accept psychological explanations for family problems as authoritative. Victimhood and dependency tend to be the result. Universalizing abuse and neglect serves a purpose. It reinforces patriarchal power within the family, and it distracts public attention from poverty and the causes of poverty. As a result, social attention is drawn away from the powerful interests that undergird structural poverty. Most importantly, an entire institutional force—child and family welfare—that greatly affects the lives of a burgeoning immigrant, African American, Latino, and Native American populace is not in solidarity with its constituency but sees them as dependents: damaged and dangerous people. Thus, the poor, racial groups, and women are rendered less powerful.

SOCIAL WORK'S CONFLICTED MANDATE

Child welfare expert Leroy Pelton and historian Michael Katz have shown that caseworkers' historically assigned dual role undercuts child welfare's policy commitment to family preservation. The friendly visitors of the Societies for the Prevention of Cruelty to Children in the late 1800s were assigned the role of helper, but the only clients to be helped were the *worthy* poor. Discerning which families were worthy and which were unworthy cast social workers into an investigative role in which they gathered information from schools, neighbors, friends, and the police about families who applied for "relief" or who were reported to the agency for neglect or abuse. Caseworkers were awarded legal authority to remove children from homes deemed unfit. Charity organizations were characteristically "centralized citywide registers of all relief recipients, maintained by a special agency; [performing] the investigation of applicants for relief for other agencies;…the supervision of the poor through friendly visiting; and the collection of data on pauperism, relief, and related subjects."[38]

Charity organization social work was thus a family regulatory system with a goal of removing children from the families of the unworthy poor—that is, families that did not exhibit middle-class standards of family morality or the work ethic. When the child-saving movement of the Progressive era, imbued with a scientific approach to children and families, institutionalized juvenile court and public child welfare authority, social work became professionalized.

Visitation workers and probation officers assisted juvenile court by investigating assigned cases. In spite of the policy triumph of family preservationist child savers, the removal of children from families actually increased from the early 1900s until the 1930s. According to Pelton, "Under the dysfunctional dynamics of the dual role, it is not surprising to find that the increase in the foster care population from 1910 on was paralleled by the growth of probation officer staff in juvenile courts, as well as, the proliferation of SPCCs and other agencies and societies involved in child welfare."[39]

Though considered scientific, casework's dual role creates dysfunction by its inevitably unpredictable results. For example, caseworkers who wish to build up a trusting relationship with parents may be less rigorous in their investigation of abuse of a child when, in fact, dangerous physical or sexual abuse is present. However, it is more likely that caseworkers' investigative behavior shuts down trust and the possibility of a helpful relationship with parents who, because of poverty, have been unable or unwilling to provide their children with needed services. Caseworkers are placed in an untenable position, in which the coercive/punitive side of their dual role is apparently deemphasized because the helper side masks this unacknowledged authoritative power.

Finally, Pelton identifies the power relations inherent in these role assignments. Whereas the state has financial, legal, and political power on its side, the parent, almost inevitably a mother, has little or no power: "No one is advocate for the allegedly abusive or neglectful parent. No one investigates and collects evidence on *her* behalf, presents *her* side of the story, presents results of psychological tests commissioned by *her* rather than the government, nor bears witness on *her* behalf. Pathologized by psychiatrists and victimized through her interaction with the agency, she stands alone and isolated."[40] Whether actually responsible for maltreatment or not, mothers should have the right to advocacy.

The inherently conflictive relationship between agency workers and the families they service shapes self-rationalizing attitudes by professionals toward parents. Caseworker class and racial assumptions that judge poor families as pathologically dysfunctional, promiscuous, or violent are confirmed when parents withhold information, lie, are hostile, and refuse cooperation. Mothers who fail to visit their children after their placement "prove" their parental unworthiness, when, as Pelton points out, the mother who has had a lifetime of victimhood simply gives in to the judgment of her as an abject failure as a mother.[41]

Pelton and Katz argue that increases in child maltreatment are linked to a need to control or regulate poor families, and Linda Gordon argues that regulation is an attempt to control the lives of the poorest women and children. However, criminologist Clifford Dorne sees the Western definition of childhood as an ideological force that permits maltreatment. According to Dorne, a definition of parent–child power relations remains culturally uncontested. Inherent in the constructed definition are the following relations:

- Adults are masters of the dependent child and determine what is right and wrong.
- The child is held responsible for the anger of the adult.
- The child's will must be broken as soon as possible.
- Parents deserve respect because they are parents, and children are undeserving because they are children....
- The way you behave is more important than how you really are.[42]

According to Dorne, if we accept a definition of children as nonpersons, what follows are "explanations" for America's child welfare practices. For example, if children are not persons, "we could expect heinous forms of maltreatment to prevail...and if children are considered fully volitional threats to social order and tranquility, as may be the case nowadays with some dominant views towards 'inner-city' youth, then panoptic law enforcement and penal measures predicated on incapacitation, deterrence and even retribution may be implemented."[43]

Whereas Dorne's insight into the oppressiveness of ideological definitions of childhood helps to deconstruct society's acceptance of dependency, it does not link children's dependency to their mothers' social and economic powerlessness or to patriarchal definitions of "normative" family life. While it is true that mothers, as well as fathers, can and do internalize definitions of children as property, with the resulting "permission" to physically discipline children to the point of abuse, powerlessness, dissembling relationships, isolation, and desperation resulting from poverty cause more maltreatment than do ideological notions about children. Also, without an analysis of gender inequity within the family, male power remains unexamined. It is the father, not the mother, whose "property rights" are legally upheld (if indeed they are upheld at all, in the case of the impoverished). Mothers are held responsible for damage to children, but they have little power to prevent state removal of their children.

Further, if both women and children are considered male "property," then male sexual abuse that coerces both mother and child into fearful silence can be expected.

SEXUAL ABUSE, TABOOS, AND RESISTANCE

The sexual abuse of children did not reach the national spotlight until the late 1970s and then only because feminists and victims organized and advocated for public exposure. The fact that the initial leadership and momentum for the public awareness of family violence came primarily from women and a few male victims is often overlooked—and at great cost. Shame, internalized guilt, and fear of hurting their families made victims keep incest a secret. Girls and young women were confronted with the need to keep silent and "acquiesce" in their violation. Telling the truth meant risking not being believed or, if believed, feeling responsible for their family's shame and possible breakup and their fathers' or stepfathers' prosecution. Boys had similar problems of not being believed, along with the "shame" of homosexual relations.

Sexual abuse accounts for the smallest percentage of abuse of children. In Illinois, for instance, although there were 24,979 cases of substantiated neglect, there were only 5,010 substantiated cases of sexual abuse.[44] But far more than in physical abuse cases, children are silenced about sexual abuse. When they do speak out, their testimonies are cast into doubt. For example, three Chicago sisters age ten, eleven, and twelve told of sexual abuse of them and of a younger brother by their stepfather, Gerald Hill (he was stepfather of two of the children and biological father of two). However, twenty-four hours later the girls recanted, and the children's original testimony was considered suspect. Only the insistence of a team of child sexual abuse professionals led by Dr. Bruce Peters of Mt. Sinai Hospital that the children's original charges were to be believed kept the children from being labeled incorrigibles. Dr. Peters stood by the original reports in which eight professionals involved in interrogations of the children said they were certain that the children had been abused in spite of their recantations. In spite of this, the parents were exonerated because the state could not prove its case once the children recanted.

It is very common for children who have been sexually abused to recant. "Recantation is common to begin with and especially when your mom and dad have ended up in the clink. They *are* your parents," claims Dr. Kathleen Coulborn Faller, a University of Michigan child sexual abuse expert.[45] According to Ellen Warren, "One study of confirmed sex abuse cases showed that 22 percent of the children recanted. More than 90 percent of the recanters later acknowledged that they had been abused after all."[46]

Women have been involved in the sexual abuse of children, but only rarely. Incest is essentially a male crime. According to Gordon, "Women do not rape,

are not often involved in sexual activity with children, and rarely commit incest with children."[47] When women are involved in sexual abuse within the
family, it is usually as a result of male coercion, according to Faller.[48] A primary inhibiting factor is their assigned role of intimacy with children. Inces-
tuous or sexually abusive males are rarely intimately involved in the child's life
and can thus objectify the child, whose interest is subordinated to their own.

According to Gordon, there is no research to support the theory that biological fathers are inhibited by the taboo forbidding sex with biological offspring. While it is true that stepfathers are more likely to commit incest, this is
not because of the lack of blood ties with the child but because stepfathers
have not internalized responsibility for the child's welfare. Biological fathers
are most likely to feel responsibility for their child's well-being. These ties of
intimacy and responsibility are the inhibiting factors. The taboo is linked to
parental care for children, not to biology.[49]

In spite of the fact that incest is predominantly a male crime, mothers are
frequently held responsible for its occurrence. State statutes cite mothers *who
knew or should have known* or who *failed to protect their child*. Closely allied to
punishing the mother's silence during male sexual abuse is suspicion regarding
the victim's silence.

A persistent myth, and one that survivors painfully struggle to exorcise, re-
gards the "acquiescence" of victims. However, children's resistance includes
silence to protect family members, as well as defiant behavior when children
reach adolescence and can exercise some power, however painful or destructive. Researchers have estimated that between 60 percent and 75 percent of
teen prostitutes are runaways who are fleeing sexual abuse. Alone and without
skills, community, shelter, or a sense of their worth, they end up selling the
one female attraction that they assume interests men—their sexuality. Whether
their defiant escape involves sex or drugs, their resistance is an effort to exercise power in a situation that had rendered them powerless.

The moral judgment that these "sex delinquents" have destroyed themselves by involvement with pimps, drugs, and, worst of all, pregnancy fails to
answer a simple question: What was their alternative? Silence and suspicion
still encircle sexual abuse. What guarantee does a victim have that she'll be believed or, if believed, that her family will not suffer from her accusations? Will
she be taken away by child protection services? Is there a safe place with other
survivors for her to be? The companionship of the streets may offer the best
of several bad options.

CONCLUSION

Following the 1909 White House Conference on Dependent Children, in
which family preservationists won the debate with the children's rights defenders of the charitable private agencies, the foster care population, ironically,
increased. Child welfare's policies supported family preservation, but the prac-

tice of child removal advanced by the charity workers continued—to the present day. In the watershed Adoption Assistance and Child Welfare Act of 1980, family preservation again won a policy victory. But the foster care population again increased. Child welfare's policies and practices are not simply at odds; they contradict each other. It is no wonder that workers, families, children under state care, and the public are confused. Nothing is as it seems in a system theoretically dedicated to protection of abused and neglected children but whose mission in practice is to monitor the poor, specifically mothers who are held responsible for family dysfunction.

The caseworker surveillance mission of child welfare was institutionalized with the passing of mother's pension laws in 1911. Maternalist child savers supported mothers' receiving these pension payments but also endorsed a dispensing system, administered by caseworkers, that was intrusive and patronizing. Unlike white child savers, black women leaders responded to poor black women's predicament not with pensions, but with the building of schools, hospitals, and day-care centers for African American children and families. Further, they advocated for better wages and working conditions.

Three critical social links failed to coalesce, and this situation fragmented social and child welfare in the twentieth century. The interests of mothers and children were separated, welfare reform and labor reform never united, and social reform activists did not make common cause with social workers.

Social work was professionalized and bureaucratized. Casework became the assessment instrument, and caseworkers had no accountability beyond a supervisor trained in the casework method. Casework is a one-sided affair that legitimates the professional's interpretation and silences families and children.

The Social Security Act of 1935, which mandated the government entitlement we call "welfare" to the indigent, also authorized entitlements to *all* Americans—i.e., Social Security and unemployment compensation. The difference between the two is that every American gets Social Security and unemployment compensation (upon losing a job), but poor people have to qualify to receive AFDC payments through "means testing." Other rhetoric to the contrary, both public assistance caseworkers and child welfare caseworkers are cast in the role of regulators of the poor, with power to discern the worthy poor from the unworthy poor. The child welfare workers' authority is the most formidable because welfare workers have the power to take a child away if the parents fail to meet the "fit parent" standards.

From the 1930s to the 1950s, the foster care population decreased, but it rebounded in the 1960s with the "discovery" of the "battered child syndrome." Maltreating parents were no longer morally defective but seen as sick. Child welfare became medicalized. Surveillance authority, while still in the hands of front-line caseworkers, was subordinated to the scientific experts—doctors and psychiatrists.

If, in the past, the poor received moral exhortations and punishment for their failure to meet class and cultural standards of good parenting, now they received treatment. Parents who refused treatment lost their kids.

Although incest is predominantly a male crime, mothers are often held responsible for not stopping the abuse. The punishment of the mother, as well as the child, is the removal of the child from the home.

Personal Narrative
Elizabeth as Told by Lamond

There is another category of outcasts beyond social lepers—the monstrous. This category includes mothers who seriously harm their children. Amanda Wallace was the psychotic Chicago mother who abused and eventually hanged her baby, Joey, with an electric cord. She became a stereotype of mentally ill "monsters." Her exceptionality not withstanding, many mothers who have mental illnesses bear the weight of both society's fear of mental illness and child welfare's hyperregulatory reaction. With associative disorders—in this case, multiple personalities—there has rarely been an analysis of the social conditions that can give rise to this disorder, which is primarily found in women who have been physically or, more usually, sexually abused.

Elizabeth's story reveals both the violent abuse that occasions the illness and the price that Elizabeth, her partner Lamond, and her five children pay for her past family abuse and the current cultural prejudice against the mentally ill. For Elizabeth to have stabilized—after a childhood of vicious abuse, homelessness, drugs, and prostitution for survival, all the while struggling against hostile multiple personalities and the vicissitudes of being a single African American mother with five children—seems incredible.

Her children have obviously suffered, but their difficulties seem as much a result of their mother's powerlessness and poverty as her illness. A defense of Elizabeth is not meant to reduce the complexity of a problem that is rarely holistically researched—unpredictable and potentially abusive behavior in parents who are mentally ill and untreated. A caseworker does have an obligation to protect a child from such potential risk if a child welfare agency lacks an effective in-home family

support system. Elizabeth's own mother was an example of a parent whose untreated mental illness prevented her from protecting any of her children from abuse, particularly Elizabeth. But what of the mother's boyfriend and the uncles who raped Elizabeth when she was four years old and again as an adolescent? They weren't mentally ill. Where is an intensive, regulatory response to male violence?

Besides her own resilience, Elizabeth's recovery from drugs and control of her mental illness have been possible because she has found a partner who knew how to access services and who, in his words, was "not awed" by her mental illness. Lamond's faith in Elizabeth results from his ability to transform the fearful (the "monstrous") into human experience. With Lamond, Elizabeth is a person with a problem, not a problem case who is secondarily a person.

My fiancée and I are recovering addicts. Myself for six years, she for four years. When I met her, she was homeless and she'd given birth to a baby girl who was born addicted. Elizabeth has four other children. After her baby's birth she sought drug rehabilitation treatment, but she was put on a waiting list. Six weeks later they found a bed for her in drug rehab. However, because she was homeless and an addict, DCFS took her children away on charges of neglect. DCFS said they'd return the kids if she successfully completed the drug program. She spent seven months in rehab and six months in a halfway house. On her release she was instructed to get therapy at the Bobbie E. Wright Mental Health

Center. She registered but had not begun when her mental disorder—she has multiple personalities—manifested.

One of the personalities began to choke her baby because the personality thought the baby was trying to hurt her. She told the therapist at Bobbie E. Wright that she tried to choke her baby, and the therapist called DCFS Hotline. The therapist did her job because the kids were in danger.

Through therapy the therapist was able to call forth some of the personalities, and she felt that Elizabeth was having a breakdown. DCFS came and picked up the children [who'd just been reunited with their mother] and took them without explaining anything to them.

The Origins of a Multiple Personality Disorder

Elizabeth was four when her mother's boyfriend began sexually abusing her. This continued for two years. When she became pregnant, they just used a coat hanger to abort the fetus, but she had to go to the hospital for bleeding. She told the authorities she was raped, but no one did anything. And this molestation wasn't the first time she'd been abused. She was sexually abused by her brother, also. Additionally, she was physically beaten, receiving traumatic blows to the head, which happened if she resisted sexual assaults. She was taken to the emergency room, but her mother stopped taking her to the clinic because she was afraid they might investigate the cause of these traumatic injuries. The mother, herself, suffered from a mental illness. The mother must have been sexually abused to allow it to happen to her child. Elizabeth's sisters were sexually abused also, but not on the scale of abuse that Elizabeth experienced.

The mother died when Elizabeth was thirteen years old. That's when she became homeless, living with friends on the streets, begging for food. She slept in abandoned buildings and cars. She

gave sex for shelter. She had her first child at sixteen.

Elizabeth has a twin brother who sells drugs. She started using. She was on drugs when she had her third child. Because of the drugs she had no money for rent, so she was constantly moving, staying with relatives or friends. She started cocaine and soon had her fourth child. She was staying with a sister and her husband—both drug users—when she had her fifth child. DCFS found out about her drug use, and they took four of the children. [One father has legal custody of the other child.]

Elizabeth created her personalities to block out her pain. She'd pretend to be someone else—someone who would absorb the pain of her trauma.

In June of 1991 I got her into a women's drug treatment center. This was the first help she'd ever received. Right now she has many, many personalities—all of whom have the personality of a child. When they come out, they think the rapes and trauma are still occurring. Each personality has to be reassured that everything is safe. Eventually, [with therapy] the personalities will merge into one.

Incredibly, more has happened to the children since they've been in DCFS custody than anything Elizabeth and I could have done to them. They were separated. They've had four or five different foster parents. The youngest kid couldn't drink water because of peeing in bed. If she wet the bed, she had to eat from a dog dish as punishment. The foster parents slapped her. One of Elizabeth's boys was physically abused. One of the older girls was fondled. An older foster mother who was in her seventies and had hip surgery beat a kid with a cane. DCFS warned her not to use the cane, but they still allowed the kids to stay with her.

Only when we kept calling and complaining and offering Elizabeth's cousin's house as a relative foster home did they take the kids out of these places. Now the children's case is being handled by a private agency contracted by DCFS. Although we've asked and asked either the private agency or DCFS to come and see our home and lives [in order to get them to return the children], neither agency has come to visit or interview Elizabeth.

Elizabeth is in therapy two times a week. I go with her one of those two times. I've done everything DCFS asked, including all the background tests necessary to become a foster parent. Now we have to go to the new agency and open up our lives once again. I think DCFS won't return our kids because of the Joseph Wallace case. They're afraid of Elizabeth, but she never abused the kids—it was neglect because of drugs.

We have a case review every six months. But there is always another requirement or hoop to jump through. When we do that, they add another one. Some of the caseworkers (not all) have been degrading and insulting. The guardian for children said, "Once an addict, always an addict." Even though we'd both been off drugs with no incidents of abuse.

I think I have an understanding of Elizabeth's mental illness because I had a mother and brother who had severe mental breakdowns. I'm not awed by it or intimidated by her illness. I'm more intrigued. There are people with associative disorders who live exemplary lives. I think this attitude helped me deal with Elizabeth. Right now she's doing great. Her personalities love the children. Even when the personalities come out, they are playful with the children.

I think Elizabeth is a champion to have suffered as much and to have come through it. The suffering she has had! I think she's a miracle! One psychiatrist told us he thought it was a miracle that she is not totally insane and locked up. I think Elizabeth is a loving mother. I watch her clean, cook, sew for her daughters. I make a decent income as a caseworker. I think the atmosphere between all of us here is loving. The kids continually ask, "When can we come home?" We have no answer. This has been a nightmare. And we want it to end. When we go back to court for custody in 1996, DCFS will have had custody for five years. We've been telling the kids, "You'll be home soon," for three years.

DCFS thinks you're guilty until proven innocent. How can a person who is poor, with a limited education, and diagnosis of multiple personality prove their innocence?

NOTES

1. Leroy Pelton, *For Reasons of Poverty: A Critical Analysis of the Public Child Welfare System in the United States* (New York: Praeger, 1989), 142.

2. Joan Gittens, *Poor Relations: The Children of the State of Illinois, 1818–1990* (Chicago: University of Illinois Press, 1994), quoting Illinois Supreme Court decision *Thomas Cowls v. Ann Cowls*, 8, Ill. 435, 1846, 17.

3. Qtd. in Grace Abbott, *The Child and the State* (Chicago: University of Chicago Press, 1938), 392.

4. Qtd. in Joseph Hawes, *The Children's Rights Movement* (Boston: Twayne, 1991), 33.

5. Gittens, 100.

6. Linda Gordon, *Heroes in Their Own Lives* (New York: Viking, 1988), 57.

7. Louise Wardner, "Girls in Reformatories," qtd. in Tony Platt, *The Child Savers* (Chicago: University of Chicago Press, 1977), 110.

8. Gordon, 83.

9. Pelton.

10. Ibid., 14.

11. Louise Armstrong, *Of "Sluts" and "Bastards": A Feminist Decodes the Child Welfare Debate* (Monroe, Maine: Common Courage Press, 1995), 42.

12. Pelton, 13–14.

13. B. Seebohm Rowntree, "A Study of Town Life," qtd. in James Jennings, *Understanding the Nature of Poverty in America* (Westport, Connecticut: Praeger, 1994), 109.

14. Gordon, 51–63.

15. Ibid.

16. Michael Katz, *Improving Poor People* (New Jersey: Princeton University Press, 1995), 44.

17. Pelton, 15.

18. Gordon, 132–34.

19. Ibid., 132.

20. Ibid., 124.

21. Ibid., 136–43.

22. Linda Gordon, *Pitied But Not Entitled* (New York: Free Press, Macmillan, 1994), 98–100.

23. Ibid., 145.

24. Katz, 24.

25. Pelton, 19.

26. Ibid., 20.

27. Gordon, *Heroes,* 172.

28. Pelton.

29. Richard Wexler, *Wounded Innocents: The Real Victims of the War Against Child Abuse* (Buffalo, NY: Prometheus Books, 1995), 30–31.

30. *A Nation's Shame: Fatal Child Abuse and Neglect in the United States: A Report of the U.S. Advisory Board on Child Abuse and Neglect* (Washington, DC: Dept. of Health and Human Services, 1995), xviii.

31. Peter and Ginger Ross Breggin, *The War Against Children* (New York: St. Martin's, 1994), xvi–xvii.

32. Clifford Dorne, *Crimes Against Children* (New York: Harrow and Heston, 1989), 85.

33. Ibid., 91.

34. Pelton, 25.

35. Ibid.

36. Gordon, *Heroes,* 166

37. Pelton, 40.

38. Katz, 38.

39. Pelton, 115.

40. Ibid., 123.

41. Ibid.

42. Clifford Dorne, "Helpless Children or Predatory Delinquents? Differential Backlash to 'Get Tough' Trends in Juvenile Justice," *Humanity and Society* 20:1 (Feb. 1994), 79.

43. Ibid.

44. Maurice Possley and Andrew Martin, "Doctors Not Backing Down," *Chicago Tribune* (Feb. 8, 1996), 1.

45. Qtd. in Ellen Warren, "Can You Take Kid's Word For It? Well, It Depends," *Chicago Tribune* (Feb. 8, 1996), 24.

46. Ibid.

47. Gordon, *Heroes,* 209.

48. Warren, 24.

49. Gordon, *Heroes,* 211–12.

PART II

Advocates and Pathfinders

6

Chicago:
A Cargo of Lost Children

The Context for
Case Study Chapters 7–9

DCFS treats its wards as if they were part of a giant shell game, moving them from placement to placement without attempting to reach into their psyches to touch their immortality, to bring forth their potential greatness.[1]

ILLINOIS PUBLIC GUARDIAN PATRICK MURPHY

T he history of child welfare in America has revealed a system that functions to regulate the family life of poor, vulnerable, and troubled families. But how does child welfare function in a particular urban context
at the end of the twentieth century? What has been the resistance of professionals to the regulatory and often punitive practice of child welfare? What is
the discourse of those who defend children's rights and who resist policies of
removal?

How is the current crisis in child welfare, particularly in densely populated
urban areas, a result of the transformation from an industrial economy to a
globalized economy, and how has that technological revolution affected Midwestern cities and the state's burden of care for affected families? How are the
disciplinary practices of child welfare inscribed on the bodies and hearts of
African American mothers and children? To answer these questions, I have
chosen to examine Chicago—the city where the child savers institutionalized
a new era of reform—in order to contextualize a particular city's response to
the crisis in child welfare.

THE CHILD SAVER'S CITY

Chicago is well-known as the city Mrs. O'Leary's cow burned down, but less
known as the city where a workers' movement rose up in the late 1800s. Carl
Sandburg's "muscled city of big shoulders" lured immigrants and later Southern blacks to its railroads, steel mills, and Back of the Yards meat packing industry. It is a bruised city that gave the blues all the sorrow it could play and
frightened Dr. Martin Luther King more than any place he'd ever marched.
Chicago's teeming tenements are where the settlement house movement
began and where America's first juvenile court sent child vagabonds, hustlers,
and thieves to reform schools.

Nowadays, Chicago makes national news because of an archaic, dysfunctional child welfare system and because of a pugnacious Public Guardian,
Patrick Murphy, who skewers the juvenile court, the Department of Children
and Family Services (DCFS), social workers, welfare mothers, and deadbeat
fathers for their failure to defend the rights of children. Another tragic distinction is that Chicago joins Los Angeles, New York, and Washington as one
of the urban centers where drive-by shootings occur once or twice a week.

In Chicago, a debate about children's rights versus family rights is intensely
contested among child welfare advocates. At the same time, the debate is publicly managed and "framed" for public consumption by media. Rarely does
the public hear the voice of child and family advocates—lawyers, caseworkers,
investigators—who work to reform a system that harms children and families.
Chapters 7–9 will let them speak for themselves. I have chosen Chicago as a
locus for these narratives because it is the city that the child savers tried to save,
because it is my home and the local base of my field research, and because of
the "lessons" of insight, hope, and stubborn solidarity that these advocates for
silenced children and families offer.

Finally, Chicago and Illinois are instructive because of the sheer magnitude of the DCFS caseload yet DCFS's obdurate failure to comply with a federal consent decree ("BH") that demands reduction of that caseload along with comprehensive reforms. In spite of the fact that the besieged DCFS administrator, Jess McDonald, is reform minded and perhaps the best hope for nudging the agency toward reduction of its foster care population, his appointed directorship has more than once been threatened by the State Senate president, James "Pate" Phillips. It seems that Jess McDonald criticized the powerful Senate president for making racially insensitive remarks about black DCFS caseworkers, so Phillips wants another director. The fate of vulnerable children rests with the retaliatory whims of powerful and vindictive state politicians. But that is nothing new.

ILLINOIS CHILD WELFARE HISTORY

According to child welfare historian Joan Gittens, Illinois' treatment of children over a 175-year history has been "underfunded, underbuilt, and undertaxed in regard to children's needs…[and] its programs are often so inadequate as to constitute downright neglect."[2] In spite of the Illinois Progressive era reformers' creation of the first juvenile court in the nation, Chicago's equally infamous patronage system undercut child welfare policy from the beginning.

Historian Tony Platt has argued that it was not simply political clout that shaped the establishment of juvenile court, but also the need of the emerging corporate "barons" to discipline potential workers. With the passage of child labor laws, swarms of discontented youth workers who were thrown into unemployment were resorting to thievery. Clusters of young men threatened good order not only in Chicago's slums but also in "respectable" areas: "While urban reformers struggled from a *moral* perspective to pass legislation against child labor and for compulsory education, corporate reformers supported such reforms out of *economic* necessity.…The child saving movement tried to do for the criminal justice system what industrialists and corporate leaders were trying to do for the economy—that is, achieve order, stability, and control, while preserving the existing class system and distribution of wealth."[3]

Platt's critique argues that juvenile court was established because of the need of the elite to control delinquents from the *dangerous* immigrant classes. However, Gittens argues that with the passage of an "Act to Regulate the Treatment and Control of Dependent, Neglected and Delinquent Children," juvenile court was established not to deal primarily with delinquent youth, but to regulate the care of the state's many dependent children.[4] A "fatherly" judge would decide children's fate. The child savers placed enormous confidence in the paternalistic wisdom of judges but had little sense of the disempowerment of families that would result from a white, middle-class, male-dominated institution deciding the fates of children and their impoverished mothers.

Dependent girls whose only "crime" was to have been so severely physically or sexually abused as to have serious emotional problems were placed in reformatories with delinquent youth because the state had no facilities to deal with their special needs. Pregnant African American girls were incarcerated at Geneva Reformatory because there was no maternity home for them. Gittens quotes a study which shows that girls who had been raped, molested, or contracted venereal disease were also sent to Geneva: "For most dependent children placed in reformatories, the justification was egregious…simple stinginess impelled counties to save the cost of probation officers and other provisions for children."[5]

In spite of the good intentions of child savers such as Jane Addams and Julia Lathrop, juvenile court increased incarceration of children rather than decreased institutionalization. Although juvenile court had legal jurisdiction over nondelinquent dependent children, 40 percent of whom were in industrial schools, the court was unable to protect them from excessively restrictive or abusive conditions.[6]

Institutionalizing Public Child
Welfare: The Department of Visitation

Parallel with the founding of juvenile court was the institutionalization of the Department of Visitation, which was the precursor to Illinois' public Child Welfare Division. The department's task was to visit children placed by the court in foster homes and institutions that received state funds. But in typical Illinois fashion, the Department of Visitation's caseload was impossibly high. When, after budget cuts, the department sought additional funds from Illinois state legislators, it received a tepid response.[7]

In 1919, following Chicago newspapers' explosive reports of horrifying conditions suffered by children in boarding institutions, the Department of Visitation was mandated to inspect and license all boarding homes. The path of regulatory oversight was thus set from the beginning. Caseworkers have trudged that weary trail for almost a century. Illinois child welfare has remained consistently reactive and investigative rather than initiatory and innovative. Its responses to children's maltreatment are driven by media exposés, political appointments, and legislative budgetary constraints.

By 1933, the Child Welfare Act required all private agencies to report to the Child Welfare Division, thus solidifying the agencies' regulatory oversight mission. Centralization resulted in less efficiency, not more. For instance, children's records were then, as now, lacking in critical information, and the narratives invariably stressed the child and family's deficits, never their potential.[8]

By 1943, a state-legislated Child Welfare Commission report found that the perennial lack of funds, lack of record keeping, and lack of communication among juvenile court, public child welfare, and private child welfare agencies created such fragmentation that virtually no central coordination or authority adequately protected children. The commission called for one statewide oversight agency to coordinate services for children. It didn't happen: "Despite half a century of effort, child welfare in Illinois was almost as random an endeavor in 1949 as it had been before the founding of the juvenile court 50 years earlier."[9]

It was not until 1964, in the restive civil rights era, that Illinois established the Department of Children and Family Services (DCFS). But centralization did not usher forth coherence or coordination. In fact, a legacy of dual service provision between DCFS and private agencies was entrenched, with inevitable confusion and slippage. Private agencies expanded their role as child placement providers and institutional caretakers. DCFS continued its licensing role and, with the passage of the Child Abuse Reporting Act of 1965, took on the provision of state protective services. DCFS also provided services to children whom the private agencies failed to place. Increasingly, those children were the sons and daughters of African Americans who had come to the metropolis during the great Southern migration of the 1940s.

Child Welfare and the Fate of Black Children in Illinois

Private agencies did not so much neglect black children—as was true of those children's legal guardian, the state—they usurped their legal privilege, as independents, to bear no responsibility for the children's care.[10] From the beginning, black children were overrepresented in the Geneva and St. Charles reformatories, overlooked by the Child Welfare Division, and ignored by private charities. Critical studies of child welfare—or even federal court decrees demanding compliance, such as the "BH" decree of 1989—have little currency in Illinois. For instance, a 1931 Child Welfare Committee Report pointed out the glaring overrepresentation of black youth in reformatories, but by 1946 the practice had expanded: "29 percent of the girls at Geneva were black, while in the city of Chicago black girls comprised only 8.6 percent of girls 10 to 17."[11]

Even when the agency began to hire African American, Latino, and Asian American caseworkers, the legacy they inherited was a process bound by restrictive procedures and fragmented services. For the last twenty-five years, DCFS caseworkers have had to search to select services from a smorgasbord of agency provisions, somehow piecing together programs and therapists that matched the needs of children and families. Workers' time is spent outsmarting—when they can—the rigid and labyrinthine procedures. If they become exhausted or discouraged, and accept the standards, then families suffer.

Social Welfare Benefits in Illinois: Undercutting the Poor

The enthusiasm that reformers held for the centralized child welfare agency waned, as did America's short-lived sympathy for the poor, during the socially eruptive reform years of the 1960s. By the mid-1970s, corporations had internationalized, with recessions and rollbacks of social gains erasing the benefits of the 1960s. Backlash against welfare reform eroded AFDC payments, which were always pitifully inadequate. In Illinois, a notoriously stingy state, AFDC benefits for mothers and children would be consistently cut for the next twenty-five years:

In 1975, the average Illinois AFDC grant was $317.00. By 1980, the grant was increased to $350.00, but adjusted for inflation the grant would be worth $227.66 of the 1975 grant. In 1990, The Center for Budget and Policy Priorities…found that benefits had declined to 48 percent of the 1970 level.[12]

It is no surprise that the combination of slashes in welfare and the shut-down of steel mills and factories resulted in devastating pressure on poor families, especially African American male heads of families who counted on well-paying mill work. By 1995, there were 100,000 homeless people in Chicago, 20,000 of whom were teens, as Illinois ranked forty-sixth out of fifty states in the availability of affordable housing.[13] The "trends" of homelessness and the reports of child neglect that emerged at the end of the 1970s are linked to the disabling effects of job loss.

However, the surge of neglect charges is not solely explained by deindus-trialization. The "battered child syndrome" that produced the 1975 Abused and Neglected Child Reporting Act gave DCFS great latitude in interpreting the ambiguous "child's best interest." The revised 1980 act broadened the net of potential abusers beyond the family and gave investigators the authority to decide on the spot if a child was in danger and take the child into protective custody. DCFS's mission seemed clearer and clearer. The department's budget and personnel expanded, more and more children entered state care, and child abuse and neglect reports grew and grew. As the department grew, so did the number of state wards. Critics pointed out this connection, but newspapers fed public outrage over the "battered child epidemic," preventing Illinois politicians (who are rarely willing to buck public opinion) from calling for a critical examination of DCFS's removal policy.

The DCFS caseload was also strained by two legal reforms that took place in the 1970s. DCFS was required to absorb "delinquent" children under the age of thirteen, and, with the decriminalization of status offenses, the depart-ment became guardian for that teenage population. Family advocates also won reforms. Patrick Murphy, and others, won some legal protection for parents (*Stanley v. Illinois* and the Burgos decree). However, the legal gains did not prevent child removal or curtail DCFS's licensing criteria for becoming a fos-ter parent, which was stipulated in a thirteen-page document.[14] Foster parents were required to provide specific square footage in each bedroom and to pro-vide each child with a separate dresser. Such stipulations were not negotiable, regardless of a family's lifestyle, cultural practice, or financial status.

Although the 1980 Adoption Assistance Act released federal funds to states seeking to reverse child removal practices and provide intensive "wrap-around services" and "individualized care" to families and children, the Illinois adap-tation—Family First—failed. It failed precisely because of DCFS's conflicted, halfhearted response, which was evident in the failure to train caseworkers in individualized care methods, failure to offer intensive six-month services to at-risk families, and the historical legacy of bureaucratic rigidity.

The 1980 Adoption Assistance Act was intended to change the foster care shuffle by requiring a permanency plan for children to be reviewed every six months. A disposition hearing would decide if the child would (1) go home, (2) be adopted, or (3) continue in foster care. Illinois has managed to incorporate the legal requirements and still have its ever-expanding foster care population mushroom. In 1996, one thousand children were entering foster care each month in Illinois.[15] An abused or neglected Illinois child spends an average of more than five years under state care—one of the longest periods in the United States.[16]

The Orphanage Debate in Illinois

As if the century's end recalled the resurrection of Progressive era solutions to the crisis in child welfare, modern Illinois child savers such as Patrick Murphy and legislator Judy Topinka are calling for institutionalized care as an answer to failing protective services and foster care services. The "orphanage" solution claims that residential treatment centers modeled after Maryville or Boys' Town's family cottage residential treatment facilities would be safer and more homelike than foster care placements. Yet such group homes are confronted with the same problems of children who have frequently been victims of sexual abuse and of the acting out of sexually abused children being placed together. The results are often disastrous.

Furthermore, an informal study conducted by the Northwestern Children and Family Justice Center found that most of the privately staffed residential/group home institutions in Illinois had rotating staffs who were not house parents permanently living with children but teams that came and went. Staff turnover is high—the average time worked at the sites by these parental figures was between $1\frac{1}{2}$ and 2 years. Not much intimate, caring, consistent nurturance is going on in these settings.[17]

Reforming Juvenile Court and Foster Care

Northwestern Law School's Children and Family Justice Center has proposed a plan to cut the time a child waits for a permanent home to two years. Also targeted will be juvenile court's tortuously long hearings, which needlessly delay termination of parental rights in cases where biological parents have abandoned children and cannot be found. Such a reform would increase adoptions, which are minimal in Illinois.

The center's objective is not to lay in place an expedited hearing process that would give the state quicker termination of parental rights. On the contrary, the center has been a vocal critic of DCFS, the Public Guardian, and juvenile court precisely because of the lack of permanent homes for children and overzealous removal of children from impoverished families. Rather, the center has identified specific cases in which termination would free a child for adoption when family reunification is impossible.

The dilemma for the center reformers is whether they can change juvenile court or whether juvenile court—in spite of the reform intentions of Chief Circuit Court Judge Donald O'Connell—will continue to meet the overarching needs of a political economy that is regulatory rather than liberatory. The Illinois child welfare history is not on their side. Nevertheless, the system's problems have created an "opening" that advocates for children can and must expand. Advocate Bruce Boyer of Northwestern's Children and Family Justice Center insists that the state must be held accountable because poor families need not less federal and state support but less punitive intervention.

Relative Foster Care

DCFS has instigated one reform of the myriad stipulations required of it by the federal "BH" decree won by the American Civil Liberties Union. DCFS has proposed a relative foster plan that would permit relatives to adopt children while still receiving assistance (approximately $340 per month for each child). By 1996, relative foster parents cared for about 60 percent of DCFS wards.[18] Such a plan, which would affect about 10,000 qualifying families, would save DCFS more than $22 million over a five-year period because the state pays approximately $6,000 to monitor and provide services to each child in foster care.[19] Critics have argued that this reform was fiscally motivated. Furthermore, relative foster guardianship is not without problems. But children are at least kept within their culture and family milieu. Relative foster care is not, of course, better than providing effective services to a troubled family or committing resources to community-based and community-run development initiatives.

As if to demonstrate the quintessential counterproductivity of Illinois child welfare, Governor Edgar announced his 1996 plan to restructure all human services at precisely the time that juvenile court initiated reform strategies. The governor's plan would draw into one superagency seven human services departments that deal with welfare, health, care of children, the elderly, and the physically or mentally disabled. Such an effort at coordinating fragmented services, though attractive in theory, has already been tried in Illinois and has failed. Rather than coordination, bureaucracy is expanded and centralized. The movement toward community-based services, which shift responsibility and control toward the communities of the poor, is thwarted.

CHILD WELFARE ADVOCATES:
NARRATIVES OF RESISTANCE

The following three chapters offer the narratives of legal experts, caseworkers, and investigators concerning these themes: (1) the family preservation versus children's rights debate; (2) advocacy for mothers and children who are among the unworthiest of the unworthy poor—that is, mothers in prison, child sexual abuse victims/children who perpetrate sexual abuse, and children languishing in psychiatric wards or filthy, unsafe, unsupervised shelters for mentally retarded children—and (3) the problems and promise of private child welfare practices.

Most of the advocates implicitly consider the reasons that the number of abused and neglected youth in DCFS custody has doubled to 45,000 between

1991 and 1995.[20] However, the advocates' analysis rarely takes into account the macro factors that cause the increased removal of children from their homes. While most, if not all, of the respondents disagree with Chicago media's blaming drug-addicted, brutal mothers, they agree that the exponential increase in DCFS caseloads is a result of Illinois child welfare politics. A number of respondents blame Chicago media hype following tragic errors on the part of DCFS workers for increased calls to the DCFS abuse and neglect hotline. Further, many blame Illinois Public Guardian Patrick Murphy and the media for attacks on family preservation in Illinois.

Virtually all the experts blame increased poverty as causal in the doubling of the child welfare population, but there is little explanation given for the causes of increased economic hardship and social desperation at the end of the twentieth century. This is not to suggest that such an analysis was the task of these advocates, only that the issue must be addressed. Implicit in the advocates' responses is an understanding of the social cost of the deindustrialization of the Midwest. But the respondents don't attribute this economic factor as overriding the more immediate political struggles between child welfare advocates and legislators/media interpreters, who shape public opinion.

Finally, although the respondents acknowledge the link between poverty and race, implicitly recognizing that 80 percent of the children and families serviced by DCFS are African Americans, only Ivan Medina, director of Child Welfare Services at Association Settlement House, directly takes up the issue of the racism of child welfare practices.

The following introductory description of Chicago's social problems is meant to provide a context within which to understand the testimonies of child welfare advocates that follow and to bring particular attention to the effects of deindustrialization on Chicago's poor and "minority" communities. Nearly 700,000 children in Illinois are living in poverty,[21] with a majority residing in Chicago. Because the child welfare system's "clients" are predominantly from poor communities, it is critical to identify the larger factors that are transforming the core city and neighborhoods of the poor.

CHICAGO: THE CONTEXT TODAY

Jane Addams's Chicago still lures immigrants and youth into its burly, punishing, and vibrant urban chaos. The skin shades of the immigrants have changed, but masses of unemployed, school dropout youth and gangs hustle and steal for survival as they did when the Illinois child savers began the juvenile court and the settlement house movement at the turn of the century. In Jane Addams's day, the enactment of child labor laws put on the streets youth who had been laborers in factories. And since the mid-1970s, the working-class fathers who worked in the South Chicago steel mills or iron works have been displaced by the closing of the plants. From 1975 to 1989, Chicago lost 142,000 manufacturing jobs.[22] According to Dave Ranney, director of the University of Illinois at Chicago's Center for Urban Economic Development, half of those who lost jobs were African Americans and Latinos, and one third were women: "Workers' informal networks of support, which sustained communities through layoffs, were lost; the system of labor market entry developed for workers' kids was lost. The results were destroyed families, families abandoned by unemployed workers who no longer turned to the unions or churches but to drugs or alcohol."[23]

Those jobs were gone and never came back. Nobody was retrained. From 1972 to 1990, the Westside lost 43 percent of its employment base.[24] If you drive through Chicago's Westside, you see the effects: burned-out buildings, huddles of young black men playing basketball in the middle of a work day, or the others, who've chosen the terrifying world of drug dealing as a way to survive—or sometimes die. Why go to high school? Where will it get you? According to Maribeth Vander Weele, 50 percent of Chicago public school students do not graduate. In two of the largest Latino high schools—Wells and Clemente—the dropout rate is 75 percent. The graduation rate at Austin High School, which is predominantly African American, is 17.6 percent. Chicago public schools ranked highest in the nation in four-year dropout rates and lowest in achievement scores among America's large public school systems in 1992. In the same year, 60 percent of Chicago public high schools ranked in the bottom 1 percent of the nation on the ACT entrance test. Although Illinois ranks twelfth in wealth, the state is forty-fifth in per-person contribution toward education.[25]

Where is there employment for even half of the city's dropout youth? A trend on the political right is to cut the summer jobs mandated by the 1982 Job Training Partnership Act. "Ten years ago Chicago had 35,000 summer jobs for youth," says Jack Wuest, the director of Chicago's Alternative School Network. "By 1993 there were 23,000 jobs. Now [in 1996] there's 14,000 left, and we may lose them. The 1.2-billion-dollar increase for summer youth jobs following the L.A. riots has been all but eliminated because President Clinton caved in."[26] In April 1996 the Clinton administration allotted $625 million for summer jobs, and Chicago got $8 million.[27] This was a drastic cut from the $28 million Chicago received in 1993.[28] In many cases, summer youth jobs supplemented family income. "This summer," says Robert Wordlaw, executive director of the Chicago Jobs Council, "we will have 14,000 additional young people roaming the streets with nothing to do."[29] The response from youth is chilling: "America don't offer us nothin'—we outlaws now, all of us," says sixteen-year-old Dwayne, who is a dropout living in Chicago's Lawndale neighborhood. "Yeah, outlaws out here with my homeboys....Don't expect nothin'."[30]

It is a terrible irony that these young people's fathers' jobs were eliminated in the 1970s and 1980s, that federally funded summer jobs for teens were eliminated in the mid-1990s, and that Congress proposed in 1995 for their mothers, who received public assistance, to find work or be thrown off the rolls within two years. Many of those mothers were also victims of deindustrialization—40 percent of Chicago's Westside Lawndale community was left on welfare as a result of job flight and job elimination.

Even before the devastating 1995 welfare "reform" plan, Illinois Aid to Families with Dependent Children (AFDC) paid a mother with two children $662 per month, some $300 *less* than the federal poverty level of $991 per month. While Newt Gingrich railed at welfare freeloaders, Chicago AFDC mothers attempted to feed and clothe children while paying 80 percent of their checks toward rent and buying children's clothes with dollars that had lost 50 percent of their purchasing power since the 1970s.[31] Proposed public aid cuts would eliminate aid to 500,000 Illinois children. Legislators who voted for this "reform" will then blame neglectful mothers when the child abuse and neglect hotline is besieged with calls.

The homelessness rate of families continues to rise. There has been little commitment to low-income housing in Chicago. The waiting list for Chicago Housing Authority (CHA) section 8 certificates has 48,000 families and individuals waiting to receive rent subsidies.[32]

In this bleak atmosphere an informal drug industry has siphoned money into these decapitalized areas. The crack-cocaine "epidemic" has received explosive coverage, but what economist Wallace Peterson calls a "silent depression" resulting from deindustrialization has been kept quiet. Even more hidden is the relationship between increased wealth and increased poverty. A transfer of wealth upwards in Chicago *increased* Northside Gold Coast residents' annual income by 65 percent between 1979 and 1989, and *dropped* the annual incomes of families living in the Southside Stateway Gardens Housing project by 42 percent.[33] The contrast is stark. According to a study by Roosevelt University professor emeritus and Chicago demographer Pierre de Vise, Gold Coast residents have an average per capita income of $82,169 per year, and a family of four in Stateway Gardens has an annual per capita income of $1,650 a year.[34] "It's getting to be like a Third World country, like India," said de Vise. "In this hemisphere, only Brazil has a higher income disparity than the U.S."[35] Indeed, the children of Chicago's Cabrini Green projects are growing up in conditions similar to those of third world countries—third world countries at war. Dr. James Garabino found that by five years of age nearly all the children in Cabrini Green had seen a shooting or had seen someone involved in a shooting.[36]

Children see horrors of war that few can imagine. What kind of desperation leads a man to burn a ten-year-old over 70 percent of his body for stealing $20 worth of food stamps while his sister ran for help? The legal description of the crime of Tony Harris—who lived with the mother of the boy who was doused with charcoal lighter fluid and rubbing alcohol before being set on fire—was *heinous* battery.[37] Children are victims in a hideous and unacknowledged war.

The skewed income disparity has made Illinois distinctly illustrative of a state that has abandoned its children. Although, as a state, Illinois has the twelfth highest per capita income, it ranks thirty-eighth among the fifty states on several indicators of social well-being for its children.[38]

Expendable Populations

The abandonment of the cities resulting from global restructuring's elimination of jobs has left a wake of rage, desperation, and despair. "If you can't pay bills because you have no job," says Jack Wuest, "you feel helpless. A job gives self-esteem. Europeans take this for granted. Why won't anybody identify joblessness as the basis of our problems? [Blaming the poor] is a well-thought-out effort by corporations who use media to 'frame' the issues."[39] According to Dr. Garabino, "A sense of abandonment and helplessness has left half the mothers severely depressed. One consequence of this depression is that they neglect their children, who (like war victims) living under threat feel the same fear and anxiety, but without someone who can soothe or assist them."[40]

Mothers and children in a war zone is the context of child welfare practice in Chicago. The tragedies mount. Chicago made *Time* and *Newsweek* in 1994 and 1995, when a DCFS worker returned eighteen-month-old Joey Wallace to his mother, who then hanged the baby with an electric cord; when eleven-year-old Robert Sandifer shot and killed a teen on gang orders (killing the wrong victim) and was then himself gunned down by his own gang members; and when nineteen children from Keystone Street were found in a dirty apartment, their six mothers were arrested and lost custody of the children.

What followed each tragedy were "get-tough" editorials that invariably attacked symptoms rather than causes. According to the *Chicago Tribune,* Robert Sandifer could have been prevented from his crime if the judge who released him from Chicago's Audy Home, a juvenile correction holding center, had a "secure facility for violent young people" to send him to. But that's not enough, went on the *Tribune* editorial; we must teach "children from the day they start kindergarten that it's wrong to have a child until you can care for it. It [reform] means adopting welfare policies that, for example, don't provide teenage mothers with their own checks, that tell all mothers an extra kid won't come with extra money attached."[41]

Money for Punishment

Jails for children—punish teen mothers—arrest mothers who are drug users, then take their children away. These were the same old solutions: increase incarceration, increase foster care, and punish welfare mothers. Had any ever worked? Governor Edgar's Task Force on Crime and Corrections reported that Illinois had built fifteen prisons in the last fifteen years but that the prison and jail system is still overcrowded and the streets are less safe. As former executive deputy director of DCFS Cleo Terry said following her resignation, "We respond to the tragedy of Robert Sandifer not with a cry to develop more early intervention programs, but with legislation to lock up 11 year olds."[42]

The "get-tough" campaign against juveniles escalated in 1980, when current mayor Richard Daley, who at the time was the Cook County state's attorney, cracked down on "youth crime." What followed was a 119 percent increase in the number of youth committed to the Illinois Department of Corrections. Yet at the time of the "epidemic" of youth crime—between 1975 and 1980—felony arrests for juveniles had *dropped* 8.5 percent.[43]

The Need for Drug Rehabilitation Centers

In 1994, presiding judge of juvenile court Sophia Hall said that an estimated "80 percent of families in the Abuse and Neglect Section of juvenile court have some substance abuse related problems…but there are not enough programs to respond to the need."[44] So does the governor build more drug rehab programs? No. Instead, a proposed $1 billion is to be spent on prisons over the next ten years. Illinois has only enough drug treatment center beds "to meet about 5 percent of the need."[45] This is a state where *"leading experts in the field have set the incredibly modest goal of serving only 15 percent of all addicted people in Illinois"*[46] (emphasis added).

Those who fill the Illinois prisons for mostly drug-related crimes are usually men of color, especially African Americans. According to the National Institute on Drug Abuse, it is not blacks but "whites who make up two-thirds of those who have tried crack and constitute a majority of the most frequent users."[47] When whites are arrested and sentenced, "a wealthy coke dealer can sell $75,000 worth of drugs and get the same 5 year mandatory sentence as a street-corner crack dealer who sells $750 worth."[48] According to House Representative Maxine Waters, "Minorities represent an average of 96 percent of those who were prosecuted for crack cocaine nationally in federal courts from 1992 to 1994."[49]

Attorney Gail Smith, director of Chicago Legal Aid to Mothers Incarcerated (CLAIM), says that the refusal to fund drug rehab programs has also increased the Illinois women's prison population. In addition, the lack of programs has helped swell the number of children removed from their homes, because addicted mothers resist applying for drug rehab programs for two reasons: First, "There's only two drug treatment programs in all of Chicago that will take mothers and children, and they have under fifty beds collectively," says Joanne Archibald, advocacy project director for CLAIM. And secondly, "The mothers hold back even applying for drug rehab programs because they're afraid DCFS will take their kids away. Unfortunately, even these programs are experiencing funding cuts, but there's no cut-off in funds to build more prisons."[50]

If mothers enter court-ordered drug rehab programs, the stipulations required to be reunited with their children are unrealistic. Mildred Williamson, who is director of the Women and Children HIV Program at Cook County Hospital, believes that juvenile court lacks an understanding of the recovery process of an addict and that children suffer the consequences:

> DCFS and juvenile court don't understand addiction and relapse. Generally, you are given six months to straighten up your life. But this [time frame] doesn't sufficiently acknowledge the triggers for relapse, the length

of the addiction, the constellation of drugs of the user, etc. The measurement is unreal also—all the way clean, or you don't get your kid back. It's too extreme. Another thing not considered in accessing recovery or relapse is the presence or absence of an abusive partner.[51]

Indicting the Powerless

In Chicago, the blame for increased reports of abuse and neglect of children is laid at the feet of poor mothers and the hulking, mismanaged Department of Children and Family Services. The high percentage of mothers who are victims of male violence is not a preoccupation of the state or of media reports. A globalized market system that creates massive inequality is never indicted. At the trial of the "Keystone 19" mothers, Judge Lynn Kawamoto declared that "poverty is not to blame. The Government is not to blame. The responsibility was with these mothers to provide the necessary care and safe environment for their children."[52]

As ACLU's Ben Wolf says, "Juvenile court is a mother blaming institution." But it's not just juvenile court. Welfare mothers—the unworthy poor—are caricatured as irresponsible mothers or welfare cheats. They are victimizers, not the victimized. Precisely 87 percent of the women who go to Chicago public health clinics live below the poverty line, and of that constituency, a Chicago Department of Health Survey found that 50 percent of the women "have experienced domestic violence in their lives…[and] one in four had been abused in the last year."[53]

Resurgent Racism

Almost 80 percent of the 45,000 children under DCFS care are African American, and although still a significantly smaller percentage, Latino children are entering the system in greater numbers. The poor black family and black community—once able to fend off mainstream cultural incursion, derision, and hatred with countercultural experiences of communal life—are trapped in social isolation and alienation, and face their "greatest crisis since slavery."[54]

Historian Lerone Bennett describes the sentiment of those within poor black communities: "There's an anger, there's a bitterness, an overwhelming disillusionment….You see broken families. You see young people destroyed by dope, an epidemic of which brings murderously high rates of violence. Rap music is the expression of the anguish of black America."[55]

University of Chicago sociologist Julius Wilson has explained the erosive transformation of inner-city black communal and family life since the 1970s as resulting from both deindustrialization *and* the departure of professional black role models from areas of extreme poverty. These socially isolated areas, said Wilson, are distinctive, insofar as they socially and economically resemble third world countries in the intensity of conditions of poverty.[56] In studying Chicago neighborhoods, Wilson found that "in 1970 only one of Chicago's so-called community areas had a poverty rate of over 40 percent, but by 1980 there were 9 such areas...all of them neighborhoods inhabited principally by African Americans."[57]

According to Wilson, the "underclass" develops as role models depart who kept participation in mainstream society alive during periods of economic depression. An eroded, dispirited community is left in the wake of the exodus of successful blacks, who signify the efficacy of such American values as education and securing a decent job, and the importance of male mentors to stable family life.

The problem with Wilson's theory, according to Carl Nightengale, is that poor blacks are not cut off from mainstream values; they have appropriated them.[58] Lack of economic opportunity and social isolation alone don't explain the tragic changes in poor black communities in the late twentieth century. The social disposability of poor African Americans is not only the result of the loss of manufacturing jobs. Social exclusion resulting from racial segregation through redlining, the construction of housing projects that concentrate poor blacks geographically, and a white-dominated municipal patronage system has marked Chicago as an apartheid city. It is the combination of racial segregation and racial hatred that has made the experience of inner-city poverty such a devastating one.

Theories of social isolation, such as Wilson's, fail to show the ways that advertising analysts have won over the inner-city market. In so doing, the poor African Americans became consumer participants in mainstream culture while remaining shut off from social participation. Confronted with the humiliation of social exclusion, African American youth have embraced American values as a compensation for their losses. According to Nightengale,

> The recent history of the ethical and emotional experience of poor African-Americans and the recent histories of their communities cannot be written without understanding how some of America's most familiar and compelling institutions, ideals, and images have helped to raise inner-city children. American ideas of social control through "law and order," American racial imagery, American consumerism, and American traditions of violence have had all important parts to play in the growing tragedy of [poor Black communities]....The age-old values of American violence...have a variety of ancestries, whether they are born in slavery, the genocide of Native Americans, frontier lawlessness, racial violence, men's violence against women, state violence against working-class people, Prohibition era gangsterism, or cold war militarism.[59]

Media's ability to promote and market these histories, images, and values has been welcomed by African American youth as a way to compensate for the shame, humiliation, and powerlessness that they experience through social exclusion. Black youth, especially boys, have developed a culture of the outsider, the outlaw, glorifying the caricature of the violent black male. In resisting their exclusion they have defiantly become the "baaaaad dude." The dangerous, oversexed black stereotype has been reinvented as a heroic ideal: "In doing so, they have not only found a way to achieve a sense of compensatory personal adequacy in the face of racial humiliation but have also created an important basis for moral legitimacy for violence derived directly from a mainstream image."[60] The virtual incarceration ritual for poor black males has taught the black male youth that he is to be feared, and, in reaction, young males have constructed a "powerful" self—one less tied to the traditional cooperative values of the African American community.

Black children compensate for the shame of poverty and the distress of racial exclusion through participation in consumer culture. Gold necklaces, starter jackets, and expensive running shoes are emblems of belonging and power. The encompassing seduction of conspicuous consumption combined with children's sense of embarrassment and shame at their poverty creates continuous stress for their parents. A mother hoping to assert control and meet the challenging behavior of a pre-teen male resorts to physical punishment, which, of course, fuels a humiliated child's rage and depletes his mother's spirit.

Nightengale uses the story of the Wilkens family to illustrate this dynamic. The Wilkens promise their children that when the tax refunds arrive, they will buy them Nintendos or sneakers. When the returns arrive and are used for intervening emergencies, this sparks dejection and yelling matches that escalate to beatings.[61] Parents, too, compensate for their eroded sense of self-esteem and parental adequacy by reclaiming "old-fashioned" notions of unquestioned authority. There is little reasonable discourse that an impoverished mother can offer to disavow the emotional anguish of a child whose only measure of worth is a material possession. American culture tells children that they don't count, that they aren't even needed except to consume. Without an "answer" for her children, the mother seeks to stop belligerence with force, hoping to demand respect.

But where is respect garnered in a city where a poor mother has virtually only one hospital to turn to—Cook County Hospital—because ten hospitals in poor neighborhoods have closed? What futility must a mother feel who has to wait up to six months for a clinic appointment at Cook County Hospital? Where is respect found if you are one of the 100,000 Chicago homeless, of which 41 percent are women with children and the majority are African American? What messages of respect does an inner-city boy feel knowing that most of the youth in his neighborhood have been involved with the criminal justice system? Eighty percent of the juveniles in the Cook County Juvenile Temporary Detention Center are black. The message from surrounding institutions is evident: these mothers and children have been written off.

The inclusion of African American youth in the mass market shapes their experience of racial and economic exclusion, which in turn effects changes in their racial, class, and gender identities. Although deindustrialization is central to explaining social alienation in an area such as Lawndale on Chicago's Westside, the parallel transfer of wealth upward is essential to understanding the demoralizing effect on the psyches of poor children living in areas of concentrated poverty. The experience of inequality in Chicago defines worth and power in terms of accumulation of material goods, but it also produces the "racial grievance" that poor blacks feel when confronted with affluence.[62]

CONCLUSION

From the beginning of the twentieth century to today, Illinois' child welfare system has been underfunded, understaffed, overextended, and undercut by political clout. Its services have been either too meager or too intrusive. Juvenile court, though intended to deinstitutionalize children from adult jails, served only to continue children's institutionalization in reform schools and industrial schools. The current DCFS bureaucracy continues the mission of administrative oversight, licensing, and protective services that was its historical regulatory mandate. Private agencies that have undergone more critical reform still continue their historical assignment to place children in foster homes or residential care.

Chicago, the immigrant's city, embraces its new immigrants with ambivalence and a need to control, just as was true at the beginning of the century. Chicago is a city smoldering from the impact of job loss, a dwindling tax base, and the resulting crisis of its public schools, hospitals, public assistance, and criminal and juvenile justice systems, as well as the problems of the public and private child welfare agencies. At the same time that low-income people—especially African Americans, Latinos, Native Americans, and the new Asian and Eastern European immigrants—struggle to pay rent and heating bills, wealthy suburban and Gold Coast residents have increased their earnings. This dynamic of flourishing wealth for some and humiliating poverty for others is critical to understanding the problems faced by public institutions and agencies, such as the Department of Children and Family Services, whose clientele are the poor, primarily women and children.

Further, the racism that mars Chicago's history also shapes child welfare policies at the end of the century. Deindustrialization, racial exclusion, and coinciding concentrations of extreme wealth and extreme poverty have transformed American cities, with devastating effects on the disenfranchised elements of the population. In summary, the African American, Latino, and Asian American poor of Chicago have to some extent joined the surplus populations of third world nations in suffering the effects of global restructuring. The policies of child welfare agencies in Chicago have not only failed to challenge that process; they have, primarily through removal of black children from their homes, facilitated the process of communal disintegration.

NOTES

1. Patrick Murphy, "When Parents Aren't Enough: Residential Care Offers Children Stability and Hope," *Chicago Tribune* (July 7, 1994), 21.

2. Joan Gittens, *Poor Relations: The Children of the State of Illinois 1818–1990* (Urbana: University of Illinois Press: 1994), 1.

3. Tony Platt, *The Child Savers: The Invention of Delinquency* (Chicago: University of Chicago Press, 1977), xxii.

4. Gittens, 34.

5. Ibid., 42.

6. Ibid., 41.

7. Ibid., 47.

8. Ibid., 50.

9. Ibid., 52.

10. Ibid., 62.

11. Ibid., 42.

12. Ibid., 65.

13. David Orr, "Overstating the State of the State," *Chicago Tribune* (Feb. 11, 1996), "Voice of the People" editorial.

14. Gittens, 74.

15. Wes Smith, "Unwanted Children Find a Haven at an Old Airforce Base," *Chicago Tribune* (Feb. 16, 1996), 22.

16. Andrew Fengelman, "Court Pushes to Find Permanent Homes for Kids," *Chicago Tribune* (Jan. 11, 1996), 3.

17. David Reed and Courtney O'Malley, *The Orphanage Debate: Making Sense of a Complex Issue* (Chicago: Children and Family Justice Center, Northwestern University School of Law, 1996), 43.

18. Sue Ellen Christian, "DCFS Proposes Guardianship Plan," *Chicago Tribune* (Jan. 15, 1996), 1.

19. Ibid.

20. Rick Pearson, "DCFS Strained Trying to Handle Record Caseload," *Chicago Tribune* (Jan. 1, 1995), 1.

21. Illinois Initiative for Comprehensive Children and Family Services, *A New Paradigm: Moving Toward Comprehensive Services* (Chicago: Voices for Illinois Children, 1995), 2.

22. Frederick Lowe, "Hiring Means Hope in Poor," *Chicago Sun-Times* (Nov. 28, 1994), 14.

23. Interview with Dave Ranney, Feb. 3, 1995.

24. Lowe.

25. Maribeth Vander Weele, *Reclaiming Our Schools: The Struggle for Chicago School Reform* (Chicago: Loyola University Press, 1994), xiv, 3, 7, 48, 88, 111.

26. Interview with Jack Wuest, Oct. 20, 1995.

27. Adele Simmons and Bruce Newman, "More Than Just a Summer Job," *Chicago Tribune* (Apr. 28, 1996), 19.

28. Ibid.

29. Nancy Ryan, "Teen Jobs Plan Is in Jeopardy," *Chicago Tribune* (Feb. 23, 1996), 14.

30. Interview with Dwayne Smith, May 15,1995.

31. William Presecky and Suzy Frisch, "State GOP Goes After Welfare," *Chicago Tribune* (Feb. 3, 1995), 1.

32. Mary Boehnke, "HUD, Quadel Take Over CHA," *Streetwise* 4:4 (1996), 1.

33. Patrick Reardon, "Rich Got Richer, Poor, Poorer, Study Says," *Chicago Tribune* (Jan. 27, 1993), 2:1.

34. Ibid.

35. Ibid., 2:9.

36. James Garabino, "Attending to the Children of All the World's War Zones," *New York Times* (Dec. 6, 1992), "Conversations" section.

37. Teresa Puente, "Boy Set Fire Over Missing Food Stamps," *Chicago Tribune* (Mar. 26, 1995), 2:1.

38. Illinois Initiative, 2.

39. Wuest interview.

40. Garabino.

41. Editorial, *Chicago Tribune* (Sept. 2, 1994), 20.

42. Cleo Terry, "DCFS Battles Overwhelming Odds," *Chicago Tribune* (Oct. 23, 1994), "Voice of the People" editorial.

43. Committee to End the Marion Lockdown, "The Criminalization of Youth of Color," *Walkin' Steel* (Fall 1995), 4.

44. Sophia Hall, "Breaking the Cycle of Violence," *Chicago Tribune* (Apr. 13, 1994), 21.

45. Editorial, *Chicago Tribune* (Oct. 1, 1995), 20.

46. Robert Boekenhauer, "Risky Cuts in Addiction Treatment," *Chicago Tribune* (Dec. 13, 1994), "Voice of the People" editorial.

47. Lynett Myers, "Harsher Penalties Remain for Crack Users," *Chicago Tribune* (Oct. 17, 1995), 3.

48. Ibid.

49. Ibid.

50. Interview with Joanne Archibald, Sept. 29, 1995.

51. Interview with Mildred Williamson, director of Women and Children HIV Program, Cook County Hospital, February 1996.

52. Susan Kuczka, "Judge Pins Blame on Keystone Moms, Not Poverty," *Chicago Tribune* (Oct. 28, 1994), 1.

53. Evelyne Giradet, "City's Poor Women Abused, Study Says," *Chicago Tribune* (Mar. 23, 1995), 3.

54. Lerone Bennett, "There's Been a Misunderstanding About the Sixties," in *On Prejudice: A Global Perspective,* Ed. Daniela Gioseffi (New York: Doubleday, 1993), 586.

55. Ibid.

56. Julius Wilson, *The Truly Disadvantaged: The Inner-city, the Underclass and Public Policy* (Chicago: University of Chicago Press, 1987).

57. Julius Wilson, qtd. in Carl Husemoller Nightengale, *On the Edge: A History of Poor Black Children and Their American Dreams* (New York: Basic Books, 1993), 64.

58. Ibid.

59. Ibid., 9, 11.

60. Ibid., 10.

61. Ibid., 58.

62. Ibid., 63.

7

❋

Family Preservation
Versus Children's Rights

Lawsuits cannot make hard problems easy but they can force
consideration of the needs of powerless people.[1]

BEN WOLF, DIRECTOR OF CHILDREN'S INITIATIVE,
AMERICAN CIVIL LIBERTIES UNION

Anumber of the respondents who follow believe that the doubling of DCFS's caseload in four years is, ironically, the fault of its main critic, Patrick Murphy. With the defeat of Illinois' family preservation practice (called in Illinois "Family First"), a policy that kept children in their homes was undermined. Murphy leads the charge against Family First because he believes that it rewards irresponsible parents: "Federally mandated child [family] preservation too often means that services are lavished on irresponsible individuals who have seriously harmed their children....Beat up or rape the kid down the block and you'll end up in the can for a good long spell. Beat up or have sex with your own child and you'll get a social worker and a housekeeper."[2]

The 1980 Adoption Assistance and Child Welfare Act, which committed federal funds for family preservation, has been continually lambasted by the Illinois Public Guardian, but never so rancorously as in the 1990s, when President Clinton's approval of the Omnibus Budget Reconciliation Act of 1993 gave states federal monies to develop family preservation resource programs.

The highly successful Homebuilders program of Seattle, begun in 1974, was the model that family preservationists presented to effect a national change in child welfare regarding families. Family preservation has been so effective in many states that they have been able to critically reduce their foster care populations. For example, Michigan's foster care population has decreased by 10 percent in two years as a result of a statewide family preservation model that serviced 22,000 families. Alabama counties where family preservation has been implemented lowered foster care placement by 30 percent in two years, and Washington State and Utah found that children in the family preservation program were less than half as likely to be placed in foster care as children without intensive family services.[3]

However, family preservation failed in Illinois because it never really started. The Homebuilders model offers families intensive short-term help (four to six weeks), in which a worker is available to a family virtually around the clock, interacting with all members, assisting with daily chores, facilitating immediate solutions to survival issues of transportation, baby-sitting, and doctor or school visits, as well as developing and implementing with the family a plan to transform (or, at least, alter for the better) the problems that are present. A key to the program's success is a process of helping the family identify its strengths as a base for problem solving, rather than rehashing failures. Follow-up is critical with families. Homebuilders insists that "the tie is never completely severed."[4] Homebuilders scrupulously screens workers and requires intensive training, supervision, and team support to encourage committed, competent family workers.

Saying that Illinois' DCFS didn't "get" the concept is an understatement. DCFS workers spent an average of thirty-two minutes per day with the family and stretched this time out over a three-month period; the "concrete" services of working with the family on daily tasks, a commitment that builds trust and emphasizes the importance of family maintenance work, was reduced to nine minutes per day; follow-up to the families was sporadic; agencies that contracted with DCFS to provide services were allowed to lower their hiring standards for workers; and families were selected for the program who were not in imminent danger of having their children removed from their homes in the first place.[5] If all that is not enough, six children died while in the program or following its completion.

It is no wonder that Patrick Murphy called family preservation philosophy "positively counterproductive, in that it harms the very people it seeks to help." However, Illinois' DCFS is not representative of family preservation. DCFS, not the family preservation model, has failed to protect children.

SUING DCFS

In 1991, the American Civil Liberties Union won a sweeping consent decree against DCFS that mandated extensive reform actions. But four years later the agency with a billion-dollar annual budget has not only failed to reduce the number of children languishing in foster care; it has doubled the number: "The [removal of children] is worse now than when we sued,"[6] admits Ben Wolf, director of Children's Initiative for ACLU.

Wolf blames much of the increase on Murphy's seizing the bully pulpit to attack and kill Family First. Outraged by caseworker judgment errors that cost children their lives, Murphy publicly railed at both juvenile court and DCFS in a rare display (for public officials but not for Murphy) of passionate, if mis-assessed, criticism. His lacerating attacks on public and private agencies won him media endorsement as the champion of children abused by state care.

A precipitating tragedy was the death of baby Joseph Wallace, who was returned in 1993 to his mother by a juvenile court judge's decision, at the recommendation of a DCFS worker and the compliance of the Public Guardian's office. This event led ABC's anchor Diane Sawyer to conclude that Joey Wallace's death had accomplished something: "in the state of Illinois, the law now reads that the welfare of the child now comes first."[7] No judge, no worker would risk returning a child to a home with the threat of incurring national public exposure. As a result, thousands of children float through the foster care and shelter system as if they were pieces of wreckage: a dangerous cargo to be kept moving.

However, Murphy's goal in saving children was the opposite of that of Ben Wolf and Bruce Boyer, the supervising attorney of Northwestern Law School's Children and Family Justice Center. Murphy wants the children in orphanages or residential treatment centers, safe from the horrors of either a dysfunctional foster care system or the perils of life in the "underclass." Wolf and Boyer (as well as the majority of the child welfare advocates who testify in the following chapters) want the kids sent home.

Both Murphy and the *Chicago Tribune* blame Wolf for not forcing DCFS's hand. Tribune columnist Bruce Dold believes ACLU has become "too palsy-walsy with the state...the ACLU captors are becoming sympathetic to their

DCFS hostages."[8] Wolf says he is less seduced than strategic, for he can't force DCFS to relate to troubled families in collaborative ways when agency culture is hierarchical, centralized, bureaucratic, and driven by procedures rather than held accountable to outcomes. Wolf's question is how to change an institutional culture that has immobilized worker initiative and creativity with the handcuffs of legal and bureaucratic procedures. Threats, fines, jail, and more reforms won't get at that inertia.

In spite of bureaucratic footdragging, Wolf is convinced that the decree has forced Illinois' legislative and executive powers to recognize their responsibility in confronting the abuse and neglect of Illinois children at the hands of DCFS. It is difficult to share his optimism, given the history of Illinois child welfare policies for the last 150 years. Nevertheless, Wolf considers initial reforms significant. Caseloads have been reduced from one hundred clients to thirty-five, there is increased access to drug treatment services, adoptions have increased considerably, there are increases in placements for special needs children, and the supervision of caseworkers has improved.

However, the Public Guardian's Office sees little change in the stream of children pouring through a system that slowly plugs its leaking boat while children drown daily. Nor is Patrick Murphy sanguine about DCFS's ability to transform a bureaucratic culture mired in an inglorious past. His preoccupation is "the culture of the underclass." As he puts it, "The problem is not racial, but neither is it economic. It is cultural. A culture of welfare-dependent individuals recycles their welfare dependency and misery to a new generation every 15 years or so, and that population, for reasons dating back to slavery and segregation, is largely African American."[9] Murphy upholds the child-saver tradition of rescuing the unworthy poor, whereas Ben Wolf and Bruce Boyer focus on fixing the rescue system's leaky boat.

One final note before the narratives of advocates that follow in this chapter, as well as in Chapters 8 and 9: the opinions of the individual advocates do not necessarily represent the philosophy of their respective organizations, although in some cases they do coincide. Finally, the narratives are in the words of the advocates, except for the opening italicized text that introduces each advocate to the reader.

Advocate's Narrative

Bruce Boyer

Bruce Boyer is the supervising attorney for the Children and Family Justice Center of Northwestern Law School. He has represented children, parents, and family members in child abuse and neglect cases and is critical of the assault on family preservation.

There is a fundamental disparity between the way in which people on either side of the child welfare debate are able to present their cause. When Patrick Murphy [Cook County Public Guardian] wants to go after family preservation programs, Family First programs, his job is a very simple one. All he has to do is trot out a couple of his stand-by cases where horrible things have been done to children and say, "If you don't listen to me, then you're going to kill children. These programs where we're supporting terrible parents are driven by dated, crazy, liberal ideas. We need to get tough with families who aren't taking care of their kids." It's a very salable type of position.

On the other side of that, people like Richard Wexler [who wrote *Wounded Innocents: The Real Victims of the War Against Child Abuse*], like myself, face a much more difficult task in trying to tell the public what the world of child welfare is really all about. I talk about Patrick Murphy a lot, less as an individual than as a metaphor for the whole world of what Wexler would call the child savers. Child savers have an assumption, which is unspoken, that the interests of parents and children are often fundamentally at odds with each other. That is, when you talk about the "best interests of the child," the debate is cast in terms of whose interests are going to prevail: the child's or the parents. In family preservation, to my mind, there's a commonality of interests. There may be some divergence of interests when parents fall down on the job, but when you're trying to figure out what's right for a child, it's not so different from what's right for a family.

You get away from this philosophy when you start talking about the children's rights movement. We all agree to protect kids, but is it going to translate into a willingness to actually do the things that you have to do to protect kids? Take a situation with the typical entrenched, complicated problems a poor family faces living in an urban environment. What are we, as a society, willing to do to respond to the needs of this family? If you believe in family preservation as something more than a platitude, then you say we need to do a comprehensive assessment of what's wrong with this family, we need to invest the time, energy, services to support that family so that the family is not broken up. If you don't really believe in family preservation, then there's a reluctance to press DCFS, or any child welfare agency, to do its job and make available the assessments and services that would really make a difference to the family.

Sensationalizing Abuse Cases

You can't take sensational cases that often have almost nothing to do with the routine of juvenile court and use them as a bludgeon to try and persuade the legislature to implement policies that might possibly prevent the next Joseph Wallace [the abused infant hanged by his mentally ill mother after he was returned to her by a DCFS worker who wanted to "preserve" the family] because in the meantime you are going to swamp an already overburdened system and send more kids who don't belong there into foster care.

Every time there's a sensational case that hits the newspaper, such as Wallace, DCFS's intake soars. Also, when DCFS blames the worker whose decision went wrong, there's another dramatic increase in kids coming into the system. Because, of course, no worker wants to be the next scapegoat.

If you have a child welfare system that is heavily oriented toward reporting abuse, toward increasing the number of mandated reporters, eventually you come to a point where you're doing more harm than good because you're processing too many cases that shouldn't be in the system.

One of the principal causes for this increase, besides the drug epidemic, is the way different kinds of harms to children follow from the way decisions are made and balanced. By that I mean the caseworker, lawyer, judge—the decision makers—have to weigh potential harms and risks. One of the problems that tips the balance toward [removal of kids] is that, for physical harms to children, decision makers are held personally and professionally accountable. The DCFS caseworker who doesn't try hard enough to get into the home, to do an investigation that subsequently gets front page in the news, gets hung out to dry. On the other hand, there are a set of harms that follow a kid in foster care even if they are treated as well as the foster care system is capable of treating children. For those kinds of harms there is no mechanism for holding decision makers accountable; the only person who suffers is the child.

The ACLU Federal Consent Decree

These are Ben Wolf's words; I can't take credit: "Litigation as a way of effecting systemic change in a government agency is the worst possible way of doing reform, except for every other way." There is so much more beyond a federal consent decree that is required in order for the decree to be effective. A critical need is for the legislature to provide the necessary financial support. The legislature is not subject to the federal consent decree. If they are not willing to give DCFS the tools needed, then the consent decree isn't going to have much of an impact. Most people would tell you that there hasn't been much positive effect as a result of the BH decree [the federal consent decree requiring massive DCFS reform following an American Civil Liberties Union lawsuit].

The problem with much of the criticism against DCFS is that it aims to dismantle the agency and to turn responsibility for making social work decisions over to the court. You can't. There has to be an agency out there to do the risk assessments, the service as-

sessments, to provide and monitor services, and to make reports to the courts. That is not a judicial function.

The Children and Family Justice Center

The center is a project of Northwestern Law School which started in 1991–1992. We said one of our objectives was to increase scrutiny of juvenile court with the idea that juvenile court had become a backwater, a dumping ground for judges who couldn't cut the standards of other courts. We took people through the courts, tried to increase exposure, etc. Well, now all of that has happened. There is no question that public attention on the court has increased....There is a much higher quality of judges down there now than five or six years ago. The new head of juvenile court, Judge O'Connell, has made [reform] his number-one priority. But where has it gotten us?

We [Illinois] have 50,000 kids in foster care, the vast majority from Chicago. The biggest public policy question facing both the juvenile court and the child welfare system is how to develop early intervention mechanisms that would deflect referrals to the court system. How can we reduce caseloads to court both at the front end [though prevention] and the back end [closing out cases]? Reduced caseloads is one measure of whether or not the increased exposure of juvenile court and DCFS is working. You build a bigger house; people will fill it. We have now, I think, if you count hearing officers, up to thirty-six court officers. This is extraordinary. It's an industry....There isn't a city in the country that comes close to having that kind of industry devoted to the processing of children who are alleged to be abused or neglected.

Where Is Prevention?

Part of the problem is the perennial inability to focus resources on the front end, on prevention. The [independent children's advocate] Voices for Illinois Children just came out with a report which concludes that we don't spend enough money on front-end assessments [preventive services and early family support services]. The frustration is that if you do that, you save money. It's not just good social policy; it's sound fiscal policy, too. If you cut down on the numbers of kids so that only those kids go into care who really need it, you don't swamp the court system, you don't swamp the foster care system. You then free up resources to expedite the processes for achieving some alternative permanency goal, whether it's adoption or whatever else.

Train DCFS Workers

The legislature needs to appropriate more funds to DCFS—it would save money, to say nothing of saving kids. In order for the process to work effectively, you have to have trained workers, you have to pay them enough to make them want to do their work, you have to give them low enough caseloads so that they devote the amount of time that good social work knowledge and understanding tells you is necessary in order to do an effective investigation and quality risk assessment. Just talking about these up-front services—if you don't do these things—you're going to bring the house down around you, which is what's happening.

Advocate's Narrative
Patrick Murphy

Patrick Murphy is Cook County's maverick Public Guardian. The New York Times, Washington Post, *and ABC's* Prime Time Live *have portrayed him as a rare public official willing to blast the Department of Children and Family Services, juvenile court judges, and social workers who fail to protect children. A target of his discontent are those who uncritically support family preservation (called Family First in Illinois).*

Murphy has three prescriptions for changing not just child welfare but also society's response to the "underclass": welfare reform, educational reform, and child welfare reform. For Murphy, the root of the problem is the underclass. He labors to define this group as distinctive but then confuses them with poor, decent people.

However, it would be a serious mistake to underestimate Murphy's capacity to hang tough. For thirty years he's been a scrapper who has defended children's rights. In the early 1970s he wrote a book, Our Kindly Parent the State, *based on his experiences*

as a legal assistance lawyer defending youth twenty-five years ago, which suggested that the way to reform juvenile court was to raze it—not a recommendation that would curry favor with officials. Yet he was invited to work to defend children's interests from within the state system. Always controversial, he has fought for children's rights with a "take no prisoners" attitude toward anyone who gets in his way. He's survived both Republican and Democratic legislatures. In some cases his high profile, as well as his willingness to take off the gloves with any comer, has protected him from recriminations. While nationally known and respected, his maverick "lone ranger" approach has cut him off from the very people—advocates for children and families—with whom he might make common cause to challenge Illinois' destructive child welfare policies.

The system is better today than it was in 1969, better than it was in 1974, and better today than in 1987 when we took over the GAL's [Public Guardian's] office. When we took over, DCFS was running horrible shelters for abused kids. Not to take credit, but we did sue them, and they contracted with Father Smyth to run Columbus–Maryville, which is one hundred times better…[although] it could still be a lot better. I think most of the reform has come because of intense media interest in the system.

Having said that, the system has many, many failures. The foster care system has probably more sexual abuse than there used to be, but most of that is in the homes of relatives—usually a cousin of a cousin—but you still get foster fathers sexually abusing kids. Kids still drift through the system, go through four or five foster homes, and when they become adolescents, they still end up on the streets for lack of alternative placements.

I think one of the most significant problems is that we are still trying to send kids back to homes that are not there, and as a result we don't look for permanency, we don't look for adoption. We hold on to parents long after we should. Obviously, it makes more sense to send the kid home as quickly as possible for three reasons: (a) in most circumstances it's better for kids who've bonded to a parent, even a marginal parent; (b) it's cheaper for taxpayers; and (c) home is better than the system, which is frequently unkind.

But having said that, what has happened is in the late 1960s and early 1970s, the majority of my clients were white, but by the time I left [Legal Aid] in 1974 the client population was fifty–fifty. Today, 88 percent of our clients are African American, and virtually all of these are from the so-called underclass.…Once you throw in the underclass, not the poor class because even amongst the poor there isn't much child abuse—I mean you have to segregate poor from underclass. If you look at

the black poor, traditionally they are a very religious and even conservative class of people. There's no child abuse or very little. But once you get into the underclass.…

Ben Wolf and I exchanged some letters, and I suggested to Wolf that the "BH" decree will always be a failure until they go over to juvenile court and see what happens. They are premising that decree on academic experts. [The experts'] view of juvenile court is premised on books like my own [*Our Kindly Parent the State*] that are twenty years old.

What we see in juvenile court is the twenty-four-year-old mom, five kids, four fathers, none involved, her mom was on welfare, her mom is thirty-eight or forty, her Grandmother is in her sixties, both are on welfare, both have had children with a variety of men. It is a culture where welfare is handed down from generation to generation. "Work ethic" isn't fair because there isn't any work or education. There's no idea of becoming educated to escape the ghetto and family; it is just assumed that when you're fourteen or fifteen you'll have a baby and the father will be uninvolved. When they say kids have babies in order to get on welfare, I disagree, but I do agree that, to a degree, it's a cultural thing. It's just like in some countries they go to sea at fifteen. It is a culture different from the predominant culture and different from black culture. It is a distinct third or fourth world culture which we can call the underclass. And until we resolve the problem of that culture, we will be inundated with these cases at juvenile court.

The problems of the underclass have become much more exacerbated because of fleeing jobs to other countries. The educational system is still premised on the fact that you're going to go through high school and get a manufacturing job, except the job is now in Thailand. I'm talking about inner-city schools. If you're a genius or very bright you can escape, but for the average student it's still geared to [preparation for a non-existent manufacturing industry].

The second problem is the need for release from the present predicament. The worse your predicament, the greater the need for release. My own personal predicament, that of a relatively well paid government bureaucrat and decently paid lawyer with two kids and a wife living in the suburbs, is that I still like to go on a vacation, I still like my Scotch on weekends, I still like to have a good bottle of wine, I still like to go to a good restaurant to eat, and I still like to see a good movie. Though I have a pretty good life, I still need that release. Now, if I have four or five kids living in Cabrini Green or Robert Taylor and have no husband helping me and I'm living on nickels and dimes that welfare gives me, my need for release is going to be much greater than Patrick Murphy's need for release. And I cannot get on a plane and go to California like Murphy can, and I can't go to a good restaurant, and I can't get a good bottle of wine—I can't even go to Michigan or Lincoln Park because it's a hassle to get there. So what do I do for release? I turn to the cheapest, most available form of release, which is drugs. It's understandable. So I do the drug of choice, crack cocaine, which is more habit forming than heroin. It's harder to get off, and when you do get off it's easier to go back on it, according to all studies.

We don't have rehab programs.... Drugs are chewing people up so that the woman loses the kids to the system and getting them back to her isn't that hot because if she increases drugs it could continue for four or five years. [Sometimes] there is no home to send the kid back to because the mom is beyond help. We don't like to say anyone is beyond help, but if you're talking about a childhood life span of twelve or thir-

teen years, I mean, if we take away three years of his life, routing him through foster homes, we're taking away one quarter of his life. If we take away five years, it's almost half his childhood.

On Ideology and Welfare Reform

I think that people on the left, people who are true liberals, are iconoclast and they will not accept conventional wisdom. The problem is that those of us from the 1960s attacked the conventional wisdom of the time and then we developed a conventional wisdom of our own. We've been afraid to attack [our own conventional wisdom]....I'm afraid sometimes we get wedded to the idea that it's not the fault of the poorest victims and we have to continually provide for them. This has shown to be horribly self defeating to the very people we're trying to help because no matter how much of a hand we try to give them, the only way out of the depths of the inner city is by virtue of your own work.

I would have incentives for people on welfare if they got jobs....Perhaps...I would reward people on welfare who in any way bettered themselves, so you'd have a whole series of incentives. Right now, the system is basically a disincentive system.

We can put ladders down there: education, adequate housing, jobs, birth control information, resources, abortion availability. There are two things I would do: (a) welfare reform so that adolescents do not get welfare at all and (b) after two kids, you don't get any more welfare....People say it's cruel—well, hey man, that's life.

Educational Reforms

The second thing I would do...is look [over] social welfare programs, eliminate many and take the money to develop the best damn school system I can...get smaller schools in the inner city at both grammar school and high school levels, starting earlier, at three or four [years old]. This would basically write off an older generation…concentrate on children coming in now and just pour everything into that.…I think we're tied to a nineteenth-century concept of education. We're no longer an agrarian country; I mean, it's goofy, my kid takes home economics, and he's learning how to embroider.

Why Assess Blame?

I think getting involved in blame doesn't serve anyone's purpose. You can say what caused segregation: slavery, the fact that the middle class pulled out of poor neighborhoods, the black middle class pulled out as soon as the barriers to segregation fell down, the fact that the factories moved out after the riots in 1968, the fact that the factories went overseas in the 1970s and 1980s when communications and transportation made it easier for them to do it in order to get much cheaper wages. I mean, there's plenty of blame to go around: the fact that we developed counterproductive programs, the fact that Republicans, who were in power for so long, didn't care about the plight of the underclass.…There are years of problems that exist.

You have to change conditions, clearly, but we cannot change conditions. If anything, the CHA [Chicago Housing Authority] mess has proven that the conditions have to be changed by the people in there. We have to give them the resources, but they have to do it. Although it has improved…the [child welfare] system will always be second class…no matter how much we try to improve it. You don't want to reward people for abusing and neglecting their kids.…One of my problems with family preservation is too frequently we give all kinds of resources to someone who's a

horrible human being whereas there are thousands of very decent women on the Westside—and some men—who are doing an outstanding job of raising their kids on nickels and dimes, but we don't give them anything. Suddenly someone abuses their kids, and they get social workers, housekeepers, money, and so on. It doesn't make any sense.…It sends out the wrong message. So my point of view is, wait a second, there is a problem, it's called the underclass.

Most underclass people don't become delinquent, and most don't abuse and neglect their kids. But they're all living in abject misery and poverty and leading horribly depressing, nonproductive lives, and we have to change that as a society. The black middle class, as [Julius] Wilson points out, have pulled out, as of course they should—who would want to remain there? So these folks are really a fourth world or third world, whatever. How do you give them the resources to get out?

My concern is that we hear DCFS now talking about community centers and so on. It's just garbage.…Social services and community…to me, if we can give a person a job I would rather do that even if it's a make-work job, cleaning streets, cleaning the prairies.…I don't think a woman with four kids who is twenty-four needs a social worker telling her she's got a bleak life.…What she needs is something to help her kids get out of the same bleak life, and maybe a job if we can figure one out for somebody who has no skills.

…We know DCFS is not the villain in this piece. They are an overwhelmed bureaucracy. But, at times, it behooves us to use them as a representative of what is wrong in the system because the media cannot grasp a complex concept.…If you come up with a kid that's killed, they understand that because of the fact that the mother's on dope and not paying attention to the kid. Well, it's more complex than that—why are there drugs, etc.—but at least you're getting the media to focus on a problem, and that is children in the inner city are being abused, neglected, abandoned, not only by their parents, but by the larger society.

The Wall Around the Inner City
...We have built this wall around the inner city which didn't exist before.... Inside the wall is violence, joblessness, hopelessness, abuse, neglect, crime, and so on. There's two kinds of people on the inside of the wall. There's the very poor, and there's the underclass. You have to distinguish the two. Financially there may not be any difference; both may be on public aid, both without fathers. The difference, I think, is the underclass is basically a family without any males, recycled through welfare from generation to generation, where education is something that isn't even considered. It's a smaller group of the very poor. The very poor...decent people, trying very hard to raise children...are afraid of the underclass who may live next door to them...so that the very poor are being preyed upon by the underclass.

I think that the statistic, to me, that's most telling is the number of kids who come into delinquency without fathers. Strapping, I don't think, is abuse, not that I subscribe to it with my own kids, but I'd rather see a kid live with a father who strapped him than live with no father at all....

You revise the welfare system to encourage people to have less children who cannot emotionally or financially afford to have them...in some ways we are blaming the victim, but I think we have to blame the victim. Because by

not blaming the victim, by not putting shame into the victim, you're letting your victim dehumanize themselves. It's dehumanizing for thirteen-year-old kids to end up with four kids by the time they are twenty. Sure, they are the victims of all kinds of other forces, but we better damn well say, "We're going to give you tools, or force the tools upon you to get out of this. No more money if you have kids."

You have to understand these are the ravings of someone who looks for a very, very tiny piece of the problem, sort of like the six blind men studying the elephant. I see only a small part... abused and neglected kids.

On Family Preservation
My only problem with family preservation is that individuals have taken a good idea and want to plug it into every goofy situation in the world. The goal of family preservation should be short-term, intensive help for somebody who is not a mean person, not on drugs, but who otherwise would lose their child. What [Illinois] started to do is use family preservation as a long-term goal for people on drugs or for people who are mentally ill. It doesn't make sense. Our office [advocates] short-term services, but you have to understand its limits.

On Critics
I can only look at one case at a time. Ben Wolf and Diane Redleaf [Children's Rights Project Supervising Attorney, Legal Assistance Foundation of Chicago] don't represent individual clients. If they did, I suspect their views wouldn't be any different than ours. It's a lot easier to talk in generality about what should be done when you don't have to deal with it daily in representing 50,000 individual kids.

Advocate's Narrative

Ben Wolf

Ben Wolf is a lawyer and the director of the Children's Initiative Project of the American Civil Liberties Union Roger Baldwin Foundation. In 1988 his team won a consent decree against the Illinois Department of Children and Family Services. The five-hundred-page document produced by thirteen experts confirmed allegations that DCFS fails to provide fundamental services—health, education, stable placements—to families. Ben Wolf and adversary Public Guardian Patrick Murphy are almost total opposites. Murphy is a tough-talking self-described street fighter who says that in the seven years since the consent decree was won, DCFS continues to violate its recommendations. So what good is it? Wolf insists that strong-arming DCFS accomplishes little beyond forcing certain compliances while leaving the bureaucratic culture that creates oppressive child welfare practices intact. Wolf wants structural change rather than piecemeal sensationalized "wins"; however, Murphy doesn't believe DCFS can or will comply.

As of 1994, it was worse. There's almost no connection between the needs of a family and services provided. What people need is money, housing, substance abuse rehab programs without waiting lists.

The reason it was worse is that the culture of the agency was backwards. They tried to force change on already demoralized workers through rules, which made it worse. Permanency planning declined while the DCFS population exploded…the number of cases closed dropped off the table. In 1987, DCFS had 14,000 cases; in 1994, they had 45,000. It's disastrous.

After Joey Wallace and Keystone, no kid went home.

Ten years ago, there were only 231 kids sent out of state to locked facilities.

Now there are 750. Late in 1995 this trend began to reverse itself. The head of the Eau Claire, Wisconsin, Residential Treatment Center says locked facilities are largely unnecessary.

We haven't gone after DCFS, who have violated the consent decree, because, well, how do you change the culture of the agency? We could mandate results—outcome-based incentives, permanency planning, community involvement—but the strategy was not the strategy of DCFS. It was a top-down strategy. It failed. We're now negotiating an alternative approach which focuses on the real problems.

A bureaucracy with services made by DCFS centrally can't work.

We don't serve and support intact families in Cook County…well, only about 6,000. Compare that to the over 36,000 kids removed from their families. We don't offer services to families in poor communities. These families and kids have reached out, but they don't get services. What's coming into the system are poor people—almost 80 percent are African Americans.

Most of the cases are neglect cases. If you have a crack habit and no money, you can't feed your kids—you'll get neglect charges. Cook County child welfare investigators don't know what else to do except remove kids—they can't figure out services, where to locate services.

The state will pay grandmothers $300 or $400 in substitute care but won't pay her to watch her grandchildren, whereas Alabama would pay Grandma or a relative directly to help a family in crisis. Illinois DCFS almost never thinks of immediate help. The resulting devastation to the kid [who is removed] is unbelievable.

How Can Child Protective Services Protect Children from Suicide?

We create a class of children who have no desire to live if they stay in the system long enough....Kids' [state wards'] suicides aren't reported as suicides but as deaths. There's no collection of data on suicides.

Where Is Accountability?

Why isn't there a study of outcomes? How many of these kids [in state care] graduate from high school? How many are self supporting? Who is not in prison?

DCFS receives one billion dollars per year—how do they account for it? Foster mothers are paid $15 per day to feed and clothe kids, but residential treatment costs $300 per day. Why is it that the guy who runs an institution is paid $150–$200 per day, but a foster mother doesn't receive that much in a week to feed the child? If we paid the foster mother, we could find adequate homes.

Mistreatment of Foster Parents

Foster parents are mistreated. They are told they'll be reimbursed for expenses for the child. They aren't. They ask for respite, for a break, a vacation. They don't get help. Those not trained to deal with troubled children need support, skills training. It doesn't happen. Emergency foster care families are treated as a bed for the night. They are given virtually no information about the child's health needs, etc. They are lost without info, back-up services.

Juvenile Court

Juvenile court is a mother blaming system—it functions to charge mothers with abuse and neglect even though most often it's a boyfriend, husband, or uncle who are the abusers. But they [males] aren't with the kid; they don't show up in court. Public opinion doesn't favor family unity. Judges who favor families get transferred.

It's a completely overwhelmed system. It's not run like any other court—routine status reports could be used rather than drag in lawyer upon lawyer and caseworkers. There's an unbelievable number of lawyers—a swarm of lawyers—in juvenile court. DCFS has a lawyer, the state has a lawyer, there are public defenders, the parents have a lawyer, and the Public Guardian has a lawyer! More lawyers don't help.

Sexual Abuse

Juvenile court orders supervised visits, but the visitation centers are not open on holidays. Parents can't see their kids on Christmas. It's bureaucratic insanity. Each child needs several hours of visitation time with a parent each day. Yet they are only allowed an hour a week at a visitation center.

It's naive to think counseling will change an adult who has forced intercourse upon a child. Yet children could be reunited with mothers who often themselves have been victims of physical abuse. If a kid is sexually abused, DCFS will blame the mother for not stopping a boyfriend, stepfather, or parent. If the kid is physically abused, DCFS will blame the mother rather than the abusive father. What's the "best interest" of a child—isn't it the bond with the mother?

Isn't the thing to do if you have to remove a child is ask the kid "Who loves you"? Let the kid go with people who love him, keep him in his or her school, people who can still work with the child's family. If you take away enough of his/her things [baseballs, dolls], they'll want to kill themselves. Why isn't this written in the casebook? Those toys, stuffed animals which are part of the child's [identity], can sometimes make the difference between wanting to live and wanting to die. Mostly, their security is about bonds with people, but it's also about what they like: after-school sports, skating, a favorite aunt, a teacher.

Bureaucracies have a different agenda than placing a kid with someone who loves them. The incentive for the bureaucracy is to fill a slot, find a placement, a bed.

NOTES

1. Michael Brody and Benjamin Wolf, "ACLU Spurred Needed DCFS Change," *Chicago Tribune* (Oct. 17, 1995), 1:18.

2. Patrick Murphy, "Preserving Chaos: The Right Ignores the Underclass, the Left Patronizes it," *Commonweal* 6 (Mar. 24, 1995), 13.

3. Richard Wexler, "The Children's Crusade," *The Reader* (Mar. 24, 1995), 12.

4. Jill Kinney, David Haapala, and Charlotte Booth, *Keeping Families Together: The Homebuilders Model* (New York: Aldine de Gruyter, 1991), 156.

5. Wexler, 12.

6. Interview with Ben Wolf, Jan. 6, 1995.

7. Qtd. in Wexler, 16.

8. Bruce R. Dold, "Kids Suffer Under DCFS Reform Efforts," *Chicago Tribune* (Sept. 22, 1995), editorial page.

9. Murphy, 15.

8

Private Agencies

The Good News and the Bad

If you become degraded, ill, criminal, then I become so.[1]

WALT WHITMAN

Words that are equal to the pain of the poor are pretty easily discredited....Even when people do accept the idea of injustice, there are ways to live with it without it causing you to change a great deal in your life....There's a kind of cultivated weariness....[2]

REV. MARTHA OVERALL, BRONX MINISTER

At their best, private agencies encourage innovation, creativity, a reduced caseload, and a commitment to children and their families. Ivan Medina, who is the director of Children's Services at Association House, Karl Dennis, who is the director of Kaleidoscope, and Denise Plunkett, who is a caseworker at Columbus–Maryville Children's reception center, typify the best.

Association House is a settlement house that continues Jane Addams's insistence that social work centers should be based in the community they serve. Both of Association House's buildings are located in West Town, a predominantly Puerto Rican neighborhood. Ivan grew up in the neighborhood, as did many of the caseworkers. The older workers, trained in casework, resist those who see their task as being organizers who help the community rebuild itself. There is tension between the two sides—one side emphasizing a clinical one-on-one approach, the other seeing a united community as a healing agent and the key to prevention of family breakdowns. However, both sides agree on a couple of things—culture is the base of a child's identity, so Latino children should be placed with Latino foster relatives if they must be removed from their homes; most importantly, every effort should be made to work with families to keep their children.

Ivan is on the side of those who believe a strong community prevents the kind of family isolation that leads to abuse, neglect, or addiction. But he administers a foster family program, and he's realistic about the need to protect kids when their family situation is dangerous, like Manuel's. Ten-year-old Manuel tells me Ivan is "sort of like my godfather." Manuel's mother was beat up by his father more than he can remember. He doesn't remember when she started to do drugs, but he hasn't seen her too much since they left a homeless shelter and then were reported for living in an abandoned building. Manuel lives in a foster home now, but he comes to Association House after school for tutoring, counseling, and sports. Sometimes Ivan takes him places. The contrast between Ivan's leadership style, his relationship with children and families, and the approaches of supervisors at DCFS central offices is dramatic.

The contrast between Ivan's office and the office of Karl Dennis is also dramatic. Ivan's is a mess—kids and workers wander in and out, and files are askew. It's not chaotic; it's more like a large family moving around on Saturday morning. Karl Dennis's office is perfectly organized, the walls and desk appointed with awards. Karl Dennis is a no-nonsense visionary and problem solver who is interested in programmatic results. For year he's been associated with one of the premier reform agencies in the country. Kaleidoscope's early distinctiveness was its willingness to unconditionally accept a child into the program no matter what the child's problem and an unconditional refusal to terminate services to the child or family unless the family or child asked for a change.

Kaleidoscope's other distinction is that the program teaches state systems how to create funding "streams" from the complex web of state and federal entitlement monies available and how to create community-based services and community/professional teams to support families in trouble. However, in spite of Kaleidoscope's innovations in the field of child welfare (or maybe because of it), rarely has Karl Dennis been consulted by Illinois child welfare officials.

But there is a private agency that DCFS does collaborate with, and that's Catholic Charities. In fact, Catholic Charities—through Father Smyth, who directs Maryville's residential center—is contracted to run the state's emergency shelter for Chicago. The Columbus–Maryville children's reception center is where all incoming children are processed for Cook County.

One of the workers there, Denise Plunkett, who works with infants, is appalled at what happens to children who are processed through the center. Plunkett allows us to see the heartbreak not only of children who go back and forth from the shelter to emergency foster care again and again, but also the grief of infants and toddlers. Hers is the perspective of a worker who witnesses the daily sorrow of children resulting from child welfare practices.

But the most alarming critique comes from a Public Guardian lawyer sent on a special litigation investigative mission to Columbus–Maryville. Pia Menon spent over three intensive months at the center examining records and interviewing staff and children. Her report was so devastating that her boss, Patrick Murphy, quashed it and took her off the case. Eventually she quit the Guardian's office. Murphy would argue that everything's a little ugly in protective services because the fate of poor children is ugly and that some agencies—for example, Father Smyth's Columbus–Maryville—are less ugly and, in fact, more humane. However, according to Menon, that's not good enough for children.

Advocate's Narrative

Ivan Medina

Ivan Medina was (he is currently on leave to complete graduate studies) the director of Child Welfare Services at Association House, a Chicago settlement house that is almost one hundred years old and that is the largest Latino child welfare organization in the Midwest. For Medina, the abused or neglected Latino (or African American) child's ability to heal is thwarted by the child welfare system's cultural ignorance and cultural imposition. Caseworkers lack an ability to discern the suffering and identity confusion imposed on already mistreated children by a system ignorant of the culture's capacity to affirm and transform.

I remember the case of Mikey, whose real name was Miguel. He came here from Mexico. It's common that a mother or father comes here alone and leaves an older child in Mexico and then remarries here. In this case the mother came here and remarried. After Miguel was seven she sent for him to live with a totally new family, new brothers and sisters. The child started having conflicts with the stepfather. Apparently the stepfather hit him and left marks—nothing where he would be seriously injured, but enough to have left marks. The school called the abuse hotline, and the DCFS took custody of him.

The child was taken to Maryville Academy, which is a big, dominant Anglo institution. He stayed there for several years. He was a very compliant kid. He seemed to do well. He was very quiet, but of course he only spoke

Spanish at the time they put him in an institution where everyone spoke English. That's when his name went from Miguel to Mikey.

When he was sixteen, they referred him back into the community, where he was sent to a group home, a Latino private agency. By then he rejected anything that was Latino. He rejected who he was, his name, his language. He wouldn't speak Spanish. Then he started delving into the occult. He'd only listen to heavy rock music. By then, this kid didn't even want to be with his family because they were Latino. He started having a lot of mental health issues, separating from reality, a type of schizophrenic behavior. But a lot of it had to do with identity confusion.

If we had been involved with this family in the beginning, we probably could have done some very simple work around family communication, some re-bonding—some in-home services to keep that child in his family. Or what we've done in some cases is send the kid back to Mexico to live with grandparents, aunts, uncles, family of origin who brought them up. Sometimes that's the best plan—to go back to where they are comfortable and secure. The state will many times fight us on that. We had a judge once who said, "I won't send any of these kids to these third world countries"—she meant Mexico and Puerto Rico. Because those countries are poor does not mean the kids wouldn't be better off with family members.

The Burgos Decree

Cultural identity is so defining of who we are. I strongly believe in permanency for children. Some would argue that it's more important to get children adopted than to have them in the same cultural setting. Even State Senator Luis Guttierez argues this, as did an African American legislator from Kansas. Well. . . .

We Latinos have the Burgos law [which mandates that Latino children must be placed with Latino families]. That allowed us to develop more [family] resources that are community based early on. The department [DCFS] reasoned—we're not going to be able to handle this population, we're going to end up in court every year being knocked on the head—so let's give the problem over to those who sued us and say, "OK, now, you Latinos, develop the resources," thinking that we would fail, too. But we had a humongous expansion of [foster] families in the Latino community. In fact, we probably have [foster] families for every single child who is not a teenager.

Where Is a Burgos Decree for African Americans?

Gaining more community-based foster family support services didn't occur because we're a more organized community than the African American community. I think it occurred because, as a result of the Burgos decree, the department was forced to say to the community, "We've got this problem [the mandate to have Latino foster families for Latino children]; if you come up with a solution, we'll fund it." So we have no problem being funded.

The problem for the African American community is lack of DCFS commitment, funds, and cultural respect for their children. For instance, there's a networking organization of child welfare agencies that's coming up with a continuum of care plan for the children of Cook County. These are the traditional, dominant white agencies saying we're going to take care of African American child welfare problems. They are never going to take care of the African American "problem" because they don't have a base or organization from within the community. For example, when Father Clements began adoption—One Church One Child—we saw dramatic increases in adoption. But that came from within the community. That's what works.

What the department needs to be doing is finding ways of empowering, helping, providing technical assistance for African American organizations to start child welfare on a community level. I can assure you that if the department did that—if they started at least ten child welfare agencies that were African American community based—in five years we would not have the problem of placing so many African American children in foster homes.

Traditional Foster Care Versus Specialized Foster Care

All the [Anglo] agencies have specialized treatment foster care, which pays a very high contract rate. But when they create resources in the African American or Latino community, they offer contracts for traditional foster care, which means for "regular" children without problems. However, 99 percent of children coming into care have special needs due to sexual, physical abuse whereas the regular child is only about 1 percent of any of our caseloads. By the very fact of taking a child out of the home, you virtually create a special needs child. The trauma of removal is that great. Even a perfectly normal child can become special needs if removed. Some kids do need to be removed from their homes. But even with kids who are abused, it's critical to recognize the damage and trauma created by removal.

Anyway, the Anglo/white agencies license these poor African American families using AFDC grants or CHA grants to set up foster families in public housing. If an agency recruits families in the African American or Latino community, the families will get a traditional rate for the children, and because they are poor they will get a monthly stipend. But this means the agency controls the money. The agency rents the apartment, puts the family in the apartment, then

places sibling groups or difficult-to-place children with this foster family. But they only pay them the traditional rate. So what does that do? It creates dependency.

It's an issue of [lack of] trust. It's "means-tested" type of care payments. If you're poor, then you can't be trusted to rent an apartment on your own and pay your bills on your own.

What our agency negotiated twenty years ago, and we had Burgos to hit them over the head with, is that we wanted all our kids to start off categorized as specialized from the beginning. We didn't allow them to give us a traditional contract. As a result, we grew. We're now the biggest Latino agency in the state.

We weren't trying to label kids, but to get sufficient funds to their families so that they could do creative things with those resources. I remember a family that we licensed who had seven children of their own. They started, as foster parents, with one child. As each of their children got married, they'd add another child. Eventually they bought a house. We know the extra part of the specialized payment of each child pays the mortgage. But they have taken eight children over fifteen years, and they were able to move from a rented apartment, which was a two-bedroom apartment, into a spacious home where kids could live comfortably. They've been excellent foster parents.

Child Welfare as Community Development

I doubt this family could have accomplished this if they were receiving traditional payments. If a family can better themselves because of the resources they receive (though it's rarely enough), that's what we want because then we're doing community development along with foster care. Right now we spend about $100,000 a month in foster care payments to our Latino community...

that money is spent by families in the community. So that's community development because they buy clothes for the children within the community, as well as other needs. If we could work with families to buy houses and invest and stay in the community, we'll be doing community development.

Dependency

If you mold the foster care program into a dependency program whereby the family lives in *your* apartment and you lease the apartment, then that's dependency. I won't have any part of it. They've come to me several times to ask me to apply for this. I said I'll write a proposal that offers every child wraparound services based on their needs and that the rate will be sufficient for the family to creatively and independently decide how to use that money to better their own family situation so that they can take better care of that child. That's how to create foster families that are independent, caring, and nurturing versus a family that has to worry about how much heat to use or whether or not they'll have enough money to pay the rent.

In this community we all grew up living three or four in one bedroom. Well, the state won't allow that for their foster kids. You have to have forty square feet per child. This immediately eliminates most families because of the lack of housing stock in this community. If we could do something about the housing stock available (to say nothing of the regulations), we'd have more families willing to be foster parents. This is a class issue also.

Tommy

Tommy's mother had diabetes, and she was a *Santerista* [a follower of a religion that mixes traditional African beliefs with Catholicism]. She was a fortune-teller, could put curses on people, etc. Tommy was a very good kid but a sort

of a wanderer, nothing delinquent. He was never disrespectful. He was used to a lot of freedom, so he wandered. Tommy was basically wandering the streets when the police picked him up. He lied about where he lived and was put into a shelter. He was kind of slow, so I'm not sure if Tommy even knew where his home was.

They filed child neglect charges against the mother. When they went to her home, she seemed weird because she dressed in a big Hispanic gown— we call them *batas*. She dressed for her clients and looked like a gypsy, but to the police she looked like a witch. They decided Tommy was better off not being at home. They moved him from foster home to foster home. Tommy ran away, but he was such a compliant kid that he'd run to his caseworker's office. He kept leaving because none of the homes could show him the kind of love and attention he really needed.

When he was a teenager, Tommy kept being moved. We finally placed him in the foster home of a single male minister. At sixteen he ran away from that home, and he refused to return. Then we got a call telling us Tommy had been shot. He'd been selling drugs with friends.

A while after that, I talked to one of the kids who'd been placed in the same home [the Hispanic minister's]. This kid told me he saw Tommy under the covers with the pastor in a sexual way. Tommy had been looking for love all those years, and when he finds "love," it's someone who sexually abuses him.

Wouldn't that mother have provided Tommy with that love? *Santerista* is an accepted part of the Hispanic community. Wouldn't a [caseworker] who understood that culturally have been able to work with the mother and Tommy so that a neglect charge would have been avoided? Tommy must have been in at least eight to ten homes in less than eight years.

Advocate's Narrative

Karl Dennis

Karl Dennis is the executive director of Kaleidoscope, a child welfare organization committed to family preservation for the hardest-to-serve children and families. Kaleidoscope was the first child welfare agency in the country to provide unconditional care for children, which meant the agency did not reject or eject any child or family from care.

In the 1970s, we started taking young people on a "no decline" basis, which means we took anyone who was referred to us. We started out with a group home, but we quickly learned we could not provide services with only one environment. I'm talking about environment as opposed to treatment programs. Usually we set up treatment programs and force people into them. Kaleidoscope makes the "treatment" surround the individual.

In-Home Services

Kids who had been sent out of state [to residential treatment centers] were returned home to their parents because there was no place for them. We went in and provided services to those families. We discovered that to be successful, the services we were providing needed to be long term and intensive. We asked the family what they needed and provided that service, whether it was washing dishes, scrubbing floors, or getting a baby-sitter—whatever it was—in this way we kept the great majority of those kids at home with their families. That became one of the oldest and most intensive in-home programs in the country.

Closing Down Group Homes

At the end of 1975 we came to the conclusion that it was imperative that we learn how to do individualized services. We weren't individualizing services by placing five kids in one place. So we closed the group homes and moved the kids into treatment foster care. We placed one child in a treatment foster home, surrounding them with [services]. The foster parent's job was to stay home and take care of that kid. We paid the parent to do that and not to take outside employment. We paid them about $700 [per month]. Today it starts at $960 up to $1,300. These children were considered the most difficult and hard to serve. This became one of the [pioneer] treatment foster care programs. Today we use that same foster treatment care process to work with adolescent parents and their children. It's been written up by the Children's Defense Fund.

Pediatric AIDS Program

Next we started our Star Program, which was the third pediatric AIDS program in the country and the first treatment foster care program for pediatric AIDS. It was different than most programs because not only did we provide services to the infants we took in, we provided services to their natural parents. In some cases we reunited the child with their parent, or the foster treatment parent has adopted the child. But in no instance have we refused to provide services.

We also work with adolescents with AIDS. "No decline" means no decline. The process we use is called unconditional care. In the early 1970s we started using this [philosophy] in the community. Instead of surrounding people with bricks and mortar as residential centers do, we surrounded them with people and services. That has come to be called "wrap-around" services. We're considered one of the pioneers in this type of service.

In 1985 we used that process in Alaska. Alaska had children in various institutions and residential treatment centers. We used this process to bring all the children back [into their communities]. We placed them in the community with foster treatment, independent living, and in-home care with supports for all those kids who had been in [psychiatric] hospitals. We brought every kid back except one, and we saved the state of Alaska literally $10 million in five years, and we changed that service system completely.

After that, the process was repeated in Vermont and Idaho. Today, based on that same philosophy, there are between 600 and 1,000 wrap-around initiatives around the country that are based on the concepts we pioneered.

That's what I do now. We move around the country helping state governments, private agencies, and foundations. I serve on a number of boards: Georgetown, South Florida University, the National Institute of Mental Health. A lot of people now see a need for moving services out of the traditional approach and into the community. It is cost effective, time saving, and it saves in terms of humanity.

There Is No Child Welfare System

One of the real issues in our country is that our services have always been categorical. I don't believe we have a child welfare system; we have a child protection system. I say that because in a child welfare system a system would come into play prior to people being in crisis and before there arose an issue of abuse or neglect, which is currently the only basis for people getting services. The criteria for what we call child welfare, which is really child protection, is neglect or abuse when people are in crisis.

One of the things that's clear is that only about 15 percent of the families and children that get involved in the child protection system are there because of neglect or abuse. [Families] enter be-

cause of poverty, because there are no other systems that will bring services in for people who come through mental health systems, for people whose private insurance runs out—the child protection system becomes the net.

The point I'm trying to make is that not all the people that come into the system are beating their kids or sexually abusing them. I used to serve on the Board of Federation of Families—it was originally the Federation of Families for children with mental health needs. Well, a lot of those families wound up in the child welfare system not because of neglect or abuse, but because they couldn't get any services through the mental health system. They run out of money. I know a lot of parents who spent all of their money on services for their children. Some were close to suicide or killing their children because the system is so categorical—there's so many criteria for people to get services. People have to be in such crisis, at their wit's end, before our systems will start to float services to them.

How Communities Can Benefit

What we have learned over the last ten years in terms of wrap-around services is that there are probably enough resources in every community, but they are held by different systems. If you are a family brought into the child protective system, you are only entitled to the resources of that particular system, not to mental health, not to special education, not to juvenile justice. Each of those systems have criteria for service, and you are only entitled to that particular line of service or resources that they control. These resources are not under community control. What we've learned is if we can pull those different systems together, then we're able to have enough resources to provide the services.

There's plenty of research on how this works—there's "Alaska Youth Initiative," the Vermont and Idaho wrap-around programs. By pulling their resources together, Stark County, Ohio, has reduced their reliance on hospitalization for children in the county by 98 percent in just eighteen months. They utilized the resources not only of the public but also the private agencies in the county.

Schools and Wrap-Around Services
There are twenty-eight school systems in this country who have become Medicaid providers, which means that they are able to bill Medicaid for treatment services. What they have been able to do is bring into their system mental health professionals, child welfare professionals, juvenile justice people, and private [child welfare] providers. Two of those school systems—I think in Pennsylvania and Ohio—brag that they haven't suspended anyone from school in over two years because they brought those services into the school.

The Cost of Psychiatric Care
One of the things we learned is that if we weren't going to be given money, at least we could use the dollars that were being spent on kids for out-of-county or out-of-state programs, or on kids in [psychiatric] hospitals. Some hospitals charge $2,000 a day for services for children. It is not unusual to find hospitals that charge $1,400 per day. Those children wind up costing whatever state they are in, in some cases, as much as a million dollars in their lifetime.

Keeping Kids in Their Communities
Most people think that the majority of kids placed in residential treatment centers are placed there by child welfare or mental health. In reality, almost 50 percent of kids put in residential placement are placed there by education. In most school districts the incentive has been that if the local school district can place a kid residentially, they don't have to pay all the money. Occasionally, they don't have to pay any of it. The state

picks it up. Thus, there are incentives to placing children.

Now many states are saying to local school districts if you place kids residentially, you're going to have to pay for it. So we see a movement toward keeping [children] in their community coming out of the educational systems. The high cost of hospitalization, which has been the backbone of the children's mental health system, can no longer be afforded. So mental health is also moving into the community and developing other services.

The large influx of children entering the child protection systems in this country, without an equal increase in the budget of those systems, has forced them also to look at other alternatives to providing services.

Graduating Youths into Prisons
Here's two statistics that are scary. In California, 80 percent of all the adults in the correctional facilities…are graduates of the state: the juvenile justice, the child welfare, the mental health and the special education systems. The Chesapeake Institute out of Washington, D.C., just came out with this scary statistic: 55 percent of all children diagnosed as seriously emotionally disturbed in special education will drop out of school; 20 percent of these will be arrested while still in school; 74 percent will be arrested within five years after leaving school.

In terms of fiscal responsibility, as much as I believe that Newt Gingrich and his crowd are on the wrong track, there is some validity in arguing that we have wasted tremendous amounts of funds in the services we have chosen to deliver.

Blending Federal Entitlement Monies
If you look at juvenile justice, child welfare, health, and education—these are all federal entitlement grants. Their dollars can be used to provide services

to areas that are held by these different categorical services. A friend of mine, Bill Underwood, along with Kathy Potter from our office, can draw a child's face on the board and show eighty-four different federal funding streams to provide services, but we don't access them. Of all the states' ability to get back dollars from the federal government, New Mexico leads. For every dollar, I think New Mexico gets back $1.76. Illinois is fourth from the bottom.

I am more respected in virtually every other state in the union than I am in Illinois. That could mean that Illinois is smarter than all the rest!

Why Family Preservation Fails in Some States

Most of the family preservation programs in this country have been short-term services: six- to eight-week interventions, three-month interventions, six-month interventions. You don't capitate services; you give people what they need. Some people may need three years; some may only need a month.

We've used the wrong [short-term intervention] family preservation model for the wrong populations. The Homebuilders model, I think, is an incredibly exciting approach, but it is a crisis inter-vention service for people who do not have direct service needs. When you have direct service needs, you need to be able to provide a longer-term service. So if you have a child who has some strong mental health needs, living with a [foster treatment] family—a child who traditionally would have been placed in residential placement for years and you leave the child at home—and the only service you provide is six months of service, what do you think that's going to do? Nothing.

When you have chronic problems, you need longer-term intervention. There's nothing wrong with the Homebuilders model; it's the use of a very good model inappropriately.

The initial issue is that family pres-ervation was sold to state legislatures as a cost-effective approach. It is a cost-effective approach. But they cut the line far, far too close. So that even some of the family preservation programs that started at three to six weeks have ex-panded to three months, and now they [have] announced six-month programs, then nine-month programs, and there are some programs with enough wis-dom to give people what they want and need.

Advocate's Narrative
Denise Plunkett

Denise Plunkett is a caseworker at Columbus–Maryville Children's Reception Center. DCFS contracted Maryville, an agency of the Archdiocese of Chicago, to manage Cook County's centralized emergency shelter. DCFS managed the shelter until June 1988, when newspapers broke the story of a retarded child's rape by another DCFS ward. It was then that Father Smyth, the director of Maryville Academy, was asked to take over management of the shelter.

Denise works on the floor with younger children, from infants through age ten. She began working at the shelter six months after it opened in 1989. She has not lost her outrage at what happens to children who enter the state system. Her deepest sadness is over the tragedy of children placed in foster care who return to the center again and again as if they were luggage.

Everything is crazy—even reforms become part of doomed practices. For example, during DCFS's current reforms [downsizing], things have never been so chaotic. During 1994 and 1995 DCFS has contracted with private agencies to do foster care placements *and* family services. It's triple the work, but there's no increase in supports, payments. The only thing certain is constant change. DCFS staff is in a state of continuous reorganization. But nothing really changes.

The changes are being driven by cost. The system is not driven by what is in the best interests of a family or child but by what is the least expensive form of care. The director of DCFS is putting emphasis on privatizing services as a way to cut duplication of services delivered in the child's community.

It's About Beds

There's pressure on DCFS to move the kids out of the shelter fast. They move them out to emergency foster homes or residential placements as fast as they can. They have to keep things "fluid" so there's a bed for the next one coming. It's about beds. They will put kids anywhere there's a bed. Placing a child in foster care is far less expensive than a residential center, which exceeds $100 a day. Foster care might be $500 or $600 a month.

DCFS caseworkers are pressed to place children in emergency foster care without assessment, and often the foster parents don't have adequate info to know what the child's problems are. So they return them to the shelter. It would seem better to first assess the child and then find a home to accommodate them and their siblings. Children feel that they are the problem—nobody wants them. They return to us again and again as they are rejected by several foster homes. Sometimes they have been abused in foster homes.

I feel more time and money should be put into helping poor families find

hope, decent housing, job skills, drug treatment. Holding families together and trying to relieve their stress should be the first priority. It would be far more cost effective down the line when you consider the cost to society of an entire group of children reaching adulthood without the ability to trust or bond with another person or without any sense of self-worth.

Working with Drug-Exposed Infants

I work with infants and younger children. The population increase or decrease is driven by politics, money, and DCFS contracts. There are medical contracts for children with health problems and treatment foster care contracts for children with behavioral problems. So if a child with cerebral palsy or severe asthma has healthy brothers and sisters, DCFS will separate the child from siblings because they don't want to pay the higher rate of special care—kids with health, behavioral, or developmental problems as opposed to traditional care for "normal" kids without these problems. We can virtually guarantee that kids entering our shelter will be separated from their siblings.

Labeling children "crack" babies or "fretful drug" babies in order to market [their vulnerability] is so wrong. These are often healthy newborns who sometimes are drug exposed. Dr. Ira Chasnoff [of Northwestern University] has the longest study in the country of drug-exposed infants. He says that by the time the babies are two years old, about 66 percent are at age level and seem to be doing everything about right. The one area that does seem a bit delayed was the area of speech development.

The terrible tragedy for the families of these children is that they live in incredible poverty and are up against the worst odds in a time of unbelievable unemployment. They can't get jobs even if they are hard workers. If you dull your senses, your kids are taken.

The Tragedy of Emergency Foster Care

There's two kinds of foster care: emergency foster care homes take the kids for ninety days, and there's long-term foster care homes. You get half the pay that the emergency foster care receives if you are long-term foster care parents. So if you are good-hearted enough to keep the kid and try to stabilize them and have them bond with you over a long time period, you'll get a 50 percent cut in payments.

These ninety-day kids go from home to home to home. They can no longer form attachments—they're pathetic. If a kid is going into emergency foster care and his record says "visually impaired," there's absolutely no likelihood that the emergency foster family will get him services, doctor appointments, etc., because it's so temporary a setup. Whereas long-term foster care takes on the responsibility of dealing with a child's particularities physically and emotionally. It's so goofy. Some private agencies have more thoughtful approaches to this. They'll have an emergency home, but after so many days it rolls over into a long-term setup.

The benefit to DCFS of having emergency homes is that they can call up anytime, day or night, and say, "Will you take these two kids?" They'll transport the kids immediately, and the emergency foster parents more or less have to say yes. Whereas a long-time foster parent will ask questions.

What Do You Do with a Child Who's Witnessed the Murder of a Parent?

There's no change in procedures. DCFS sends children who've witnessed the killing of a family member to emergency foster care. I remember one kid whose baby brother was killed, and we received the five-year-old. Kid is sent to emergency foster home. So you know the kid is not going to get counseling, ther-

apy…nothing. Can you imagine the child's grief having seen his brother killed? I can't remember the story of what happened.

We got a four-month-old and his five-year-old brother after their sibling had been killed just last month. The brother went out; the baby stayed on. But then this baby of so much grief was sent to a foster home which is unlicensed with nine other kids in it! So they were all sent back to us because the foster mother wasn't licensed. I don't understand it—isn't it terrible?

Now that baby has been sent out again. I don't know where he's gone. Imagine besides a sibling killed in his home, the baby is not with his five-year-old brother—who knows where his brother is?

One kid who'd been in a home where a sibling was killed was taken by a relative, but the relative wanted him removed because he would break the air conditioner, pound on the walls, and he was suspended from school. But look at what this kid has been through. I think they put this kid on quanadine to help control his behavior. By the time many of these kids are seven or eight years old, they are so disturbed.

Top-Down Reform

One day a DCFS honcho came and called a meeting with an agenda handed out re: "substance affected infants." This guy was hyped.

"I'm sent here by DCFS second in command. Let's begin. Agenda point #1. Why are these infants in residential centers? There's just been a study done, and the clinical results are that these children are better off in foster homes than residential care." We just stared at him in disbelief. Then he ticked down the list of his agenda making point after point—no discussion. When he finished, he asked if there were comments.

I said, "I'm completely shocked at this suggestion. Nobody can find a foster home that will take an infant. That's why these residential centers don't discharge kids. It's like pulling a train uphill to find homes. This shelter is completely overcrowded. In fact, your office is trying to prevent caseworkers from sending more kids here. If you empty these centers, where are you going to put these kids...on the street?"

Then another worker piped up and said, "I called twenty-five agencies last week, and not one had an opening for a baby. I asked each one when they anticipated an opening, and none of them knew when."

The guy was taken aback, but it didn't stop him. He went back to repeating what the study had said about babies in residential settings. I said, "I'm curious to know—what does the study point out? Does it point out that institutionalized babies are more prone to depression than kids in foster homes? Finally, what is the alternative? Do you have foster homes? Does anybody have them? Did the clinician measure the emotional damage done to children sent to five emergency homes?"

It's completely crazy. The top level is ready to move on something, and it makes no sense. I know one of the clinicians involved in the study, and they're no fools. They're bright.

What happens is there is a federal appropriation of money for an "abandoned babies project," and Illinois applies for the money based on a study. But the study is coming out of space. It has no connection to the issues. This guy just comes in and announces a new program!

Most people don't want adolescents; they'll take younger kids. A family, for instance, will say, "We'll take two girls."

The worker says, "Good, we have two sisters, two and three years old."

Family says, "Are they toilet trained?"

Worker says, "Only the oldest."

Family says, "OK, we'll take her."

And, by George, they separate the kids. Renny, the kids scream and cry when they are separated. It's a nightmare. One of the DCFS women that transported the kids to foster homes told me that 85 percent of the time her heart was broken.

I talked with one guy who did the transporting for Maryville, and he told me about a time when he couldn't find an address for the kid he was transporting. He found out that to get to this "home" you had to go through the grocery store, go to a next set of doors, knock on some back door, then a scuzzy guy came out, and the child had become hysterical, begging for the worker not to leave. But he had his orders. Still, this guy said he felt so bad for this child that he told the child to wait, and he went and made a phone call to Maryville on behalf of this kid.

"I can't leave this kid," he tells the supervisor. "He's hysterical."

He had to tell the kid on the way back to the shelter, "Listen, I did this once; don't think this is a way to get out of going to placements."

Advocate's Narrative
Pia Menon

Pia Menon was an attorney with the Public Guardian's Office, where she was assigned to a special litigation unit to investigate Columbus–Maryville Children's Reception Center, under the direction of Father Smyth and Catholic Charities. DCFS contracted with Catholic Charities and Father Smyth after a scandal pushed demands for a reform in the way that children were warehoused by the state. Public Guardian Patrick Murphy spearheaded the push for Catholic Charities to take over sheltering, processing, and placing of children for DCFS. Although Murphy recognizes problems at Columbus–Maryville, he believes it is the best, and probably only, alternative to a state shelter. Murphy's father grew up in a Catholic orphanage, and Patrick Murphy was a seminarian. He believes in the discipline and devoted attention of the nuns and priests of those institutions.

Pia, who is originally from Singapore, had none of these sympathies when given the task of investigating the institution. She simply reported what she saw and documented the treatment of children. In a bittersweet way, both Murphy and Menon locked horns over their own fading ideals: Murphy denying the Catholic institution's questionable treatment of children and Pia's realization that crusader Murphy, and the Public Guardian's Office that she believed in, would not intervene. Since Pia's investigative work in the early 1990s, Columbus–Maryville has reformed some of its practices, but structural reform has not taken place because it requires changes in the whole system, beginning with DCFS.

I was a DCFS licensing representative before I went to law school....Adults who are needy should never become foster parents. If you're missing something in your life, don't use a child for your needs. I was so disillusioned by the people they were licensing that I decided, well, maybe the law is the way to go. So I completed law school and landed a job with the Public Guardian's office. This was fantastic...my chance to make a difference. For five years I thought I was making a difference, until I got to the Columbus–Maryville shelter as an investigator.

Even my experience as a DCFS worker and as a Public Guardian lawyer in juvenile court for four years did not prepare me for what I experienced there. The court is professional; it has no flesh and bones. You have no sense of what awaits the child. You can't glimpse the

raw feelings of a child left in a stranger's home. You don't know if she/he cried or was hysterical. It is clean in court. You and I can not even conceive of what it means to a child to be removed from an environment he or she is familiar with and then put in a strange home...or shelter. Once that door is closed, they're isolated. No one knows what's going on.

Investigating Columbus–Maryville

I was supposed to identify the problems in the shelter. The shelter is a seventy-two-hour placement for a child in temporary custody before being placed in a foster care home or residential treatment center. That little wait...well, let's put it this way, it can take a year. Here's how that works—when, say, for instance, a child says, "I'm leaving" and steps out of Columbus–Maryville premises, he is considered technically not in the shelter's population. When he/she returns, even in fifteen minutes, it's considered a new admission. They come back; they constantly come back. When I reviewed some of the records, some of the children had been there for two and more years.

What I also found disturbing was that many of the staff members would encourage children to leave. But the children became wise to the system— they knew that Columbus–Maryville has a contract with DCFS not to turn anyone down. For this "open door" policy contract, Columbus is getting up to a million dollars.

The first thing that I did when I was assigned to the shelter was to review Columbus's contract with DCFS, to learn basic contractual provisions. I realized provisions were being violated. There's supposed to be a 1:4 ratio of staff to child. The reality was often ten kids to one staff. These are children who are terrified, yet caseworkers are cynical, and they treat children as objects—giving them a place to sleep in and then ignoring them. If you looked at the ratio of the staff to child, you understand why it's physically impossible for them to look at each child as a special case. It's not possible—it's a warehouse. Yet Columbus–Maryville's million-dollar contract with DCFS promises counseling, therapy for special needs children, and a myriad of services to these vulnerable kids.

The population at Columbus–Maryville oftentimes defies imagination. They have admissions coming out of psychiatric hospitals, children just released out of a crisis situation, or children with handicaps and children who are mentally retarded. Investigation was a slow and tortuous process because of the reluctance of staff to be frank with me, perhaps fearful of jeopardizing their jobs. There was a tug of war to get factual records and logs. When I did, I realized that DCFS chooses to believe staff members rather than their wards. DCFS has to maintain their contract with Columbus–Maryville because there is absolutely no other institution that is going to provide that kind of "care" for troubled children. So they look the other way.

How Children Are Silenced

When a child in placement calls the hotline to report an abuse by a worker, foster parent, etc., the silencing process is initiated because it is DCFS that is investigating themselves. It is perplexing to me that such a conflict of interest has never been challenged. Who believes kids? So in spite of serious injury to the child—for instance, broken bones—injuries would eventually be labeled accidental or reported as unfounded. Once a report is unfounded, it is destroyed. There is no way to challenge it.

Columbus–Maryville contracts with Columbus Hospital to provide emergency medical service to the children in the shelter. I went through the accident reports…it's called unusual incident reports, which, by law, are supposed to be

directed to DCFS and the Public Guardian's Office. The Public Guardian's office would get these reports perhaps nine months after the incident happened. Yet broken bones were common.

I began to speak to my clients and find out what happened in each of the incidents reported. What I discovered was that the staff members were usually undertrained and they were using certain "restraint methods" as a means of punishment. Notably, teenagers who were "troublemakers" ended up with broken bones. Children reported a staff member who put them into an armlock and started twisting. The more they'd resist, the likelihood was that they would hear the snap. It is such common practice. Circumstances relevant to these incidents were not being reported to medical personnel. The doctor would speak to the staff person who brought the kid in, and the caseworker would say, "Kid fell and hit the table, an accident." It's ludicrous.

Drugging Down the Teens

Many teenagers are on psychotropic medications. Almost every child who comes into the system ends up on some kind of psychotropic medication—we're talking about four- and five-year-old kids who are on Prozac and Ritalin for symptoms of blah, blah, blah. Give me a break—it's to quiet them down. But, unfortunately, when a child leaves an agency and goes to another agency, there is this gap in which she/he doesn't get to continue medication. This is not medication to treat an illness; it is just something that is systematically convenient. Generally, psychotropic medications take the place of nurturing.

When you suddenly cut a child off from medication—to send them to a placement—you're going to see a lot of side effects. Foster homes are not prepared to deal with a kid who's having drug-induced nightmares. If foster parents cannot handle this child because of their many "problems," there is always the haven of Columbus–Maryville to return them to.

I know some brave caseworkers—daring to be kind and conscientious. But basically there are few who will question. A child told me about a worker who taunted him, saying, "Does this hurt, is this pain enough for you?" This after he had broken the child's arm. For some strange reason, some men feel disrespected when a child doesn't cry. Drug-induced behavior is so different from normal behavior. I don't know if the threshold for pain is higher or what.

"Oh, so you are asking for pain?"

"No, I will not cry. I will not scream."

This is how they survive. There is this subtle attempt to break the spirit, you know. I don't know if this is a macho thing or what.

Useless Evaluations

There appears to be a battle of wills between the staff members and the teenagers. Psychological and psychiatric evaluations on these kids are an exercise in futility. Caseworkers who have minimal biographical information and, oftentimes, misinformation will be the primary source that the psychologist, psychiatrist relies on.

So, for instance, the caseworker says, "Oh, the child was reported to have been seen with his hand down some other child's underclothing." So the immediate assumption is that we're talking about a sex offender here. Do you know that all it takes is just for that kind of a statement to be made with absolutely no reliable context? The damning effect of either innocent or malicious misinterpretations perpetrates the misery of these unfortunate kids.

As far as I'm concerned, the majority of these evaluations are baseless. Caseworkers prefer that the child is medicated. It helps the foster care parents, who may not be qualified to deal

with a disruptive child. Staff often have no idea what a drug does to the child. They dispense it like aspirin. There is absolutely no one to monitor kids on multiple meds.

What this is all about is a systemic assault on children who've already been assaulted, been removed from home, medicated, coded, misdiagnosed, therapized....I'm not blaming the professionals; it's not really their fault. We are talking about cases where there are time constraints, information channels are restrained. How can you rely on the parent when the parent is hardly ever there? Many substance abuse/addicted parents have no concept of what's going on. So where can you get reliable information to provide to the assessor? So you've got a whole system that is based on misinformation. No one really ever talks to the child. The reliance is on adults and the case record.

Ludicrous Case Records

My God, these case records are ludicrous. I often went to Columbus–Maryville in the middle of the night for a particular record. Half the stuff in there is simply not true. Information that ought to be there is not. If a concerned caseworker wanted to go back to the child's record, he or she is still not going to have anything to rely on.

The child is not seen in any way as special...there's a kind of "I've seen it all before" attitude that is very scary. This contributes to the ongoing miscategorization. If one foster parent says the kid was a troublemaker, that's going into the record, the residential assessment, future placement [consideration]—wherever the child goes.

I know for a fact how often adoptions fail. It is because of lousy record keeping and useless evaluations of children. You can't give the caregiver a good assessment of what's wrong with the child without a good case history. People adopting children assuming everything is OK, and then the problems start coming out and they can't deal with them.

Juvenile Court

Juvenile court has an aura about it of goodness and great sensibility. There is a sense that we have to win—the public defender wants to win; the public guardian wants to win. We all assume, like gods, that we know what is in the "best interests of the child." There's this mass production mentality that we can treat all families alike. There have been drug-addicted mothers who I felt were capable of taking care of their children. Yet the drug programs I'm familiar with are so dismal that I don't know how anyone would chose to stay in them. [However,] Haymarket is decent.

The other thing the court can do is order parenting classes. But who checks what they learn—what the classes are like? So you stay off drugs for three months, attend classes, and you get your children back. So what? We all know what's going to happen...relapse. Instead, why not put the services in the home for the parent? Providing it outside won't help. You have to protect the child where they're going to be at greatest risk.

Facing Reassignment

Eventually I realized I would not be backed up; my "special" unit was not going to do anything about this. I was reassigned by the Public Guardian. I became extremely disturbed about what I was seeing. I couldn't do anything. Staff from Columbus kept calling me even after I was reassigned. I felt that I had lost an important battle, not only for the children but staff who put their jobs on the line. Immediately after Murphy reassigned me, those staff members were targeted as the troublemakers.

I felt as though I really failed the children and those staff. I tried to continue because I have children of my own. I didn't want to work just to earn a paycheck. I tried to carry on [in the new assignment], but it became clear that I was just wasting time. Of course, it was humiliating for me, but what was most painful is that I was hearing from Columbus that everything was back to "business as usual."

NOTES

1. Walt Whitman, *Leaves of Grass* (New York: Mentor, 1954), 184.

2. Rev. Martha Overall, qtd. in Jonathan Kozol, *Amazing Grace: The Lives of Children and the Conscience of a Nation* (New York: Crown, 1995), 189.

9

Advocates for
the Unworthiest
of the Unworthy

Lepers in terror of the terrified.[1]

W. H. AUDEN

When crimes begin to pile up they become invisible.
When sufferings are unendurable the cries are no longer heard.[2]

BERTOLT BRECHT

T his chapter only begins to name America's social lepers. Here are a few of those who experience the social isolation of children and adults who are shut away in institutions: sexual abuse victims, some so repeatedly sexually abused that they develop resulting mental illnesses or become perpetrators of sexual abuse; mothers in prison, the majority of them addicts who lose their children to the state; and retarded children who become state wards. They need not carry bells, as did lepers, to warn us of their coming. The youth are locked away, often for their childhood. The incarcerated mothers do return to society, but too often their children are not returned to them.

In theory, most Americans and child welfare workers would not "blame" sexual abuse victims, but in practice they are the children whom the system offers little sympathy. If the children repeat what has been done to them and become, in casework lingo, "perps" of other children, or if they become disturbed and drug therapy does not control their behavior, child welfare will turn from them. The deeply violated child is too often headed for delinquency court or a locked psychiatric facility. Few foster families can handle these damaged children. They end up in residential care centers or hospital treatment wards, which Public Guardian Special Litigator Peter Schmiedel calls barbarous. Child psychiatrist C. A. Cowardin also questions the "treatment" these children receive:

> There is this strange group of residential facilities that is not hospital...not under medical supervision. But for somehow, for some strange reason, requires psychiatric diagnosis to get into it. And where what is called treatment is not treatment at all. It's usually behavior modification. But all these places bill themselves as "treatment" centers....And there's pressure to get children who don't do well in a foster home into a residential placement.[3]

Dr. Cowardin enumerates the more common reasons youth don't do well in foster homes: loyalty to parents, rebellion at having been sent to numerous "placements," fear of attachments that can be disrupted by an agency decision, personality differences, and, occasionally, a foster mother who becomes too ill to continue care. None of these typical reasons requires "treatment."[4]

Often, teenagers are sent to psychiatric treatment centers not because they have mental problems, but because they have behavioral problems. After enough time in state care some rebel, but the price they pay is high. Cindy Clark, an investigator with the Public Guardian's office, says, "There's no investment in youthful wards....If they don't follow the rules to a 'T,' they're kicked out of both residential treatment centers and foster homes."[5] Once they've "disrupted" too many times or, more precisely, when they rebel, they're often headed for a locked facility. If a state prohibits locked facilities, as does Illinois, the way to get around that is to send the kid out of state.

For example, in March 1995 Cindy was part of the Public Guardian team that helped close Palm House, a Florida psychiatric ward in Horizon Hospital that took Illinois kids between the ages of eleven and seventeen. There was no therapy, no counseling, no teachers or school, and the undertrained staff used mechanical restraints on the young people. "They called them snug bags," Cindy said. "They are mesh bags more encompassing than straitjackets because they cover the entire body."[6]

Another reason that children are sent to in-state residential treatment centers is if they are designated as "special needs" cases. What drives these particular residential treatment placements, says Public Guardian attorney Peter Schmiedel, is the increased payments that are available once a child is labeled "special needs." "Kids are commodities," Schmiedel says.

Peter's office filed a petition on behalf of nine children that accused DCFS of neglect and abandonment; by "allowing children to languish and deteriorate in unnecessary institutional placements, by failing to remove children from inappropriate psychiatric hospitalizations despite…knowledge that they are ready for discharge and are regressing, and by failing to remove the children from inappropriate placements, [the DCFS Guardianship Administer] has neglected and abandoned children in violation of 2-3 (1) of the Juvenile Court Act."[7] Peter narrates the story of his investigations of "treatment" centers for these children and the tortuous fate of a boy named Didrich.

SEXUAL ABUSE AND
MULTIPLE PERSONALITIES

The majority of people with multiple personalities are women. Psychotherapist Aggie Brown, whose clients are women with multiple personalities, has found that many young girls, often intelligent and imaginative, "split off" parts of themselves in order to bury or lock away memories of rape or sadism too traumatic for the personality to acknowledge.[8] Reintegrating the personalities is a lengthy, intensive, and painful process. For women who can work through their buried anguish, the integrated self is often deeply insightful and empathetic. But what of the sexually abused children of the state sent to residential treatment centers, where therapy consists of drugs, "quiet rooms," and "psychotherapy" from a psychologist who comes once a week and invariably deals with reports of behavior problems rather than the underlying psychic pain of abuse?

WHEN MOTHERS AND
CHILDREN BOTH DO TIME

Mothers convicted of drugs and who lose their children while in prison are probably the most typical of the "unworthiest" category. The state response to the highly reported increase in the number of drug-addicted infants has been to criminalize pregnant drug users. State prosecutors seek arrest, convictions, and incarceration on charges of use of illegal substances and child abuse for mothers who use drugs during pregnancy. The officials who report these mothers to the police are doctors and health professionals, thus expanding the net from child welfare to criminal justice to the medical professions. According to Drew Humphries, legally defining the use of drugs as child abuse "only shifts the burden from the criminal courts to the family court, breaks up families, and produces boarder babies, half of whom go into congregate or foster care. The boarder baby crisis makes a mockery of claims that the statutes protect children."[9]

Rather than provide drug treatment programs for mothers with children (in a recent New York study of seventy-eight drug treatment programs, 54 percent refused treatment to pregnant women, and 87 percent had no services available for Medicaid patients who were both pregnant and addicted to crack[10]), the state has chosen to treat drug addiction as a criminal problem rather than a problem needing both medical and family support services. This "crackdown on the epidemic of crack babies" has resulted in increased imprisonment rates for women (between 60 and 70 percent of women imprisoned are mothers incarcerated for drug-related crimes), and children are placed in state custody where they also "do time" and are often not reunited with either their mothers or other siblings for the rest of their childhoods.

Because the chasm is so gaping that separates the majority of Americans from the anguish, catastrophe, fear, and humiliation faced by women without economic or social power, it is impossible to imagine how a mother could risk destroying herself and her children through the use of drugs or the commission of petty economic crimes. This is not to imply that the process is a conscious choice as much as the tragic outcome of a life out of control or in despair. Gail Smith, the director of Chicago Legal Aid to Incarcerated Mothers (CLAIM), and Jane, who lost her children when she was imprisoned, speak of the problems faced by mothers in prison.

Advocate's Narrative
Peter Schmiedel

Peter Schmiedel is a supervising attorney of the Special Litigations Team in the Office of the Public Guardian. Peter's team investigates institutional abuse of children and brings the problems to the attention of DCFS. If DCFS doesn't make changes, Schmiedel's office brings a lawsuit for damages or files for an injunction. Peter has an intuitive insight into the ways children resist the self-annihilation that results from institutionalization, especially the damage done to children who have been sexually abused or who have become sexually reactive or aggressive as a

result of their own sexual exploitation. These children are the discards of the system. Tragically, their "treatment" benefits only those who win the contracts to service them.

Well, how do kids resist institutionalization? There was a kid, I'll call him Didrich. He was three years in the system. He was taken from his mother's home because of physical abuse and put in foster care with his grandmother. I think the grandmother allowed the mother in the house, and therefore

Didrich was taken out and sent to a shelter a year ago. From the shelter he was sent to Indian Oaks, a new private residential treatment under contract with DCFS. It's out in Manteno, Illinois, on the grounds of what used to be the state mental institution. Indian Oaks occupies one building, but the rest is desolate, empty, broken buildings. It's something out of a bad, eerie movie.

They have a program with an emphasis, supposedly, on juvenile sex offenders, and another program for sexually abused kids who have become sexually reactive. They have twenty kids from six to twelve in one wing, three girls out of the twenty. The girls' rooms were directly across from the boys' rooms. This wing was for sexually aggressive kids, as well as kids who've been sexually abused. I don't know that they've made a distinction [between sexually abused and sexually abusive kids].

Kids twelve to eighteen who are adjudicated delinquents for juvenile sex offenses are in another wing. Supposedly these two groups don't interact.

In January of last year, the Public Guardian's Office filed a lawsuit called "Catherine M." The suit was about the fact that DCFS would place kids who are sexually aggressive with kids who have been sexually abused in the same treatment [center]. But the court responded that, because of the "BH" case filed by ACLU against DCFS, you can't bring this lawsuit because it's precluded—it's covered under the broad provisions of the "BH" consent decree. But it did identify a problem, and what happened was last January DCFS began to look for programs for sexually abused and sexually aggressive kids.

Treatment for Sexually Abused Children: A New Market
[Private agencies who wanted to take advantage of funds] were looking for beds and treatment centers. They get so much money. I mean, it's children as

industry. Say DCFS has identified a need for space for treatment. Then people say: "Hey, I can do this. I've got twenty beds; I'll hire a director. Start sending me your kids."

Here's how Indian Oaks picked this kid Didrich. Once they had their beds and their license they said, "OK, let's go get the kids now." So they went to shelters and looked through files. The clinical director of Indian Oaks, who had come from a mental health hospital, went to the shelter where Didrich was and picked him out of the file!

Didrich didn't have much choice; he was at the shelter. If you ever want to see something terrible, go to the DCFS intake shelter at Columbus–Maryville. Go downstairs where they keep the teenagers. The place used to be a morgue. It's a room without windows, crowded, wall-to-wall beds. It's not a locked facility, so the kids come and go. Supervision is minimal. These kids are some of the most troubled kids in the system. That's why they are there, because foster families couldn't handle them or other placements can't handle them, so they dump them on the shelter, and there they stay without the services they need.

Didrich and the Quiet Room
Going back to Indian Oaks and Didrich. It isn't clear if Didrich was sexually acting out or a victim of sexual abuse. His grandma, who had him, denies both. There seems to be some indication he had problems in school; it was more behavioral problems.

According to Indian Oaks, Didrich started having behavioral problems. So they put him in the "quiet" room, which is the size of a large bathroom...no furniture, nothing in it. They put the kid there for up to eight hours a day. This is a violation of DCFS regulations as well as state law. They did this forty times in a four-month period. It was punitive rather than a temporary need to calm down or separate a child. For instance, Didrich would be placed in the quiet room on consecutive days.

They complained that Didrich was acting out in school and preventing teaching from going on. The clinical director gave us a copy of the rules of the quiet room. Unbelievable. You get eight hours in the quiet room for running down the hall from staff, any kind of sexually acting out behavior, inappropriate behavior.

Once in the quiet room, Didrich's behavior deteriorated. He would tear his clothes off with his teeth. He would strip naked and sing, scream, yell. It was his resistance to being locked in this room.

The Indian Oaks people didn't think this was really seclusion because supposedly a staff member was in the room at the same time. But, interestingly, staff was only permitted to be in the quiet room for two hours at a time in order to avoid burnout for the staff. But kids could be kept for eight hours.

Once the lawyer from our courtroom found out this was going on, he had Didrich removed. He had two orders: one, that Didrich couldn't be at Indian Oaks, and two, that he couldn't be at the shelter. Because the DCFS caseworker, who had only seen him twice in the course of three years, couldn't find any place to put Didrich, he went home to his grandmother's house! His grandmother agrees that Didrich needs help at this point. But apparently he's been doing OK since a little before Christmas at his grandmother's house.

I went out to Indian Oaks with investigators when we heard about this. I gave a University of Illinois consulting psychologist the policy on the quiet room. He was appalled, said it was Byzantine. I mean, if you have to keep a kid in a quiet room for eight hours, wouldn't you realize after the second time that whatever you were doing was wrong, the kid couldn't handle it? How could anyone leave a kid sometimes

four days a week in the quiet room? It's shocking. The rules are if you have to go to the bathroom and they determine it wasn't an emergency, you get fifteen more minutes tacked on to your time.

DCFS regulations say if you have to keep a child secluded for more than two hours, the child has to be taken to a psychiatrist immediately. No "ifs, ands, or buts." To Indian Oaks, this was deep therapy.

These kids are the most vulnerable people in the culture. They have no power. You can advocate for them, do your best, but they have no voice. They are at the mercy, at the mercy....I told the story of Didrich to show a kid resisting: "You want to deal with me like this. I'm going to make you put me in this room." He escalated his outrageousness in response. He understood this. He knew how to send them off. It was interesting; they brought in an outside worker who evaluates disruptive kids to determine if the kid needs hospitalization. Here's Didrich locked in a room, taking his clothes off, singing hymns, smearing his feces on the wall, and they finally, after forty times of this, bring an evaluator out to do an analysis on him. What they concluded is that Didrich was so clever that he was doing this stuff to get out. He wasn't psychotic or mentally disturbed. They knew he was being purposeful.

Old Orchard

It's called a residential treatment center, but it's really just another wing of Old Orchard Hospital. They have twenty kids on a floor. The kids are six to twelve. DCFS went to Old Orchard a year ago and asked them to open up a wing for sexually abused and sexually reactive kids. They said fine.

I went out there in December and talked with eight kids. The place was awful—everything bad about a hospital, but rundown. No privacy, windows facing Northshore Hospital. They, too, had a quiet room with a bed bolted to the floor and no furniture. This quiet room was about the size of a shower with holes in the wall, electrical sockets coming out of the wall.

One of the kids I talked with who had been terribly abused told me he was put in the quiet room because he and some other boys had kicked holes in the wall. Another incident was a night when they had only three staff on duty for twenty boys. The basis of their funding is that they have one-on-one coverage. That night the understaffed workers put three sexually acting out boys together in the quiet room to sleep. According to the story in the morning, the boys were acting out: running the halls, exposing themselves, urinating on the floor. The kids had engaged in anal and oral sex. So they removed two of the kids to other programs and put one into the shelter.

Again, these beds were created in direct response to DCFS saying, we need beds for this population. It's market-driven forces, children as industry. They'll promise treatment to receive payment of between $140 to $170 a day per kid as an average. DCFS has a billion-dollar budget. There are people who are willing to take their money. There's been an enormous influx of children into the system. In 1985 there was, I think, 17,000; now it's 50,000.

The Shelter Shuffle

There's terribly damaged kids sitting in those shelters without services; they don't attend school. Then they are sent out and revolve back into the shelter again. I remember the first time I went to Columbus–Maryville shelter. I saw this kid who must have been the age of my daughter, who is six. This little girl was sitting there crying with a coat and a little bag, sitting in an intake room being processed. Someone was trying to comfort her. But this was her introduction into the state system.

Then if you go upstairs to the dorm rooms, well, I was frightened. I've been

around, I've been to Pontiac Prison, but I was afraid to go down to the basement with those teenage kids. They've got kids who are twelve years old in the same downstairs section where they have eighteen-year-olds. Imagine a twelve-year-old walking into this place or a six-year-old girl who, through no fault of her own, is just sitting there. [Peter throws up his hands, shakes his head, and looks down.] It's a terrible place.

Anyway, going back to how [the system] deals with needs of all these kids pouring in. They don't have the resources to be able to monitor places like Indian Oaks, Old Orchard. One of my jobs is to go through the unusual incident reports. We must get two or three hundred a week. These could be runaways, an accident, but then there are serious reports of physical and sexual abuse of kids in treatment centers, in foster homes…it's mind-numbing. I've got three investigators; I don't have the resources to investigate all of these things. It's frightening—we don't know which cases are the most serious. We take five or ten to investigate a week; then we give the rest to their calendar [juvenile court] lawyers. But you have to understand these are young lawyers with 400 cases representing 1,200 kids each on an average. It's overwhelming.

You see what some parents do to their kids, but then you see what happens to kids who are removed from their homes and put into foster homes. It's shocking…I mean, the stories are grotesque. Two days ago a kid was removed from a foster home where she was raped twice by somebody who lives in her building. What DCFS does is have different workers servicing different kids in the home, so one worker takes this child out because she was raped, but they leave the other two or three kids in because they are not their case. There's no communication. Workers are so desperate for foster parents they don't monitor them properly, screen them properly. They put too many kids in the homes—six or seven kids.

So many kids are suffering from post-traumatic stress syndrome. They've watched or heard youth get shot. The outside world is abusive. Then often the inside worlds of their homes are abusive. Then the kid gets taken by the state. It's traumatic just to grow up in many poor communities.

Sure, everybody's afraid to have a Joseph Wallace case, but I'm saying there are countervailing pressures in the system to discourage sending kids home.

A lot of these issues are poverty issues. A lot of the kids within the system are seventeen and eighteen, with the stress of raising two or three of their kids. You're not going to resolve that by cutting off welfare for people after they have two kids. This is something that is being talked about, and I vehemently disagree....What they need are housing and jobs to give people a chance to raise kids. Those things are the hard social issues that aren't getting addressed now. Instead, what's getting addressed is all the hysteria about the problem.

Advocate's Narrative
Gail Smith

Gail Smith is a lawyer and the executive director of CLAIM (Chicago Legal Aid to Incarcerated Mothers). One of her tasks is to prevent the state from sending the children of incarcerated mothers into the foster care system. It is harder for the mothers to reunite with their children once they become state wards. Gail's work is to prevent, whenever possible, the breakup of families when Mom goes to prison.

Gail struggles against the stereotypes about "bad" mothers, the poor, and women of color that have shaped laws and sentencing patterns. Almost 63 percent of the women locked up had Class 3 and 4 felonies—petty offenses that used to draw probation. Simple possession of a drug is now reason enough to be sentenced to prison. Women's incarceration rate has exploded. Between 1980 and 1993, the female prison population increased 313 percent.[1] Of those incarcerated in state prisons, 67 percent are mothers with children under the age of eighteen.[2]

For Gail, the most critical question is why women turn to drugs. In too many cases, she says, the women have been victims of sexual abuse who self-medicate their pain with drugs.

The federal mandate in child welfare is to *prevent* kids from being removed from parents. Illinois doesn't. What's needed is to provide services at the *front end*: substance-abuse rehab programs, community-based programs, homemaker services (what extended families used to do). The state doesn't support prevention the way it supports crisis intervention. The urge is to remove the kids and ask questions later. This floods the system, and cases such as Amanda Wallace [who hanged her infant son Joey] are created. One overwhelmed caseworker can misidentify a serious case.

Policy makers have an insufficient understanding of why people are poor, so they blame the victim. There's a rescue ideology—we'll save kids from bad parents.

How the State Punishes Children
We do a lot of cases to prevent foster care. Sometimes it's too late to do that—kids are already in foster care either because Mom was "using" before she was ever arrested and the kids got into the system that way, or because

upon her arrest there was no one to step forward to take custody of the kids. The patterns we see:

- Almost always the separation of siblings.
- Lack of visitation because the DCFS system is too overwhelmed to provide a long ride to visit Mom. The child–mother relationship inevitably breaks down. Even once a week isn't enough for a two-year-old. Once a month breaks the bond.
- Lack of services for the mom.
- Lack of joint counseling for kids and the mother.
- There is a terrible lack of services for the mother's reentry into her family and community. DCFS services are abysmal.
- Mothers' and kids' reports of abuse in foster homes are ignored. The mother's credibility in reporting her child's abuse is absolutely zero. We've had teen girls report sexual abuse [to their mother], and the worker refused to believe the mother. The kids are stuck, so they run away and end up in Audy Home or a group home or on the streets.
- Caseworkers act like the mother is temporarily dead.
- While sentences for nonviolent offenses are getting longer, the system is moving to terminate parental rights much faster. From a perspective of permanency for the kids, this can be a positive thing if they are actually in an adoptive home already. But when you have a mom with kids who are bonded with her, who is doing four years for possession—simple possession, I'm not talking about someone who is dealing drugs—the tendency to move fast can destroy viable families.

There's no room for error on the mom's part. If you look at a family where the children are bonded with the

mom and she has been a pretty good caregiver for a few years, and then you look at the disease that addiction is, most people don't make it on the first try. People giving up cigarettes don't make it on the first try. We expect a crack cocaine addict to make it through treatment and never, ever use again. Well, most people have to go through treatment several times before they're going to succeed.

That's where there's a real conflict between what's perceived as the child's interests and the mother's interests. You have a kid who needs permanency and a mom who needs time. I don't know the answer, but to buy the kid permanency by cutting the mother out of their lives isn't good for anybody. Yet that's the norm.

We don't have a system that requires the cooperation of foster parents and biological parents. If the system were more nurturing of the family, if it were more cooperative—if the question asked was "How can all the adults in a case cooperate to make sure the kids have some continuity and have their needs met?"—if those were the questions we asked in setting up foster care, we'd come out with very different results.

What we're trying to achieve when we keep kids out of foster care in the probate division is to find a grandma or aunt who is supportive of the mom while understanding her imperfections. It is important that the guardian does not try to set the kids up against the mom or put a loyalty conflict on kids. In effect, she co-parents with the mother, which increases the mother's chance of success in addressing her drug problem. So that if she's involved with the kids, her guilt is reduced, the kids' sense of alienation is reduced, and her sense of responsibility continues. This makes family reunification and reentry a very different process than if she is completely cut out of the picture for a couple of years.

Johnny Jones's Eighth Birthday

Let me give an example of what happens. Jane Jones was a drug user serving a long sentence for being an accessory to a murder. She had three kids staying with their grandmother. They told the mother that they had black-and-blue marks on them, that their grandmother was hitting them, and that she used drugs. The mother called the DCFS abuse hotline several times, but DCFS didn't investigate. She begged the grandmother to give up the kids to another relative. She wouldn't. Finally, a neighbor called the police. The kids were removed and placed with a friend of the mother. However, because this woman was not a relative, she could not receive relative foster care benefits. CLAIM wanted her appointed guardian through probate court, but we couldn't because this woman had a previous felony for a bar fight. We told her not to request financial assistance from DCFS because they would discover her record. We helped get her food stamps, but that wasn't enough.

The kids seemed happy and well cared for. But DCFS, upon discovering the woman's record, picked up the kids and immediately took them to a shelter. Johnny was seven. The two younger kids were placed in separate foster homes. Johnny was placed in a series of group homes.

CLAIM requested visitation, the kids requested visitation, the mother requested visitation. Nothing. They promised Johnny three times that they'd take him to see his mother, but the caseworker never delivered. He was promised he could see her on his eighth birthday, but it passed without his seeing her. Up to that point Johnny had been exemplary in every group home where he was placed. On the birthday he was refused a visit with his mother, he locked himself in the bathroom for five hours where he banged his head against the wall repeatedly. Johnny went from being described as "sweet, polite, and a good student" to being a problem child within three months.

These kids are still in three separate foster homes, and they are looking at long-term care. Yet those children had spent eight months or more with the mother's friend, together, and doing quite well. The mother's friend went to court to fight the Public Guardian, DCFS, and juvenile court for custody. She couldn't possibly win. This indicates the lack of common sense and slavish following of rules which the system [engenders]. Yes, it's a good rule not to place children with felons, but you also have to consider what the children *need and want* and make exceptions when they are safe and thriving.

Those children were grieving, not only the loss of their mother but each other. When Johnny became disruptive, the school and caseworker blamed him. The caseworker said, "This child gets on my nerves. I'm not going to drive $2\frac{1}{2}$ hours [to the downstate women's prison] when he gets on my nerves." So they are basically punishing this kid, withholding his mother from him because his grief is causing him to act out.

The problem is that once the kids are removed, the process is almost irreversible.

Why Are These Mothers Locked Up?

We have a lot of clients locked up for nonviolent crimes, and not only drug abusers. There are nonviolent property crimes: deceptive practices [forgery, shoplifting when the theft is committed enough times that it becomes a felony]. In Illinois, 63 percent of women are locked up for Class 3 and 4 felonies, which are mostly petty offenses that used to draw probation. Of the 37 percent remaining, many are accomplices to crimes who, in my opinion, take the rap far, far too often. There are women within that 37 percent who fought back against male abusers and therefore committed a violent crime; others were sentenced for armed robbery who didn't, in fact, commit bodily harm but included a threat of bodily harm. Since 1985, the number of women in prison has quadrupled. There's overcrowding. There were about 250 women in Cook County Jail in 1985. In July 1995 there were 900.

Some women are in prison for simple possession; these are women who had drugs for their own use, not women who were dealing. Domestic violence is a big reason they use drugs. Sometimes they are first injected by male drug abuser companions. Also, you have to look at young women's sense of self—where do they get self-esteem? You have to look at education, housing, and job opportunities. They may not be able to support their kids [and they give up]. You have to address drug abuse in a much more holistic way than anyone has ever addressed this problem.

Another stereotype is that if a woman is in prison, it must be for child abuse. That is absolutely not true. There was a study done in California which found that less than 1 percent of women prisoners were there for child abuse.

Even economic crimes can be a result of battering. We had a case in which a mother of five kids tried to leave her abusive husband. She decided to leave for her sister's house. She had no money at all. She bounced three checks for a total of $187. In 1984 the amount for a felony of deceptive practices was $150, so she was sentenced to eighteen months for $187! One of her kids had Down's syndrome. Her sister couldn't handle all the kids. The twelve-year-old was babysitting for her siblings as well as for her three cousins.

The grocer who the mother bounced the checks on said he'd be happy for her to make restitution. But no. The judge could have sentenced her to probation and restitution. Nowadays, the mandatory minimum sentencing laws force judges to impose prison sentences.

It was totally unnecessary to hurt that family. The children were traumatized enough to have seen their mother beaten by the father. Her Down's syndrome child suffered terribly in her absence. She did regain her children after her release eight months later.

Blaming Mothers

If we had a system that didn't vilify mothers, we'd have an open adoption system where mothers can see their kids. If the concept of a foster family and adoptive family were not so polarized, we could approach the family in a more realistic way. Both the foster parent and the biological parent could co-parent. The "rescuing kids from bad mothers" ideology pervades the legal, political, and social systems. We have to stop treating children as property and stop treating mothers as if they didn't exist.

Notes

1. National Women's Law Center, Washington, D.C., and Chicago Legal Aid to Incarcerated Mothers (CLAIM), "Women in Prison," *Walkin' Steel* (Fall 1995), 9.

2. Ibid.

NOTES

1. W. H. Auden, in *Collected Poems*, Ed. Edward Mendelson (New York: Vintage, 1991), 294.

2. Qtd. in Adrienne Rich, *What Is Found There* (New York: Norton, 1993), 213.

3. Qtd. in Louise Armstrong, *Of "Sluts" and "Bastards": A Feminist Decodes the Child Welfare Debate* (Monroe, Maine: Common Courage Press, 1995), 282.

4. Ibid.

5. Interview with Cindy Clark, Public Guardian investigator, June 7, 1995.

6. Ibid.

7. Notice of Emergency Supplemental Petition in the Circuit Court of Cook County, Illinois, County Department, Juvenile Division—Child Protection Division, *Minors' Emergency Supplemental Petition for Findings of Neglect and Abandonment Against Their Guardian, DCFS Guardianship Administer, and for Other Relief* (May 23, 1995), 4.

8. Interview with Agnes Brown, Feb. 12, 1995.

9. Drew Humphries, "Mothers and Children, Drugs and Crack: Reactions to Maternal Drug Dependency," in *It's a Crime: Women and Justice,* Eds. Ted Alleman and Roslyn Muraskin (Englewood Cliffs, New Jersey: Regents/Prentice, 1993), 142–43.

10. Ibid., 140.

10

❀

Delivering Services
or Building Community?

The fundamental political conflict in the opening decades of the
new century, we believe, will not be between nations or even the new
trading blocs but between the forces of globalization and the territorially
based forces of local survival seeking to preserve and redefine community.[1]

RICHARD BARNETT AND JOHN CAVANAUGH

It is not the condition of being poor or being a single parent that
produces dysfunction. It is the lack of a surrounding community
structure that is so detrimental….[Poverty] is the site of material
deprivation. With a communal ethos it can also be a marginal
space where people can make alternative ways to live their lives.[2]

BELL HOOKS

Poverty does not lead to violence, crime, and maltreatment of children. The shredding of community does. As best as they could, African American slaves built a wall of resistance to protect their children from slavery's brutish violence. Dancing the African ring shout or later singing spirituals in forbidden "churches" made of pine branches, slaves reconstituted a solidarity with one another deeper than the reaches of lash or law. In the 1960s it was the beloved community of black America that rose from Southern bayous and cotton fields, and Northern ghettoes, colleges, and factory floors to face attack dogs, billy clubs, hosings, and even death for the sake of freedom. Community is the weapon that the powerless wield. It does not guarantee triumph, but it does carry forth a people's hope and dignity.

A war against the majority Mayan people of Guatemala in the 1980s decimated the highlands, taking the lives of 50,000. Guatemalan military carried out a massive scorched-earth policy. Yet twelve years later, 20,000 Mayan Indians came down from the Ixchan and Sierra mountain areas where they had hidden, farmed, and raised children. Seemingly defenseless against marauding Guatemalan armies, continual strafe bombings, and aircraft surveillance with infrared sensors that could identify the movement of even small animals, the peasants had survived and built bases of resistance that outsmarted modern warfare's best technology. Their weapon was ancient—*comunidad* (community).

This book argues that global political and economic transformations (as well as the disinvestment in core city areas and redlining of the 1970s) have severely wounded the traditional extended family and communal networks that formerly sustained poor communities. Isolated as never before, poor families now lack the neighborhood and cultural support systems that offered both concrete "services"—such as an aunt, uncle, neighbor, or church or temple member who could watch your children, help out in a family crisis, lend money—and a sense of belonging and safety. Social clubs, unions, block clubs, and community organizations have been decimated by structural unemployment, the scissoring of the "safety net," and massive cuts in social spending.

Without a connection to a community of support, people give up hope. Yet the despair, rage, and isolation of the poor are invisible. Michael Harrington argued, over twenty years ago, that the poor are invisible because suburbanization separated the middle class from seeing the problems of the urban poor. The majority don't see the elderly poor's desperate struggle to pay rent and live alone in a studio or one-room apartment. Poor people in America aren't "recognizable" because "it is much easier in the United States to be decently dressed than to be decently fed, housed or doctored."[3]

If poor people are not seen, then how much more invisible are poor children who are taken from families whose major descriptive characteristic, according to all studies, is isolation? Both the children and the families served by state welfare agencies lack political power. Confronted with social invisibility, poverty, and lack of political voice, these struggling families encounter child welfare, possibly their only link to mainstream society. Yet their concrete needs are still not addressed. The services provided focus on their deficits, not their strengths. Their political and economic powerlessness is not addressed. Instead, both the child and the family become "therapized," "medicalized," and regulated.

Social workers are not trained to identify the social forces that break down families. Thus, services target individual or family system "pathologies." Such an individualized approach dislocates the ongoing cause of dysfunction and substitutes services that reinforce families' and children's victimhood.

When poor neighborhoods are organized, powerlessness is collectively confronted. An organized neighborhood does not guarantee that all poor families will be drawn in, particularly if a family has been marginalized for generations. Some parents will still physically or sexually abuse a child. However, a focused community effort to build relationships between neighbors and to win a political voice for collective needs ensures greater hope in depressed urban areas and increases the possibility of networks that can reach out to isolated families close to breakdown. Most of all, rebuilding communities confronts directly social and political powerlessness. A strong community may not solve all its social problems, but it will provide members with bonds of solidarity to confront their individual and collective problems. The services that people need are collaboratively identified by families in need and by community-controlled child welfare service systems.

Identifying community as the agent of change, reconstruction, prevention, and healing calls for liberal reforms and offers the potential for radical change. At a minimum, centralized child welfare systems must decentralize and move into neighborhoods, with services made available to community institutions, such as the schools, day-care facilities, churches/synagogues/mosques, shelters, and youth programs.

WHAT IS COMMUNITY?

Community is not so much a description of people's closeness to one another as it is about their collective commitment to self-determination. Community forms as people struggle to take back their lives from passivity, powerlessness, and victimhood in any of the areas where they are denied social power—jobs, housing, responsive institutions such as schools, hospitals, and the criminal justice system. Community transforms powerlessness. As people form associations to identify, strategize, and act to solve their problems, they enter into relationships that authenticate their own authority rather than the authority of experts.

Community is the true vessel of citizenship because the relations it fosters are relationships among historical actors. Citizenship without a commitment to grassroots democracy is inevitably undemocratic and elitist because it trades belief in people's ability to solve their own problems for the authority of experts. People claim their authority when they discover the power they have to solve their own problems by (1) analyzing and identifying their problems and needs, (2) setting a plan to overcome these problems, and (3) acting to change their situation.

What, in contrast, are the empowerment and healing offered by service systems—in this case, the child welfare system? According to John McKnight of Northwestern's Center for Urban Affairs and Policy Institute, "for 36 years...I have never seen service systems that brought people to well being, delivered them to citizenship, or made them free."[4] McKnight delineates three reasons. First, social service systems receive enormous amounts of federal, state, and city money, but rather than the money going to the poor, it goes to salaries and benefits for the service providers. For example, McKnight's research team found that of all the federal, state, and county money earmarked for low-income people in Chicago, 63 percent of the money was for services, and 37 percent went to income for the poor people being serviced.[5]

Second, service systems focus on people's weaknesses rather than on their strengths. Vibrant communities build on people's capacities in spite of the areas in their lives where they have failed. Social service systems are organized around identifying and treating people's weaknesses. What these service systems produce are dependent clients rather than citizens.[6]

Third, social service systems legitimate professional expert authority and undercut the authority of clients. Social solidarity is displaced by dependency on psychologists, doctors, caseworkers, and diagnosticians: "The proliferation of an ideology of therapy and service as 'what you need' has weakened associations and organizations of citizens across the United States."[7]

Social work's micro-management focus on psychosocial family dysfunction doesn't address the expanding social problems that confront the end of the twentieth century. Professors Mark Lusk and David Stoesz suggest that the social work profession needs to learn community building from third and fourth world populations, which although materially impoverished have upheld a practice of community solidarity aimed at strengthening the common good: "As we in this country face the growing community and national level problems of homelessness, urban and rural collapse, hunger and chronic unemployment, we must look to those who have dealt with these issues in greater extent and depth than we....Instead of increasing the dependency of excluded groups on an indifferent public bureaucracy, the mission of post modern social work is to reinforce the self-sufficiency of marginal groups by developing culturally sensitive programs...post modern social work would look to the indigenous abilities of marginal groups, rather than the state, for program development."[8]

COMMUNITY-BASED SERVICES
OR COMMUNITY-BASED SOLUTIONS?

Rebuilding community as a goal for social and child welfare organizations would require that the money directed toward professional administrators and managers of the poor be cut, rather than cutting jobs or subsistence payments to the poor. Services—such as drug rehab, family or individual therapy, job and organizing training, services to developmentally delayed or disabled children, youth empowerment programs, workshops in parenting skills, infant nutri-tion, family and children's legal rights—would be offered in a community-based program. However, *local community councils, agencies, and organizations, rather than centralized bureaucracies,* would identify and facilitate the services that fami-lies need.

Investing in community building is very different from the way federal monies, in conjunction with corporate monies, have created enterprise zones in poor communities. Targeted enterprise zone monies bypass the community-identified leaders and organizations and are funneled through powerful city hall "community" leaders or loyal "community-based" political interests.

A current trend in child welfare is to develop "community-based services." At its best, this reform effort seeks to decentralize maligned, overwhelmed child welfare urban bureaucracies as well as to form management teams with existing community services and organizations that could respond to the needs of chil-dren and families under duress. At its worst, the reform-minded "community-based services" will simply change the location of child welfare's control center to an office in a poor neighborhood. It will not change practices of child re-moval, and it will continue to focus on family deficit and on regulation of family life according to white, middle-class norms. Even if the community-based case managers are of the same race as the clientele, the programs will not work if the relationships remain regulatory rather than emancipatory. Ac-cording to Ruth Massinga, "In a real sense, system reform can be a slick, tech-nologically supported recasting of triage arrangements, or it can begin with a courageous rethinking of societal institutions and values."[9]

Transformation of social service systems must address the critical issue of power—who has it and who is kept from having it. Changing that equation calls into question all the social institutions that reinforce inequality and an economy that produces stratified social status. Progressive or radical social ser-vice advocates insist that change will remain ameliorative rather than transfor-mative unless a larger analysis targets the globalized economy that is producing increasing structural inequity. In any case, the catalyst for change must be com-munity based and community directed.

Liberal reformers believe that child maltreatment can be prevented with-out such radical change. Liberal reformers believe in creating a series of pro-grams that, if constructed effectively, effect change. Child welfare scholars James Garabino and Kathleen Kostelny refer to this model of change as "patch-work prevention."[10] No one program in itself has emancipatory capacity, but when added together the programs can effectively change at least child wel-fare's regulatory and/or punitive response to families and children of the poor-est classes.

Both radical advocates and liberals work for child welfare reform. Radicals endorse programs that change the power equation between families and pro-fessionals even though the proposed programs may not target the structural roots of poverty, which spark social and family disintegration.

The liberal reformers' scramble for federal, state, and foundation funding is often engaged in the name of the poor but lacks an awareness of the effects

of the competitive "victories" on the people who are served. Social transformers such as Kip Tiernan, of Boston's Poor People's United Fund and co-
director of the University of Massachusetts Ethical Policy Institute, hold
service providers accountable for appropriating poverty and human service
funds:

> Service system lobbyists and advocates see the competition for limited
> public resources as a competition between various service providers and
> systems. They rarely acknowledge, however, that the net effect of their
> lobbying is to limit cash income for those they call needy and increase
> the budget and incomes of service programs and providers. The results
> become a piling up of publicly funded services and a stagnation in com-
> mitments to income. Poor people need income, choice, and economic
> opportunity, not service, therapy and labels.[11]

However, both the radical "social transformers" and the liberal "patchwork
preventers" agree that community-based programs are a critical first step in
dismantling centralized control and rebuilding shattered community networks
of support for families.

Ironically, the conservative "family values" proponents also support community-based services. But their motivation is not change but maintaining the
status quo. Dismantling government-supported social welfare bureaucracies
frees government from social responsibility for the problems of the poor and
marginalized. Slashing federal social welfare and giving block grants to individual states to dispense as they wish in an economic climate that is spinning
downward is an attempt to "save" America. But the America they are referring to is not the majority but the powerful corporate few. The defenders of
an elitist America intend to reverse the liberal reform legacy of New Deal legislation and to discipline women who deviate from white, middle-class standards of family life. Community-based programs fit their agenda of eliminating
subsidies to the poor (federal entitlements) while supporting taxation "reform"
that will subsidize corporations.

The community-based programs that congressional conservatives advocate
are based on delivery of services instead of *community economic development* models. There is no commitment to job development in economically depressed
areas. Instead, treatment services are offered in lieu of economic opportunity.
Without such ameliorative services, the urban concentrations of surplus populations might become eruptive and unmanageable.

The national policy consensus of progressives, liberals, and conservatives
has created a reform opportunity. Communities can and must take advantage
of this "opening," which would refocus monies and policies at the local level.
At the same time, the danger of this opening—the impulse to privatize—must
be addressed. *Privatization* does not refer to historical private social agencies in
the tradition of settlement houses, but it can include not-for-profit entities
whose services are determined by the available federal or state categorical
monies. Largely, the term refers to an economic model (named neoliberalism
or structural adjustment policy in third world nations) that transfers state publicly funded social services to the corporate-for-profit sector. The current

move toward privatization absolves Americans from social responsibility for the common good. The marginalized become serviced by the corporate sector that co-produced their marginality.

Within the arena created by the current trend toward community-based social and child welfare services, innovations and alternative models of youth and family advocacy have emerged that foster social and self reliance. What follows are descriptions of some of these paradigms and programs.

Homebuilders

The Homebuilders model described in Chapter 7 is a model of successful family support intervention at the point where foster care placement of a child is imminent. The Homebuilders' practice—of going to the home of the family to provide intensive relational support, of affirming a family's strengths, of collaboratively identifying what's needed to overcome problems, and of offering traditional services such as therapy as well as nontraditional services that tap community resources—has worked: "Since 1988, 88 percent of the families served by Homebuilders [in Washington State] were still together a year after intervention...in the South Bronx (in 1987) after one year 74 percent of the families they worked with were still together."[12] It is cost effective. Foster care placement in Washington State costs more than $7,000 per year and residential care more than $22,000, whereas Homebuilders costs $2,700 for family preservation intervention for an intensive six-month period.[13]

Other private agencies, such as Kaleidoscope, have adapted intensive in-home family preservation models similar to that of Homebuilders and have translated those models to a statewide level. These initiatives emphasize the critical importance of developing family support and reunification practices within community-based settings in recognition of the environmental conditions that give rise to family breakdown and crisis.

Community-Based Individualized Services
and "Wrap-Around" Services

Those who resist changing child welfare's programs, processes, philosophy, and practices often do so out of a sense of the "impossibility" of the task rather than as a defense of the system. Some workers carry an investment in the theoretical psychoanalytic or psychodynamic therapeutic models they learned in the university. Even when experience teaches that those models are, broadly speaking, ineffective, child care professionals assume that the failure is theirs, the family's, or the child's, rather than that of the service model.

Analyzing the most challenging child welfare population—children and youth who are severely maladjusted—demonstrates the effectiveness of alternative models that are results oriented. Some child welfare advocates have challenged the practice of sending severely troubled youth to out-of-state residential treatment centers or psychiatric hospitals. An official impetus for creating alternative programs for these children came with the creation of the Child and Adolescent Service Program (CASSP) in 1984 by the National Institute for Mental Health. And such programs as Kaleidoscope in Illinois and Youth Empowerment Project in Texas have developed a model of services that stands the traditional model on its head. In response to the disempowering results of professionals deciding what is in the child's "best interests," *individualized care and wrap-around services* make the services match the child's needs rather than making the child fit into the service programs provided. Individualized care deals with the family and the child's concrete reality and needs, and *sets a plan to provide the services the child and family identify.* Wrap-around services are the array of services necessary to reunite the troubled youngster and family. Services could include getting a refrigerator, finding a youth mentor, tutoring, and providing an after-school worker who could spend time with the child until dinner.

The philosophy of individualized care begins with the assumption that families have strengths, not simply deficits. The assessment process upends the child welfare model: "While traditional assessments tend to emphasize pathology and service needs, assessments for individualized care emphasize the child's and family's assets as well as their deficits."[14] The ideal program is based on collaboration with the family and has as its objective returning the child to the family unless that is utterly impossible. The individualized care approach insists that it is critical that a child be kept within the community and that services provided be culturally and ethnically appropriate. Even when it is not possible for a child to be returned home, the program recognizes culture as a deep aspect of "home" and belonging, broadly speaking, and places children within their cultural milieu, whether that is a foster family or a group home.

Case managers must have a commitment to a philosophy of strength-based individualized services but also to cultural competence. This later competency is more difficult to ensure in a dominant culture that is fundamentally racist and with academic programs that emphasize therapeutic competencies and *multicultural appreciation* but require few cultural competency *practice* requirements for child welfare or social welfare agency work. For example, how often do academic programs tackle racism as part of a multicultural curriculum? How are the links between culture and power addressed—the connections between subordinate cultures and internalized powerlessness, as opposed to the privileges afforded Caucasians?

Finally, and perhaps most importantly, individualized care provides unconditional care to the child. This philosophy—developed in the 1960s by Browndale, a Canadian agency, and adapted by Kaleidoscope in the 1970s—admits children on a "no eject/no reject" basis. The program promises the child and family not to give up on them no matter what happens. Children who are referred or apply are accepted, and none are ever terminated. This is a radical commitment because it addresses directly the issue of responsibility, which child welfare does not. Individualized care says this: here is a support system that will not abandon you (as often family or professionals have) no matter what you do—including drugs, attempts at suicide, violent acting out, and being sexually or physically abusive.

Implementation of the Individualized
Care Model: The Process

Interagency Collaboration/Comprehensive Services In order to provide individualized care, a collaborative process must be developed, beginning with an agency's commitment to collaboration with the child and family but extending to interagency collaboration in order to provide the array of services that the child and family need: "The current system is described as fragmented; an individual child may receive services from multiple agencies such as child welfare, special education, mental health, and juvenile justice."[15] An interagency team approach, on the other hand, draws multi-service community organizations together to share workload, responsibility, and creativity in responding to the needs of children with serious behavior problems. The team approach draws together all the people familiar with the child, along with new team members, and allows a more comprehensive assessment of how to meet the child's needs.

Reframing A critical task of the team is to reframe the child's life and experience. A child with emotional/behavioral problems often has a multi-agency case record that has come to represent his or her life. The reframing process occurs with the entire team, including child and parents, collectively articulating a knowledge of the child/family and their strengths, potentialities, and limits. The creative power of reframing can't be underestimated: "The parent and child have literally exposed themselves to a room of people...[their] vulnerability is immense, the intrusion obvious. This charged atmosphere communicates humanity and vulnerability."[16] The process deepens the stakes and draws participants into a more profound collaboration—the infrastructure of a team.

Coordination of a Plan Case management, which is critical to coordinating a plan of services, is team based, advocacy oriented, and immersed in the child's immediate family and cultural community. The case manager is able to draw upon an array of both formal and informal services available in the community—from traditional therapeutic programs to informal programs such as the Boys' or Girls' Club gym for basketball or boxing, health clinic services, coach or tutorial volunteer assistance, and summer job training programs.

Wrap-Around Services Critical to the success of wrap-around services (surrounding the child and family with services) is access to flexible monies. Individualized, unconditional care cannot occur within traditional budgetary constraints—that is, child care driven by funds available for services that match categories (special needs, medically complex, etc). A pool of flexible funds available to follow the child's need for services rather than to sustain existing categorical services is essential. Children with serious behavioral problems have fluctuating needs, and funds must be fluid enough to respond to the changing needs of both child and family. Funds may be necessary to pay off phone bills, repair a washing machine, provide for a bilingual therapist, pay for dental care, hire a crisis worker or family friend to assist the family at a critical time, or purchase gifts for Christmas:

> Strategies include creating a pool of blended funds from the various child-serving agencies which can be accessed by case managers and/or interagency teams to pay for individualized intervention plans. Additionally, an increasing number of service programs across the country (such as home-based service, day treatment, therapeutic foster care, and other programs) are budgeting various amounts of flexible funds to purchase wrap-around services and supports for participating youngsters and families.[17]

Blended, Flexible Funds Some team member must develop funding source literacy in order to access the web of government, state, and private funds and entitlements that could be blended to serve a particular child and family. Having access to "streams" of funds greatly increases the chance of establishing pools of flexible monies. Without this competency, the process stalls and becomes compromised.

Nonnegotiable Process Components Dr. John Whitbeck summarizes and enumerates the critical *process* components that make or break an individualized care program:

- **Access:** Do the child and parent have actual inclusion in the decision-making process?
- **Voice:** Were the child and parent heard and listened to throughout the process?
- **Ownership:** Are the child and parent in agreement with the plan about their lives?

These process components are nonnegotiable—without them, individualized care is invalidated and the process fails.[18]

Where Have Individualized Care Models Worked?

Washington State A study conducted by the Mental Health Division of the Washington State Department of Social and Health Services under the direction of John Whitbeck, using interviews with children, families, and administrators from formal and informal child-serving agencies and community organizations of nine counties, found that "the process of providing individualized and tailored care for children with complex needs in their communities is robust and workable...the elements involved in this process are known and can be replicated."[19]

The Alaska Youth Initiative (AYI) In 1985 the Alaska departments of Education and Health and Social Service, under pressure to send children with serious emotional/behavioral problems into out-of-state residential care, chose instead to integrate individualized services into their child welfare system. With the objective of bringing 117 youth back to Alaska, and where possible into their family homes, state mental health, social services, and special education agencies launched an individualized care program titled "The Alaska Youth Initiative." After two years, all but one of the children returned to Alaska and were in considerably less-regulated home or residential placements. No children who participated in the program were sent out of state again.[20]

One reason for the success of AYI was that the planners recognized the political forces that would be aligned against innovation, so they built a base of support among sympathetic politicians and policy makers to fend off destructive criticism and threats of funding withdrawal. Another dimension of their success is that villages and remote communities that lack formal services have had individualized care workshops, reinforcing a community's ability to develop team-based services that support families in dealing with troubled children.

Vermont With the assistance of federal monies provided by a CASSP grant, Vermont passed legislation that would provide an individualized care model with wrap-around services for families/children with serious emotional problems. Unlike Alaska, Vermont targeted a broader base of children than those who had been placed in out-of-state care. The objective has been to reunite children with their families—a task less demonstrably attractive to legislators because it doesn't save the state as much money. (Out-of-state placements, for instance, cost Alaska $70,000 a year for each child.)

Vermont's success, like that of Alaska, was its ability to convince legislators to codify individualized care for troubled youth. Further, Vermont has managed to package federal monies such as Medicaid, rehabilitation services, and Title IV-E. Vermont opted to use existing state and federal monies, unlike Alaska's interagency pooled funds, "because the state has learned to use Medicaid in innovative ways through its Home and Community-Based Waiver."[21]

Pennsylvania A joint project by Pennsylvania's Council of Children's Services, the Presley Ridge School, and the Center for Research and Policy has created an "outcome-based" program of individualized services for severely troubled children and their families. Thirty-one not-for-profit agencies with combined client populations of 5,000 volunteered to become part of the program, which measured its effectiveness by gathering data that evaluated the child and family's quality of life following services. Outcome indicators, evaluated at two- and five-year intervals, were education, employment, recidivism, and drug and alcohol use. The thirty-one agencies used this method of evaluation with such effectiveness that it will be transferred to the remaining seventy not-for-profit state agencies that have plans to be implemented by the Pennsylvania departments of Public Welfare and Education. The process of testing an evaluation process with agencies working at the community level first and then transferring an effectively demonstrated process to the state level reverses the top-down model of program implementation.[22]

Wyoming, Arkansas, Washington, Maryland, and Montana These states are in various stages of implementing adaptations or modifications of the Alaska Youth Initiative model of individualized care.

Chicago and Bloomington, Illinois Karl Dennis, executive director of Kaleidoscope, promotes the practice of outcome-based individualized services in Illinois by saying, "It is what you would do for youngsters and their parents if you really liked them, what you would do if you were given the tools that would allow you not to give up on them, and what you would do if you could break free from the constraints that both our professional training and agency structures place upon our desire to do what makes sense."[23]

The Chicago Hull House Youth Initiative program, started in 1995, has adapted an individualized care model to work with youth returning from out-of-state residential treatment programs. The Hull House settlement house, which continues the legacy of Jane Addams, has a contract with the Department of Children and Family Services to implement the program. The advocacy program assigns an advocate who works intensively with each young person to help the client establish an independent living arrangement, get a job, enter training or college programs, and learn how to budget, etc. Young people are provided food vouchers, transportation tokens, weekly allowances, and rent. In addition to the special advocate, they are provided with a back-up case management team that supports their transition into mainstream society and personal independence.

The program is cost effective for the state because DCFS has to pay up to $500 per day for out-of-state residential care, whereas the Hull House program, though staff-intensive, costs $260 per day. The program lasts nine months.

The young person's service plan is not imposed upon him or her. Instead, the social work advocate brings together the youth's family and friends as a support team to assist the young person in following through on the goals that he or she has set. During this process, in which the support community is present, the young person may change goals, accept feedback, and set new priorities. All those present commit themselves to very specific support actions. In this way, a support contract is forged.

The program is already being reassessed and adapted. "We're learning that the program has been a little too loose," says Seth Donnelly, a case manager supervisor. "We have to more effectively communicate our expectations so that kids don't assume our unwillingness to kick kids out translates to 'anything goes.' But what's good about this program is that it's open, supportive, oriented toward reuniting the family, and that helps rebuild self-esteem and belonging."[24]

Although the program is possibly one of the best support systems for very troubled youth, Seth feels that it still doesn't go far enough because it doesn't question the larger causes of family breakdown: "The philosophy encourages young people to assimilate into society and become independent. But what does independent mean? There's no critical examination as to why youth or their families are in trouble. It seems to me that young people need to know what they're up against. Hull House is an assimilationist/maintenance organization rather than a transformative organization. In spite of saying this, I hesitate to impose my perspective....I do see good coming out of this program."[25]

Home Visiting: A Traditional Approach
Effective for the Future

A model of care not categorized precisely as individualized care but that practices the individualized philosophy of building on strengths is the practice of home visiting. Visiting home nurses' early support of families with newborns has amplified an "at-risk" family's ability to recognize and develop its strengths. The visiting nurse of the nineteenth and early twentieth century who extended the work of settlement house social workers by offering health care and support to immigrant and poor families in their homes was a healing liaison to the isolated. Unlike immigrants' fear of and, at times, hostility towards caseworkers, the visiting nurses were welcomed. Similarly, young mothers of today are less threatened by a nurse who offers prenatal or postnatal care for their newborns. The resulting relationship has fewer obstacles to overcome in order for the nurse to be trusted by parents.

Healthy Start: Hawaii's Home Visiting Program

Hawaii's approach to child welfare focuses on earliest prevention of problems by using a home nursing plan that assists newborns and their mothers. Begun in 1985 as a prototype project to prevent abuse and neglect, the program targeted an impoverished area, Leeward, Oahu, that had an array of problems related to poverty—unemployment, substance abuse, mental illness, and child maltreatment. By 1988, an evaluation revealed that not one case of child abuse was reported among the 241 families involved. As a result, in 1991 Hawaii's Maternal and Child Health Branch of the Department of Health institutionalized the program, funding several Healthy Start community-based agencies throughout the state.

What appears as an anomaly—Hawaii's annual legislative support appropriation of $7 million—is actually the result of a well-planned strategy, begun in the 1970s, to enlist legislative support. The program does not rely exclusively on state funding but uses Medicaid and some Title IV federal funds. Healthy Start's effectiveness is that it reaches families not typically "serviced" by child welfare by providing immunizations, general health care programs, and prenatal care programs. Visiting nurses provide a nonthreatening service, creating the opportunity to develop a relationship with the family over a five-year period. Whatever parenting, nutrition, budget, stress reduction, or job counseling assistance families identify as needed (through their developing trust in the health care worker) continues throughout the child's formative years: "Among 2 year olds in the program, 99 percent are immunized, 85 percent are on target development...a recent review of children hospitalized because of abuse found 97 percent were from areas not served by Healthy Start programs."[26] Healthy Start has become "a systematic and multi-purpose network of community based maternal child health services [that] reaches approximately 52 percent of the families with newborns throughout Hawaii."[27]

Home Health Visitor Program of Elmira, New York

David Olds and his research team charted the effect of nurses' home visits to "high-risk" (poor, teenage, unmarried) mothers during a two- to three-year period following a birth. They found that only 4 percent of the mothers were reported for child maltreatment during the first two years of the baby's life, as opposed to 19 percent of a group that did not have pre- or postnatal home care.[28] A dynamic that ensured the program's effectiveness was that the nurses offered not only nurturing support to the mothers, but also feedback on their parenting skills. In addition to preventing child maltreatment, the home health visitor program "reduced prematurity rates, increased birth weight, decreased smoking during pregnancy, decreased accidental ingestion of poison in the first year of life, and improved the mother's attitude and perception of the child."[29]

New Zealand: National
Community-Based Family Preservation

One child welfare program based on communal and family strengths has been institutionalized nationally. New Zealand has legally mandated a national program that draws families into a participative community-based process of resolution and care. In 1989, New Zealand enacted legislation, based on the indigenous Maori communal decision-making processes, that profoundly changed child and family welfare policy and practice. Unlike in the United States, where child welfare decisions are made by casework professionals and the courts, the New Zealand Children, Young Persons and Their Family Act requires that the extended family play the most prominent decision-making role in all child welfare decisions referred to the Department of Social Welfare: "The new law…formalized a developing change in social work practice that embraced processes of family decision making, and it made a radical attempt to address, legally, issues of family disempowerment and alienation.… Family responsibility is reinforced, welfare agencies having a secondary role of enabler in terms of facilitating this family responsibility."[30]

The family group conference (FGC) is the formal procedure by which the extended family and invited community members, brought together by a care and protection coordinator, develop a plan of response in cases of maltreated children or "delinquent" youth. In conflicts of interest, the child's or young person's interests are the deciding factors. Fears that families might make decisions detrimental to children were allayed after a first-year evaluation. More than 5,000 family group conferences were held, with 2,000 of these cases involving child care and protective services: "In only one or two cases has the department had to exercise its statutory powers to not agree to the plan because of concerns about the safety of the child or young person....Diversion has increased: arrests make up only 6 percent of the cases reported by the police now, compared with 29 percent in 1984; and it is estimated that only 10 percent of cases appear in court compared with 45 percent in 1984."[31]

The family group conference involves three steps:

- Information sharing, in which professionals share their information and assessments.

- Extended family (and invited friends) meeting together privately to decide what to do to protect a maltreated child.

- Plan of action presented to the coordinator and caseworker—at this stage there are "give and take" discussions that may revise the plan.

Once the family completes its plan, the referring agency must accept the plan, and the Department of Social Work then provides needed resources toward the plan's success.

Strengths and Weaknesses New Zealand Department of Social Welfare child welfare worker and researcher Ann Barbour has analyzed the family group conference's strengths and weaknesses.[32] Its strengths:

- Reduces removal of children from their homes and communities.

- Demands cultural competence skills.

- Offers greater affirmation of family/community wisdom.

- Encourages family initiative and creativity rather than dependence on the authority of experts.

- Decentralizes government services and statutorily mandates community-based solutions that involve the parties affected.

- Creates a working link between caring professionals and local communities.

- Produces a nonadversarial process (as opposed to U.S. courts' adversarial decision making) that involves cooperative planning.

- By involving a wide range of family members, pressure is lifted from the nuclear family, and the possibility of one or two stable and responsible members emerges even with severely dysfunctional families.

- More effective follow-through on the part of the family because they have had an investment in the decision making.

- Monitoring of the plan is more effective because family members are invested in its success and have more immediate access to the ongoing process than does an overworked caseworker.

- Improves families' problem-solving skills and provides a social framework for solving future problems.

- In situations where a parent has a drug problem, a community of support is activated that can help the parent maintain his or her resolve or encourage his or her recommitment if drug use is resumed.

Here are the weaknesses of the family group conference:

- Successful conferences depend upon the cultural sensitivity, process skills, and values of the plan coordinator, but there is, as yet, no ongoing training process that can produce new coordinators.

- Occasionally, an extended family is a group of strangers who have not had enough interactive ties to work together in order to create an effective plan of support for a child and family.

- Occasionally, but not always, sexual abuse situations so divide families that resolution plans are not feasible.

Provisional plans have been made to adapt such a model in the United States. For example, Illinois child welfare policy researchers have proposed using the FGC as a way to build a family support base for the single mothers who are the majority of its parental clients. Although the Illinois model would be only a partial adaptation of the New Zealand model, it would, at least, dramatically alter the Department of Child and Family Services' focus on family deficit and child removal.

Programmatic Disadvantages of
Individualized Care in the United States

There is a growing consensus at the policy level that punitive, deficiency-oriented service models of child and family care have failed and must be changed to individualized care models that develop family capacity. Nevertheless, there are two criticisms of individualized care. One says the initiative doesn't go far enough; the other says it's too demanding. Seth Donnelly's criticism of individualized care's failure to question the reasons that poor families are at risk places him within the tradition of radical social work advocates who focus on community building within a framework of social transformation of the structural obstacles to empowerment. But there are other criticisms of individualized care that come from the ranks of reform-minded liberals as well as conservative defenders of the status quo. The following are some of their criticisms:

- Because it is staff-intensive, individualized care is difficult to duplicate in states with densely populated urban areas requiring large pools of caseworkers.

- Categorical services, though largely ineffective, are easier to initiate with a large numbers of clients.

- Therapists, psychologists, and caseworkers resist innovations and continue to use particular psychoanalytic theories of intervention or program models with which they are familiar.

- Few have learned the skills needed to creatively "blend" entitlement monies into funding streams needed for wrap-around services.

- Administrators of large child welfare state agencies fear programs that legislators would describe as "coddling" children (even when the administrators know the program is demonstrably better than massive categorical services).

■ Overwhelmed agency administrative directors can't see a way to create collaborative models between agencies. Their fear of legislative censure (or of not being reappointed) keeps them from risking programmatic change.

Although individualized care has been presented as focusing on severely maladjusted children and families, the same approach has been used in Vermont as a prevention model that can offer wrap-around services to children early on in order to avoid removal from their home and community. This application demands a comprehensive evaluation of the family in distress and a family/agency collaboratively developed plan of service that meets the family's needs. Also constructed is an intensive school-based service program that draws together the caseworker, family, teacher, school nurse, and/or special-ed teacher. This emphasis on using communal institutions as part of a partnership expands the community's capacity to effectively support its membership.

YOUTH DEVELOPMENT AND COMMUNITY DEVELOPMENT: A NEW PARADIGM

Beyond family services provided by innovative state child welfare or private agencies are initiatives that focus on youth or family development as a preventive, empowerment-oriented approach to child and family welfare. In the case of youth, the shift to a development model is profoundly simple: assume that young people are capable and possess potential and creativity rather than treat them as deviants or outsiders. This may seem deceptively easy, but in a political climate that targets young people—especially youth of color and poor teens—as the source of America's moral decline, it is difficult. According to Luis Rodriguez, award-winning poet and former Los Angeles gang member, dumping responsibility on youth for a culture that careens toward violence and apathy is what is "easy." "I know from experience," says Rodriguez, "that it doesn't take guts to put money into inhumane, punishment driven institutions…such policies make our communities less safe. It's tougher to walk these streets, to listen to young people, to respect them and help them fight for their well-being. It's tougher to care."[33]

Distanced from the life of youth in the core cities, mainstream America accepts the "family values" political attack on minority youth and media's caricature of "underclass" youth. Youthful defiance confirms our fears and justifies a punitive response. Rarely do we interpret youth's rage and pain as a response to betrayed hopes. Rappers, gang-bangers, punkers, and taggers represent both a rejection of, and appropriation of, white mainstream America's violence and material acquisitiveness: "Even when the gritty facts of urban life are intellectually understood, it is impossible for an outsider to know what it *feels like* when siblings are murdered, abuse occurs daily, crime and violence are the norm, and messages of rejection are everywhere."[34]

Programs that treat youth as a problem fail: "Youth vote with their feet… [they] experience many so-called prevention or remediation activities—substance abuse prevention, remedial education courses, boot camp for juvenile offenders—as downright demeaning and punitive."[35]

So what "works"? Researchers Milbrey McLaughlin, Merita Irby, and Juliet Langman studied sixty neighborhood-based organizations with membership of 24,000 youth in three cities, and they identified characteristics of people who effectively inspired young people to become part of community-building projects affecting their neighborhoods and peers. They called these leaders "wizards." The "magic" that the wizards wield is *not* that they develop dazzling programs, curricula, or organizations.

Wizards

Wizards believe in young people, and they believe in their own ability to make a difference in young people's lives. What "works" is not programs or services, but putting youth as a priority: "In everything to do with their organizations [wizards] are unyieldingly authentic….They see youth organization technology and the models that policy-makers focus on and try to replicate only as vehicles for turning commitment into a practical reality….They have a passionate commitment to young people, particularly to underserved and disadvantaged youth. This trait is so strong as to constitute the most elemental aspect of youth organization leadership."[36]

Wizards see in youth a potential to be developed rather than a population to be fixed or regulated. Their advocacy is not codified as a service as much as it is a commitment to "be there" for young people. Wizards broker institutions that should serve young people, and they act as job counselors, academic advisors, financial/budget coaches—as buddies, parental figures, and friends.

There is no uniform program that wizards promote. However, characteristics of successful programs are the following:

- The youth organization is a safe haven.

- Young people are invited to be part of the youth organization's decision-making process.

- Young people are invited to be part of organization building, which is a key to building trust, responsibility, accountability, and investment.

- There are few rules, but they are collectively forged and clear-cut, and the consequences for transgressions are predictable and consistently applied.

- Through volunteer or salaried community-building, young people gain a sense of cultural and personal dignity.[37]

Wizardry works. To those who insist that there are no formulas that "work" in transforming youthful alienation in the postmodern world, wizards reply, "You're right. There is no formula, but what must be done is simple:

we have to trust young people." According to Luis Rodriguez, "We must reverse their sense of helplessness. The first step is to invest them with more authority to run their own lives, their communities, even their schools. The aim is to help them stop being instruments of their own death and to choose a revolutionary service to life. We don't need a country in which the National Guard walks our children to school, or pizza-delivery people carry side-arms, or prisons outnumber colleges....We can be more imaginative."[38]

More than anything else, wizards are imaginative. They believe in the potential of young people who have been rejected, mistreated, and betrayed, even when the youth themselves no longer sense their own worth. Such faith and imagination can't be codified.

The limitations that wizards confront are precisely that they have no well-articulated programmatic proposal that wins ongoing funding. Other limitations wizards struggle with are the following:

- Their organizations are dependent on volunteers who turn over every couple of years.

- Funds for neighborhood-based work have dwindled.

- Abandonment of core neighborhoods, lack of paid jobs for youth, crumbling inner-city infrastructures, poor recreational opportunities, indifferent and volatile neighborhood schools, and inner-city decapitalization and neighborhood drug economies all contrive against efforts at creating youthful self-determination and commitment to community building.

- Wizards' unwillingness to label youth or make them fit categories in order to procure funding leaves them in a precarious financial position.

- Where funding does support the initiatives of inner-city youth, it is given to traditional programs such as Headstart, and it targets young children.[39]

Community Mutual Aid Groups

Other community-based groups that receive little funding are mutual aid groups such as Parents Anonymous. Groups of parents who have been stigmatized because they have had children removed on charges of neglect or abuse form their own support groups: "These organizations provide [families] the opportunity to take on new social roles, to become leaders, and to forge new and positive conceptions of themselves."[40] The groups become a subgroup within the community that, through development of a social network of support, endorses people's collective creativity in solving their own problems.

Studies indicate that mothers who were part of a welfare rights organization had an enhanced sense of self-confidence because they demonstrated to themselves their capacity to affect history rather than to be passive recipients. The mothers' involvement and support of each other were the catalyst that produced community investment and leadership. Further, a study of a mutual support group of former mental patients found that they had significantly less need to return to psychiatric hospitalization than did a control group without such a social network.[41]

Organizations such as these remain unfunded by child welfare agencies because "informal social support strategies seldom place the paid service provider or professional at the center of the helping process. Indeed, such methods assume that there are many problem situations common to child welfare clients in which professionals or other formal helpers are not the best sources of assistance."[42] Such a prospect can threaten those invested in the professional (psychiatric or medical treatment) model. But this process requires development of the community or special interest group's capacity. It is not a quick fix, and commitment to a support group is a long and precarious process.

In recommending the development of mutual support groups, child welfare researcher Ray Thomlinson insists that the first priorities are to deal with the instigating causes of neglect and abuse. Nevertheless, says Thomlinson, "it would be unjust and repressive to ignore the economic and social correlates of child abuse and neglect. The strongest family support measures undoubtedly would be to provide many of these child welfare families with access to decent employment and adequate income, good housing and safe neighborhoods, and opportunities to gain self-respect."[43]

To Heal the Family, Heal the Community

Researchers Garabino and Kostelny found that child welfare workers in deteriorating, unsafe neighborhoods reflected the despair and chaos of the inhabitants in much the same way that overwhelmed, understaffed refugee support workers functioned in war-torn nations. In visiting a large urban housing project, the researchers found parallels with a refugee camp in war-strafed Cambodia. In both situations the workers did not live among the populations they served: "After dark, the setting was controlled by the gangs (in Cambodia, they were more clearly political gangs)…any decisions made or actions taken during the day had to be reconciled with the realities of who was in charge at night…for this reason, it will not be enough simply to introduce family support programs in a very limited way…it will also be necessary to link them to massive peacekeeping and socioeconomic development efforts."[44]

The researchers distinguish "high-risk" poor neighborhoods, with levels of violence and depression characteristic of people living in war zones, from "low-risk" poor neighborhoods, where social networks exist. The social welfare staff in both neighborhoods reflected their environment. In high-risk settings the staff delivered few services, and in low-risk neighborhoods they enhanced and serviced the communal networks. Even the rate of child abuse deaths mirrored the environmental conditions of the two poor neighborhoods. Of the twelve deaths that occurred during the study from 1984 to 1987, eight of the deaths happened in the high-risk neighborhood and four in the low-risk neighborhood. This is a tragic but instructive statistical verification of the argument for changing the social conditions that give rise to family disintegration and child abuse: "Anyone with an appreciation for the depth and pervasiveness of the social impoverishment in contemporary high risk neighborhoods understands that social support must be part of a sweeping reform of the neighborhood and of its relations with the larger community."[45]

Family and Neighborhood Residents as Resources

A model that demonstrates trust in families' ability to diagnose their own problems was developed by the Minnesota Hennepin Community Service Department in 1992. The "Family Options" demonstration project provided 600 "at-risk" families with a family service account of $3,500 for a year to purchase whatever services they felt they needed. Such a reform project has as its goal not community development but a 15 percent reduction in child abuse and neglect.[46] Although this is a modest goal, its effectiveness saved the lives of a number of children and initiated an altered relationship between a public child welfare agency and troubled families.

Programs that try to develop indigenous or "natural" family helpers from local neighborhoods also express trust in the wisdom of community members. Researchers have found limitations with this approach because families with complex physical or psychological problems need expertise that paraprofessionals, no matter how relationally skillful, may not have the ability to offer. However, trust in the wisdom of natural allies and helpers can be supplemented with consultation workshops without undercutting the informal network of care provided by paraprofessionals and without "professionalizing" care.

In Chicago two programs, an Ounce of Prevention and the North Lawndale Family Support Initiative of the National Committee for the Prevention of Child Abuse, brought their concerns about the difficulty of natural helpers' ability to reach past families' reluctance to deal with issues of sexuality or aggression. The program workers brought their concerns to open community forums that opened up the hidden issues of aggressive parental physical punishment and teenage sexual behavior.[47]

The Bienvenidos Family Services Program in the Latino community of East Los Angeles is a good example of a community-based agency whose strategic objectives were forged for and with community residents. Its center-based programs and in-home services respond to comprehensive communal needs by providing the following:

- drug rehab programs
- immigration services and support
- housing advocates and job counselors
- culturally respectful and diverse staff
- support and family education groups for parents and teens
- prenatal and well-baby care[48]

The philosophy of Bienvenidos believes that families can develop creative problem-solving abilities if given proper support. Plans of service are collaboratively designed by family members and caseworkers. An in-home family-centered program provides a family support worker who spends between five and twenty hours per week for a period of three to six months working with family members on concrete issues of homemaking, child care, and family dynamics. The family support worker is part of a team of two caseworkers and a supervisor that offers consultative support.[49]

This intensive in-home family preservation model "teaches" family members new competencies. Once the family overcomes its powerlessness and can act on its own behalf, family members enter a "maintenance" relationship with Bienvenidos. In this stage they may offer support to other families entering the program by becoming phone "buddies," welcoming new families to the center, or co-facilitating parent education support groups. This provides the maintenance families with the following:

- an opportunity to give something back to the community
- practice in using their newly acquired skills
- ongoing involvement with the Family Center's support programs
- practice in accessing social services on their own[50]

Bienvenidos is a community-based model that is "family centered, community based, comprehensive and collaborative...culturally sensitive and non-judgmental...and allow[s] for flexibility to address each new situation."[51] In effect, Bienvenidos practices programmatic implementation of the values that child welfare programs such as individualized services, wrap-around services, youth development, and health home care programs uphold.

EFFECTIVE MODELS ALREADY IN PLACE

The family preservation programs exist, the wizards exist, and the communities exist that have shown the way. We know how to prevent child abuse and neglect through emphasis on community and youth development projects, job training linked to actual attainment of jobs, social centers, mentoring programs, after-school programs, Headstart, programs for dropouts, school- and community-linked initiatives to give children and youth a stake in community building, and employment linked to community development, such as housing rehab, construction of playgrounds and recreation facilities, and social service and health care preventive programs.

There are models of community redevelopment projects that have been successful for over twenty-five years, such as the New Community Corporation founded in Newark, New Jersey, in 1967 by Father Bill Linder. This not-for-profit housing development enterprise resurrected neighborhood hope and vitality by constructing housing for 6,000 people, establishing day-care facilities that serve 700 children, and providing 2,800 meals daily. The project employs 1,400 neighborhood residents.[52]

There are also recent community development projects, like the Dudley Street Initiative in Boston (which will be discussed in Chapter 11), that have resurrected a shattered community.

We know there are stories of successful community redevelopment projects that can assist communities in chartering the complex tasks of creating democratic governing structures, of building human and social capacity, of learning fiscal and funding skills, of coalition and alliance linking, of winning the services that families need, and of crossing the racial and ethnic borders that divide and fracture a community. Not every project answers every question a particular community has because each initiative will be different. But there are some common problems faced by poor and working-class communities that are culturally diverse or homogeneous. Researchers have documented these stories and offer some "nuts-and-bolts" suggestions about the promises and pitfalls of community building and delivery of social services that enhance the community by strengthening troubled families.

The American Youth Policy Forum offers a series of booklets, a few of which are listed below:

- *Children, Families and Communities: Early Lessons from a New Approach to Social Services,* by Joan Wynn, Sheila M. Merry, and Patricia G. Berg. An analysis of eight comprehensive community-based initiatives in poor and culturally diverse Chicago communities. The analysis identifies issues that community residents and governing councils have raised in their journey toward community redevelopment.

- *What It Takes: Structuring Interagency Partnerships to Connect Children and Families with Comprehensive Services,* by Atelia Melaville with Martin Blank. Suggestions for how schools, social welfare agencies, and community-based organizations can collaborate.

- *Thinking Collaboratively: Questions and Answers to Help Policy Makers Improve Children's Services,* by Charles Bruner. A checklist to assess if local collaboratives are change agents.

- *Contract with America's Youth: Toward a National Youth Development Agenda,* American Youth Policy Forum, Center for Youth Development and Policy Research, and the National Assembly of National Voluntary Health and Social Welfare Organizations. Twenty-five authors write on what is to be done to build youth and community development projects.

- *Opening Career Paths for Youth: What Is to Be Done? Who Can Do It?* by Stephen F. and Mary Agnes Hamilton. Cornell University's Youth Apprenticeship Demonstration Project.

These pamphlets are available at a reasonable price from American Youth Policy Forum, 1001 Connecticut Avenue, NW, Suite 719, Washington, DC 20036-5541 (202/775-9731).

- *Employment Strategies for Urban Communities: How to Connect Low Income Neighborhoods with Good Jobs,* by Neighborhood Works, with Support from the Ann E. Casey Foundation. Chicago: Center for Neighborhood Technology Publications, 1996. Describes economic development and job training strategies. Shows that the largest employers in poor neighborhoods are health and social service agencies. This booklet gives examples of how a 1995 initiative to connect youth from poor communities to jobs is operative in six cities: Denver, Milwaukee, New Orleans, Philadelphia, Seattle, and St. Louis.

- *Working Neighborhoods: Taking Charge of Your Local Economy,* by Neighborhood Works, with Support from the Ann E. Casey Foundation. Chicago: Neighborhood Technology Publications, 1996. Shifts focus from Wall Street to local communities.

Available at a reasonable price from Neighborhood Works, 2125 W. North Avenue, Chicago, IL 60647.

- *The Extra Economic Development Potential of Social Service Delivery,* by the Woodstock Institute. Identifies social service agencies that have moved beyond temporary solutions—the same services that are provided to communities can be a source of jobs for community residents.

Available for a reasonable price from the Woodstock Institute, 407 S. Dearborn, Suite 550, Chicago, IL 60605.

- *Settlement Houses Today: Their Community Building Role.*

Available for a reasonable price from the Chapin Hall Center for Children at the University of Chicago, 1155 East 60th Street, Chicago, IL 60637.

- *Facing Racial and Cultural Conflict: Tools for Rebuilding Communities,* by Lester Schoen and Marcelle DuPraw. Available from Program for Community Problem Solving, 915 15th Street, N.W., Suite 600, Washington, DC 20005.

Also note the following two books:

- *Forsaking Our Children: Bureaucracy and Reform in the Child Welfare System,* by John Hagedorn. (Lakeview Press, Chicago).
- *The Quickening of America: Rebuilding Our Nation, Remaking Our Lives,* by Francis Moore Lappe and Paul Martin DuBois. (Jossey-Bass, San Francisco).

As important as are resources that share the experiences of groups involved in community building, no "blueprint" is possible that a community can follow. Moreover, the critical ingredient is not competencies in dealing with government, agencies, foundations, and regulatory officials. The critical ingredient is a community's willingness to define and solve its own problems. This is important to repeat lest the new *language* about community-based, comprehensive initiatives overwhelm the *practice* of community building. Guidelines for community building should not overwhelm or distract neighborhood residents from their most critical task: organizing and getting the people involved.

NOTES

1. Richard Barnett and John Cavanaugh, *Global Dreams* (New York: Simon and Schuster, 1994), 22.

2. David Trend, "Representation and Resistance: An Interview with Bell Hooks," *Socialist Review,* 24:1, 2 (1995), 120.

3. Michael Harrington, *The Other America: Poverty in the U.S.* (New York: Penguin, 1986), 5.

4. John McKnight, "Thy Servanthood Is Bad," *The Other Side* (Nov.–Dec. 1995), 56.

5. Ibid.

6. Ibid.

7. Ibid., 58.

8. Mark Lusk and David Stoesz, "International Social Work in a Global Economy," *Journal of Multicultural Social Work,* 3:2 (1994), 103, 109.

9. Ruth Massinga, "Transforming Social Services," in *Putting Families First,* Eds. Sharon Kagan and Bernice Weissbourd (San Francisco: Jossey-Bass, 1994), 96.

10. James Garabino and Kathleen Kostelny, "Public Policy and Child Protection," in *Children at Risk in America,* Ed. Roberta Wollons (New York: State University of New York Press, 1995), 276.

11. Kip Tiernan, "Homelessness: The Politics of Accommodation," *New England Journal of Public Policy* (Spring 1992), 600.

12. Richard Wexler, *Wounded Innocents: The Real Victims of the War Against Child Abuse* (Buffalo, NY: Prometheus Books, 1995), 254.

13. Ibid., 254–55.

14. Judith Katz-Leavey et al., *Individualized Services in a System of Care* (Washington, D.C.: CASSP Technical Assistance Center, Georgetown University Child Development Center Publications, July 1992), 3.

15. Albert Duchnowski et al., "The Alternatives to Residential Treatment Study: Initial Findings," *Journal of Emotional and Behavioral Disorders,* 1:1 (1990), 17.

16. John Whitbeck et al., *A Report From the Field: Individualized and Tailored Care: What Makes It Work,* draft report of research in progress (Washington State: Mental Health Division, Washington State Department of Social and Health Services, 1995), 6 .

17. Katz-Leavey et al., 10.

18. Whitbeck et al., 3.

19. Ibid., 2.

20. J. VanDenBerg (in press), "Integration of Individualized Services into the System of Care for Children and Adolescents with Emotional Disabilities," sponsored by *Administration and Policy in Mental Health* (1991).

21. Katz-Leavey et al., 33.

22. John VanDenBerg, Shirley Beck, and John Pierce, *Outcome Project for Children's Services.* Unpublished monograph, 1989.

23. Qtd. in Katz-Leavey et al., i.

24. Interview with Seth Donnelly, Nov. 27, 1995.

25. Donnelly interview.

26. Tino Ramirez, "In Hawaii, Healthy Start for At-Risk Families," *USA Today* (Apr. 11, 1994), 10.

27. Gail Beakley and Betsy Pratt, "Healthy Start Home Visiting: Hawaii's Approach," *The APSAC Advisor,* 6:4 (1993), 7.

28. Garabino and Kostelny, *Children at Risk in America,* 281–82.

29. Ibid., 282.

30. Marie Connolly, "An Act of Empowerment: The Children, Young Persons and Their Families Act (1989)," *British Journal of Social Work,* 24 (1994), 87, 90.

31. John Angus, "The Act: Year One," *Social Work Review,* 3:4 (1991), 5.

32. Ann Barbour, "Family Group Conferences: Context and Consequences," *Social Work Review,* 3:4 (1991), 18–19.

33. Luis Rodriguez, "Turning Youth Gangs Around," *The Nation* (Nov. 21, 1994), 608.

34. Milbrey McLaughlin, Merita Irby, and Juliet Langman, *Urban Sanctuaries: Neighborhood Organizations in the Lives and Futures of Inner-City Youth* (San Francisco: Jossey-Bass, 1994), 5.

35. Ibid., 7.

36. Ibid., 95–96.

37. Ibid., 98–110.

38. Rodriguez, 609.

39. McLaughlin, 161, 200, 218.

40. Ray Thomlinson, "Uses of Skill Development and Behavior Modification Techniques in Working with Abusing and Neglecting Parents," in *Child Maltreatment: Challenges in Expanding Our Concept of*

Healing, Eds. Gary Cameron and Michael Rothery (Hillsdale, N.J.: Lawrence Erlbaum, 1990), 160.

41. Ibid.

42. Ibid., 166.

43. Ibid., 167.

44. James Garabino and Kathleen Kostelny, "Family Support and Community Development," in *Putting Families First: America's Family Support Movement and the Challenge of Change* (San Francisco: Jossey-Bass, 1994), 315–16.

45. Ibid., 312.

46. Massinga, 101.

47. Garabino and Kostelny, "Family Support," 306.

48. Gail Huntington, Lorraine Lima, and Irene Nathan Zipper, "Child Abuse: A Prevention Agenda," in *Risk, Resilience and Prevention: Promoting the Well Being of All Children,* Ed. Rune Simeonsson (Baltimore: Paul Brookes, 1994), 177–79.

49. Ibid.

50. Ibid., 179.

51. Ibid., 180.

52. Lynn Curtiss, "Investing in What Works," *The Nation* (Jan. 15/18, 1996), 18.

11

❋

Community Building

Resurrecting the Disposable

Delivery of services is not enough. Someone has to build community.[1]

JOHN GARDNER, FORMER SECRETARY OF
U.S. DEPARTMENT OF HEALTH, EDUCATION AND WELFARE

As the power of the professional service systems ascends, the legitimacy, authorship, and capacity of citizens descend. The consequence of this professional persuasion is devastating for those labeled people whose primary "need" is to be incorporated into community life, not isolated from it.[2]

KIP TIERNAN, FOUNDER OF ROSIE'S PLACE, THE NATION'S
FIRST SHELTER FOR HOMELESS WOMEN, AND CO-DIRECTOR OF
THE POOR PEOPLE'S UNITED FUND AND THE ETHICAL INSTITUTE
OF THE UNIVERSITY OF MASSACHUSETTS AT BOSTON

COMPREHENSIVE COMMUNITY-
BASED INITIATIVES: WHO DECIDES?

Many of the community-based programmatic initiatives and youth or family agencies discussed thus far exemplify effective models of care, but few have developed comprehensive community infrastructures and governing processes that have long-term viability and that are community controlled. What is critical to the success and duration of these initiatives is not simply communally responsive programs, institutional funding, and social agency collaboration but that a democratic governance process represents neighborhood residents in all their diversity. Such a process is instrumental in building individual and social capacity as well as providing the needed political power to reconstitute communities that were devastated in the Reagan and Bush years of the 1980s, when industrial jobs were eliminated and social spending was cut.

Such a demand is rigorous because it challenges virtually all of the professional agendas of social and child welfare, and because diverse communities must struggle to incorporate voices of difference—racial, ethnic, gender, ability, and age. Community building, like community organizing, is hard work fraught with power struggles, setbacks, and tensions. There is no blueprint for how to develop governing structures that can hurdle challenges to community governance and empowerment. But there are principles that can be identified:

- The local community, not outside experts, possesses the collective knowledge to solve its problems and the political power to agitate, organize, or negotiate for change.

- Such a recognition that the neighborhood and the community are the locus of knowledge and power does not mean that the local community has power until, and unless, it organizes itself and marshals both the formal and informal networks of local power and knowledge to solve the many social problems affecting the children and families of the community.

Table 11.1 is a paradigm developed by Francis Moore Lappe and Paul Martin DuBois that illustrates a new model of social services based on these principles.

The fundamental issue that differentiates the service model from what the authors call a model of "living democracy" is governance. In the service model, the power to decide is in the hands of professionals. In the living democracy model, decision-making power is collaboratively shared among the people who will be affected by the decisions.

It is the process of self-governance that develops both individual and social capacity as individuals and groups gain skills and competencies in forging strategies and collaborative programs. Through strategic planning and actions (whether through organizing campaigns, elections, protests, and demonstrations or through coalition and alliance building with social service or community organizations), local residents discover and exercise political power. But building a communal democratic process is not a smooth path.

Table 11.1 The New Emerging Model in Human Services

At Issue	Service Model	Living Democracy Model
Who's in charge?	Professionally driven	Citizen/client driven
Contribution of professional	Professional provides answers	Professional is resource
Process	Diagnoses single cause/cure	Understanding multiple causes and seeking change
Procedure	Bureaucratic	Informal
What's valued	Credentials	Experience
Communication	Largely one-way	Collaborative
Focus of problem solving	Individual deficiency	Capacities developed through interaction
Exchange	Limited to fee for service	Includes mutual benefits

SOURCE: Francis Moore Lappe and Paul Martin DuBois, *The Quickening of America: Rebuilding Our Nation, Remaking Our Lives* (San Francisco: Jossey-Bass, 1994), 156.

University of Chicago researcher Robert Chaskin and Sunil Garg of the Chapin Hall Center for Children have identified three challenges that neighborhood governing councils must address: (1) they must broker the relationship between their emerging local governing council and local government or the state; (2) they must decide who they represent, to whom they are accountable, and how their community authority is legitimated; and (3) they must address strategic questions about long-range staying power.[3]

First, both local government and state welfare systems subcontract more and more service provision to private, not-for-profit agencies that in turn provide services to local communities: "Thus, because responsibility for service delivery is increasingly based with private agencies, the link of accountability between citizens and government for the delivery of such services is diffuse. Further, as contracting arrangements increase, non–profits become more and more a part of the governments's social service system—dependent on it for revenue, destabilized by cut-backs, with an increasing exchange of personnel between the public and private sector—and are less able to play a role as political advocates for change in government policy and practice."[4] The local neighborhood or community governing authority must address these contradictions by developing coordinated services and agency collaboration. Such a task is rich with tensions.

Chaskin and Garg also identify three types of relationships that community governing councils can make with federal, state, or local authorities: they relate as *alternative* local governing institutions that provide services that local government has not provided; as an *incorporated extension* of the local government's service provision; or as an *oppositional* local governing council that seeks to implement policies challenging resource allocation and provision of services.[5]

The issue of representation of the community is tied to the issue of relationship with the local government. The community governing council that

has incorporated into local government structures does not have the autonomy that the *alternative* or *oppositional* community council has, nor does it have
the same freedom to represent dissident or oppositional voices within the community. More unencumbered space to work toward representation of diverse
class, racial, and ethnic constituencies is possible for community councils that
maintain degrees of autonomy from municipal or state governments. Circum-
venting local government's efforts to appropriate grassroots governing councils, particularly when the issue of delivery of services becomes an issue of
negotiation, is difficult, but never more so than when funds, resources, and
access to city hall are part of the offer. Another seduction for governing councils in impoverished or lower-working-class communities is the corporate or
federal offer of grant money, which only later reveals the funder's interest in
gaining legitimation, political capital, or public promotion.

The issue of representation and communal authority must be tackled by
both the alternative and oppositional groups that, at least in the beginning,
have yet to develop an accountability or feedback process. In neighborhoods
where organized community groups are established, the issue of who represents the community is hotly contested. Further, established community social
agencies often see themselves as the representatives of the community, particularly when the issue of services to children and families is raised. Forging working alliances with these groups with the objective of constructing a democratic
process that works toward communal restoration, effective services to families
and children, and transformation of social powerlessness requires creativity, pa-
tience, and the conviction that the process is as important as the product. The
community building path is, in the words of the poet Antonio Machado, not
made: there is no road, the road is made by walking it.

Alternative community governing councils more or less take the position
that neither grassroots initiatives nor the current government and current
foundation enthusiasm for community-based social service reform can rebuild
communities. Outsiders lack legitimacy, and poor communities lack resources
and access. What is needed is an alliance in which the authority of the community is acknowledged and responded to by local or state governments and
by foundations seeking to support community initiatives.

Chaskin and Garg delineate a spectrum of community governing councils:
incorporated groups such as the New York state-legislated Neighborhood Based
Alliance; the Roxbury, Massachusetts, *oppositional* Dudley Street Neighborhood Initiative, which has no government involvement; and *alternative* groups
such as Maryland's Community Building in Partnership, in collaboration with
the Baltimore city government and the Enterprise Foundation, New York's
Agenda for Children Tomorrow, partnered with the Tides Foundation and
the Mayor's Office of New York City, and the Neighborhood and Family Initiative, supported by the Ford Foundation and with local government representatives sitting on the community governing councils.[6]

This book has argued that the way to heal troubled families, and therefore
protect children from harm, is to heal the wounded and fractured community.
The rocky path to community development of a particular neighborhood, ge-
ography, and history must be made by the community participants, not by ex-

perts. Otherwise, what results are programs and projects that lack community ownership or that are "owned" by sectarian or professional entities. The principle which insists that the residents have the knowledge, power, and right to create a process of governance that will address its problems is far more demanding in practice than in theory. Not only do professionals, local officials, liberal philanthropists, and academics fail this trust, but the people who have been marginalized or overwhelmed also fail to trust their own social capacity. Rescuing them when they falter or lose confidence reinforces their dependency. However, partnerships can be forged that don't compromise community authority but support it.

What are those partnerships? How does a community governing council structure itself? What is its relationship to local government and to service providers furnished by the state? As Chaskin and Garg illustrate, "While a strong, recognized neighborhood organization (or unified coalition representing, in the aggregate, the neighborhood as a whole) may be able to promote a certain level of change and successfully advocate to government for particular policies and practices, it must still ultimately rely on government for significant funding, jurisdictional approval, and the provision of basic services. Conversely, directly connecting such governance structures to government presents the possibility of cooptation, in which the fates of neighborhood organizations and governance structures are so tied to the structure of authority that they are unable to effectively advocate a minority position."[7]

THE DUDLEY STREET
NEIGHBORHOOD INITIATIVE

While many of the child and family reform initiatives named thus far are excellent examples of family preservation in community-based settings, there is one model that rebuilt both the physical and human infrastructure of a fractured inner-city community. That is the Dudley Street Neighborhood Initiative (DSNI). The story of the resurrection of a diverse multicultural Boston community in a neighborhood cluttered with dump sites, junkyards, and burnt-out buildings is told by Peter Medoff and Holly Sklar in *Streets of Hope: The Fall and Rise of an Urban Neighborhood*. What follows is a brief summary of their account of the Dudley "miracle."

In 1981 two community organizations, La Alianza Hispana, a multi-service agency, and Nuestra Comunidad Development Corporation solicited MIT's Department of Urban Studies and Planning's research and technical assistance in assessing community needs. With a neighborhood study in hand, leaders of the organizations asked Boston's Riley Foundation for funds to repair La Alianza Hispana's dilapidated center. But the Riley Foundation, which had spread its funding among numerous inner-city community projects with feeble results, decided that renewing one community agency when the whole neighborhood was falling apart made no sense. So Riley Foundation chose to concentrate funds on a community revitalization plan. Agency leaders and

MIT researchers identified the community's needs as renovation of the land and environment, empowerment of the people, and a community building process that would be driven by residents rather than by the Riley Foundation's funding requirements.[8]

A Dudley advisory group, composed of not-for-profit health and social service agency directors, small business leaders, religious leaders, officials from the city and state, and representatives from the four major ethnic groups—African American, Latino, Cape Verdean, and white—set up a provisional governance structure that, it was assumed, would be the elected governance council. But an intervening threat by Boston's Redevelopment Authority (BRA) to gentrify Dudley by turning the area into a "new town" upscale condominium neighborhood galvanized community residents to attend the next meeting of the DSNI's governance council. Although the BRA plan promised resident participation, an advisory committee, and a beautified community, Dudley residents, long a socially disposable group, were suspicious of dislocation.[9]

The first DSNI community meeting was explosive. Residents refused to accept the governing board, most of whom they pointed out didn't live in the community, and they challenged the right of Riley Foundation to have made deals with professionals without their input. Che Madyun said it was not a community-based initiative if the residents had no control of the process: "How can we nominate people to represent us when we don't know each other?...I don't know if I should vote for them or not."[10]

The meeting surfaced festering fears that this initiative would be like so many government failures, like Model Cities or other outsider programs that targeted an aspect of Dudley's problems but eventually left. Blacks feared that the Latino agency leaders would not defend their interests. One common agreement was that the initiative would work only if there was resident participation and leadership.

The Dudley Advisory Group scrapped their plans and opened what was to have been the election confirmation meeting to all community residents. Rather than a governing board with four seats for community members, the governing structure shifted to a majority of resident members, with equal representation from each of the four racial/ethnic groups. There were two co-chairs, one from the community and one from an agency. The Riley Foundation pledged financial backing for the initiative and did not request board membership.

Community Control: The Heart of the Matter

Two more "tests" occurred over the issue of community control rather than agency control acting in the name of the community. The final candidates for director of DSNI were a Latino agency director and a white community organizer who believed in resident control. Although still being silent listeners in many of the board meetings, it was the community residents who voted for the organizer, in spite of their hesitancy to trust white male leaders, because they believed he was more committed to resident control of the process of community renewal than the agency professional.[11]

Another milestone was passed when, in spite of the tradition of electing board presidents who were agency officials, a community resident, Che Madyun, was elected president. That's when residents began to believe they would be represented, and they bought into the process. When DSNI led a successful campaign to force the Mayor's office to kick out corporate dumpers of asbestos and other dangerous substances, residents began to believe they had some power to effect change:

> DSNI…turned the traditional top-down urban planning process on its head. Instead of struggling to influence a process driven by city government, Dudley residents and agencies became visionaries, created their own bottom-up "urban village" redevelopment plan and built an unprecedented partnership with the city to implement it. DSNI made history when it became the nation's first neighborhood group to win the right of eminent domain and began transforming Dudley's burnt out lots from wasteland to wealth controlled by the community. Launched with the strong backing of the local Riley Foundation, DSNI developed a growing network of public and private sector supporters."[12]

An aspect of Dudley that separates it from so many efforts of reformers is that the constructors of the initiative really are community residents in partnership with agencies and foundation supporters. Leaders from the community are not simply "advisors" to programs. Before DSNI, the usual situation was that even those reform initiatives based in the community, with the goal of preserving and strengthening families through intensive comprehensive services offered through agency and local government assistance, rarely engaged a process of ownership by the residents. Reform-minded professionals from agencies, universities, government, or foundations would support initiatives of community-based leaders or councils only *if* the funding proposals and governance structure met their criterion. DSNI, on the other hand, rejected Mayor Ray Flynn's proposal for the city of Boston to fund the revitalization plan because the city staff insisted on "collaboratively" directing the initiative.

To fully understand Dudley, one has to understand the community development project as it unfolds from the hearts and imagination of the participants. This is radically different than reading the often formulaic language that describes the goals and objectives of community-based local government or foundation-supported partnerships. Too many times the initiatives peter out because the community leaders "empowered" by project funders lack trust in the creative capacities of local residents.

To speak of *comprehensive community-based development initiatives, of services that support family preservation through agency collaboration, and blended funding/creative use of foundation and entitlement funding streams to meet the needs of individual families and children* is reform language. When these initiatives are more than simply community based, when those who will be affected by the changes develop the capacity to implement their vision and to have ownership of the community development process, then community building enters the path of transformation. DSNI is on a transformative path.

The primary strategy of Dudley's community revitalization plan was to provide housing along with a town common with a park, shops, and a community center—an "urban village"—and to do so without displacement of residents. But it was not the housing and commons development projects that resurrected the community. It was the commitment, in practice, to an inclusive *process* that called forth the creativity and ingenuity of Dudley's diverse residents. The process of placing trust in the people of Dudley built the community—its hidden and unrecognized (often by the residents themselves) capacities, talents, and competencies were tapped, releasing not only a community development labor source but an increased human capacity to solve difficult community problems.

When two urban planning consultant firms (the two finalists) bid to consult on DSNI's comprehensive community development plans, Dudley residents rejected the one with an exemplary record of quality physical design and chose instead a consulting firm whose stated philosophy was to serve the goals and objectives set by residents from lower-income areas with the same respect as those from higher-income neighborhoods, and to uphold the community's inclusive process of decision making rather than interject its own.[13]

Community ownership of the process was not accomplished by making an announcement. It was an organizing project. Both the urban planners and the DSNI leadership council believed that community participation in the process had to be developed through the tenacious work of organizing. One example of the Dudley planners' confidence in community residents' actual or potential competence is the faith they had in youth. Twenty-six youth between the ages of nine and sixteen, in league with friends and family who gave suggestions, began a wish list for what the Community Center should be like. Then, with the support of volunteer architect Gail Sullivan, community leaders, and urban planners, the group grew. Forty-five young people who wanted to be members of the Young Planners and Architects were divided into groups and assigned a project leader. They learned how to make designs, use surveyor's tape, and to draw to scale. Each group developed a vision of the center, designed models, discussed issues of accessibility, learned how to use trees as part of the design, and drew floor plans. Their decisions were reached through consensus.[14]

As a result of organizing drives that solicited more and more residents' identification of community needs, key committees formed to deal with land, environment, housing, and human services. The Human Services Development Committee called for the formation of an agency collaborative among the child welfare/social welfare agencies, community centers, after-school tutoring and recreation programs, three youth service centers, the Dudley Library, a drug treatment center, a job training center, the Urban League, legal services, shelters for the homeless, and a housing office.

There was agency reluctance to share information and collaboration resistance based on a fear of losing a competitive edge in the scramble for scarce resources. Arnaldo Solis, who is deputy director of Children's Services of Roxbury, saw the resistance as a failure of the agencies to understand community empowerment. Though agency leaders were located in the community, they still bought into a top-down style of leadership, and they didn't share the goal of building human capacity and ownership among the residents. According to Solis, agency directors hesitated to trust nonprofessionals

> because it down-played their importance within the community...it's also a threat, because if you give the community residents that kind of power, it means that then you are open to criticism by these same people if you're not rendering the type of services that you have identified as needs within the community, or that the community itself identified as needs. And I don't think agencies are all too receptive to that.[15]

What brought the agencies to collaboration was the same process that was "teaching" Dudley residents, agency workers, and academic and foundation advisors that cooperation was possible and that faith in community members' development was as important as the development of Dudley's physical infrastructure.

In 1992, Dudley residents attended an economic development summit in which they made an account of the labor and clerical skills of residents, of the land and building holdings accomplished through their Community Land Trust project and successful use of the right of eminent domain, and of their small businesses. They assessed job development plans and investment opportunities, and they formulated strategies for winning public works contracts. In 1993 the Economic Development Committee held another summit called "Economics with People in Mind" to which were invited Dudley residents and businesspeople, government contractors, Boston employers, and community service and development organizations. More than a job fair, the summit challenged residents to make connections between job loss and corporate disinvestment strategies, downsizing, and deindustrialization, and to recognize that economic development must be comprehensive, visionary, and long term. The committee targeted the job needs of mothers who were single heads of families along with their need for child care in order to upgrade their jobs without having to either use their salaries for child care or stay on welfare. A Youth Build Project aimed at developing rehab housing jobs for youth was also developed.[16]

What is unique about the Economic Development Committee's summit conferences is not that they "solved" the problem of job loss in inner-city areas. But they initiated an inclusive process that faced the magnitude of the underlying causes of unemployment, they made the connection between themselves and other displaced workers nationally and internationally, and, while developing an analysis of the economic crisis, community residents (not economic experts) assessed their strengths and collectively developed ways to create more jobs.

Dudley's Greatest Accomplishment

Perhaps the economic development process most deeply exemplifies the power of the DSNI. DSNI faces globalization's devastating effects on poor communities soberly, but with hope and an economic development plan. Dudley's people aren't giving up. This distinguishes Dudley from most impoverished areas and, for that matter, from most middle-income or working-class neighborhoods. What the Dudley residents cherish is not their programmatic, environmental, or project successes—that is, not what outsiders or foundations or officials see: the revitalization of the physical infrastructure of the neighborhood. Dudley's pride is that it has rebuilt shattered lives, the broken and wounded human infrastructure. Dudley has constructed a process that too often is merely rhetoric—empowerment. DSNI accomplished this by organizing the people. There was nothing romantic about the determination to remain open and bring everyone in even when distrust might have sunk the boat. No accomplishment or product—job training programs, a cleaner, safer environment, collaborative and intensive services to families, the construction of low income housing, sustainable development—is as critical as the accomplishment of a relationship-building process that values the contributions of everyone.

Dudley's greatest accomplishment is that the residents rebuilt the community. Therein lies protection for vulnerable residents, children, and youth. This will not eliminate the need for services for the troubled or the unemployed, but the capacity for relational care and a process that draws in, rather than isolates people, are guarantors of protection. Community is the one initiative the corporations can't commodify. The physical changes that community organizations produce can, and will be, co-opted, but genuine community is the expression of people's trust and hope in one another and in the creative capacity of the human spirit. It can't be bought or sold. The powerful are stumped by its force and resilience, and its criteria for success elude them entirely:

> "We're learning how to be a better community together," says DSNI's Sue Beaton. "But whether we look perfect at the end is really, not to me, the issue. It's how many people participated along the way, who gets the benefits of whatever we can accomplish together, and how do we hang together and not get co-opted in the process of doing what we're doing."[17]

DSNI has an "answer" to the process that is creating disposable communities and disposable children. The answer is creating community among the diverse cultures of disenfranchised surplus populations: "The people of Dudley are pathfinders, guided by a vision of the future in which no one is disposable."[18]

ACCOMPANIMENT: THE ROLE
FOR PROFESSIONALS

This book has critiqued the failure of child welfare to protect children and families from harm and to reveal the state's role as a regulator of family life according to the class, race, and gender norms of the dominant culture. However, the narratives of child welfare advocates present examples of professionals who have worked to subvert or change agency practices for the cause of dispossessed children and families. Finally, this research has argued that community transforms the alienation and powerlessness that give rise to, or exacerbate, social isolation, dysfunction, and maltreatment. If the power and creativity necessary to solve social problems are in the hands of local community residents, what is the task of professionals who wish to be advocates for children, families, and communities?

The characteristics of successful advocates, wizards, or pathfinders are the following:

- They focus on strengths, both individual and collective, rather than deficits.
- They place genuine trust in a family or community's capacity to solve its problems.
- They treat children with unconditional regard.
- They understand their social task as accompaniment.

Accompaniment is a term that can seem to connote almost a passivity. Yet accompaniment—in which the professional sees his or her role as standing or "walking" with the family, child, or community in the journey toward independence, health, and self-determination—demands rigorous discipline. Accompaniment insists that the advocate walk neither ahead of those who struggle to rebuild shattered lives or communities nor behind them. The temptation of those in the legal or helping professions is to solve people's problems, to rescue the fallen, to fix the broken. The accompanier is simply and radically present during the people's process, willing to provide the services, support, and resources needed but not willing to usurp the initiative that must come from the people.

Accompaniment is an act of solidarity with people who have been written off as too damaged, too dependent, too dysfunctional, too wounded, or too powerless to take control of their lives. At times, children or families have been so damaged that the most that can be offered is the solidarity of presence. At other times, accompaniment allows a partnership between poor people and professionals that can transform devastated communities. Professionals can offer much needed access to systems, services, and resources that families or communities need. But more critical than the professionals' service or resource power is their stance of solidarity. Without a deep and unambivalent belief in people's ability to solve their problems and reinvent their lives, the temptation to "manage" people or to speak for them is irresistible.

DR. KORCZAK: THE ACCOMPANIMENT OF CHILDREN

Few of us could emulate the total solidarity that Dr. Janusz Korczak exemplified in his accompaniment of Polish children after the Weimar Republic fell and Hitler rose to power. His story is told as an inspiration for those professionals who walk the rocky path of advocacy for children, families, and communities. Dr. Korczak's narrative seems particularly instructive for advocates and communities facing the shredding of the already tattered social safety net, constant attacks on mothers, youth, and children from impoverished areas, structural unemployment, and an increase in the number of people whose lives have been written off. Korczak's children and their families were also disposable.

The Children's Republic

Korczak's initiative enjoined children and adults to an exercise of moral responsibility and called upon adults to stand with and for children even when trust was difficult and racial hatred did not distinguish between children and adults.

Janusz Korczak's legend as a defender of abandoned and destitute children began during the Nazi liquidation of the Warsaw Ghetto. A famous pediatrician and author of *The Children's Right to Respect,* he was well connected with the Polish intellectual elite. In 1941 they implored him to leave Poland or, at least, the Warsaw Ghetto, where the orphans' home he founded was located. The children were doomed, they argued, and he could do nothing to stop the Nazis from cordoning off the Warsaw Ghetto for its pending annihilation. While there was still time, he could save himself and his philosophy of child care. That was his responsibility to the world, his colleagues and friends argued. But Pan Doctor (Good Doctor), as the children called him, insisted that his responsibility was to the children: "You do not leave a sick child in the night and you do not leave children at a time like this."[19]

Korczak, whose real name was Henryk Goldszmit, was a Polish Jew who founded both a Catholic orphanage and a Jewish orphanage for children who were considered incorrigibles, delinquents, prostitutes, or cultural outcasts. These were not orphanages in the traditional sense because most of the children had parents who were either too poor to care for them or who could no longer handle them because of encounters with the police and courts. A few children were simply abandoned.

Korczak lived in the "orphanage" with the children and wrote stories for them about maverick and impoverished children who triumph, and, in the process, teach lessons of moral courage to disbelievers. He encouraged their writing, and the children produced a weekly newspaper. He organized the orphanages on the basis of children's republics in order, through the practice of living in a just community, to give the children a voice in deciding their own destiny and in reclaiming their shattered dignity. It was their powerlessness, he felt, that led them into mischief, cruelty, and rage.

The children's court of peers was the centerpiece of the republic. More than Korczak or the dedicated caretakers and teachers of the orphanage, the children themselves taught one another accountability, fairness, discernment, and justice through their participation in court. Rotating child judges conducted hearings and meted out punishments for infractions of rules or suits brought by children against each other (this practice was abandoned because of the chaos of children bringing suits and countersuits). Korczak, himself, was brought up on charges along with other staff whom the children felt had wronged them:

Korczak felt that within each child there burned a moral spark that could vanish the darkness at the core of human nature. To prevent that spark from being extinguished, one had to love and nurture the young, make it possible for them to believe in truth and justice. When the Nazis materialized out of that darkness, with their swastikas, polished boots and leather whips, Korczak was prepared to shield his Jewish children, as he always had, from the injustices of the adult world.[20]

Korczak did not lose his faith in truth and justice even as those qualities were trampled under Nazi boots. Against every plea to the contrary, Korczak stayed in the Warsaw Ghetto Orphan Home from 1940 until 1942, desperately struggling to keep the children from starvation.

His presence was an act of accompaniment. He could not save the children, but he could walk with them on their journey. Faith in children was his source of hope when social hope was lost. Such faith—not the national Silver Cross awarded by the Polish Republic, not the medals he had won as a Polish major in three war campaigns—was his badge of courage.

When German guards came to evacuate the orphanage, Korczak had the children put on their best clothes, carry one favorite toy, and line up for the journey. With Stefa Wilczynska, his collaborator and unsung supporter for thirty years, he passed through the children's columns, encouraging them to not be afraid and to hold each other's hands. Then he picked up five-year-old Romcia in his arms and marched through Warsaw's streets, trailed by almost two hundred children.[21]

Where they boarded the boxcars, the terrified children saw SS squadrons snap whips at families who'd become hysterical or who tried to bolt. Nahum Remba, an official with Judernat, ran to Korczak to ask him to go with him to the Judernat office to get a possible stay order. Korczak refused. The children might panic, he said. The SS might take them away while he was gone.[22]

For the last time, Korzcak chose the children's journey. His solidarity never faltered. Korczak boarded the cattle cars with quiet dignity, soothing the children. They filed in orderly, school-like fashion, with Stefa and Janusz restraining their own terror for the sake of the children. As their line moved forward,

> the Jewish police cordoning off a path for them saluted instinctively.
> Remba burst into tears when the Germans asked who that man [Korczak] was. A wail went up from those still left on the square.[23]

Korczak and the children rumbled on toward Treblinka concentration camp, where they were killed and then burned in the crematoria.

The children and Janusz Korczak's story didn't end, of course, at Treblinka. Korczak's memory gives hope and meaning to a time of unimaginable horror and despair. Nor did his life take on meaning just because his solidarity cost his life. It was his daily, ordinary faith in damaged children's potential that made him exemplary. *Unworthy* poor children, especially those who are belligerent, promiscuous, delinquent, ungrateful, or unresponsive, have few advocates.

The story of Korczak is not intended to join the chorus of child welfare reformers who would repeat the nineteenth-century orphanage "solution," which would remove the poor to institutions. Nor is his story intended to promote a group home model that only tangentially involves the children's impoverished, often widowed, or single parents. One of Korczak's errors was that his utopian vision of a children's community free from the insensitivity of adults kept him from involving parents enough in his experiment. He was always determined to return children to their families, unlike the removal practice of today.

The unique contribution that Korczak's project of communal responsibility with the children offers is a model of solidarity with, and trust of, children. Korzcak presents an extraordinary example of solidarity with the poorest, despised sector. Confronted with social annihilation and his inability to save the children, Korczak refused safety and offered a simple willingness to be present. Such an act is not passive or nihilistic but the opposite—an affirmation of life and care over and against the forces of death.

Finally, Korczak's gift is that he constructed a system that led children to a greater sense of their own power through a collaborative effort to build community. Korczak made no distinctions between the worthy family or child and the unworthy. He sought to be in solidarity with the child who suffered. In Poland in the 1940s, to practice that ideal with impoverished Jewish children was a dangerous act of solidarity.

The myth of the unworthy poor in our technologically developed nation protects us from facing the terrifying notion that masses of people, often those racially scapegoated, are poor through no fault of their own. The persistence of the American belief in a distinction between the deserving and the undeserving poor elucidates a child welfare practice that stigmatizes families whose "fault" of neglect may be no more than their inability to meet standards of class or race worthiness. As wards of the state, children who respond uncooperatively to their placements soon enter the ranks of the unworthy dependents. These young people do have an attitude. And they have reasons for it.

NOTES

1. John Gardner, qtd. in *Urban Sanctuaries: Neighborhood Organizations in the Lives and Futures of Inner-city Youth* (San Francisco: Jossey-Bass, 1994), x.

2. Kip Tiernan, "The Politics of Accommodation," *New England Journal of Public Policy* (Spring/Summer 1992), 660.

3. Robert Chaskin and Sunil Garg, "The Issue of Governance in Neighborhood-Based Initiatives," discussion paper, *Chapin Hall Center for Children at the University of Chicago* (December 1994).

4. Ibid., 8.

5. Ibid.

6. Ibid., 14–15.

7. Ibid., 26–27.

8. Peter Medoff and Holly Sklar, *Streets of Hope: The Fall and Rise of an Urban Neighborhood* (Boston: South End Press, 1994), 38–42.

9. Ibid., 49–50.

10. Ibid., 55.

11. Ibid., 62.

12. Ibid., 4–5.

13. Ibid., 97–98.

14. Ibid., 220–24.

15. Ibid., 177.

16. Ibid., 187–89.

17. Ibid., 286.

18. Ibid., 5.

19. Betty Jean Lifton, *The King of Children* (New York: Schocken Books, 1988), 4.

20. Ibid.

21. Ibid., 338–45.

22. Ibid., 345.

23. Ibid.

Index